THE
SIMPLE TRUTH

BY
JIM LEDDY

The Simple Truth
by Jim Leddy

Printed in the United States of America

ISBN 978-1-60647-828-8

Unless otherwise indicated, Bible quotations are taken from The Holy Bible Authorized King James Version.

www.xulonpress.com

I would like to say thanks to my son Steve for the encouragement to write and publish this book and for the help with stuff that goes along with working a computer.

TABLE OF CONTENTS

Introduction

THE SIMPLE TRUTH

Come and let us reason together I believe is a better way to begin than to say, listen to me, or let me tell you, because those phrases make it sound like I know it all and you don't. That is not the impression I want to make. What I would like to do is to share a few things with you that I have learned through the years.

Chapter 1

LEARNING

Learning can be a very complicated thing and it can be misunderstood, but on the other hand it can be quite simple. One way we learn is precept upon precept, precept upon precept; line upon line, line upon line; here a little, there a little. That is not the way we would choose, but if we stop and think about it that is the way it works, probably most of the time. We would like to read it and know it, or hear it and remember it. They tell us that the way it works is that we have some knowledge and we add to that original knowledge. Many speakers and teachers and preachers seem to think that everyone gets all that they give out. And they are disappointed when they find out that is not true. As we proceed, I trust that you receive a little here and there that will be of benefit to you as you proceed through life.

In the Readers Digest, years ago I read something interesting about intelligence. It went like this, you draw a circle and write idiot at the top. As you go around the circle intelligence increases until you have a genius just across from the idiot. I don't how true that is, but it sounds like it could work that way. Another possibility was expressed by the Apostle Paul, when he said, "ever learning and never able to come to the knowledge of the truth." (2 Timothy 3.7) We are living in a time where much learning is taking place some of it good, and some not so good. It is needful for all of us to be extremely careful and look for the truth in everything we hear and read. As you know that is a large order. There is so much deception, and so many people trying to persuade us to do things their way. In some circles honesty is in short supply. Learning means to gain knowledge of a skill in a subject etc. by study or experience or by being taught. There are other terms connected with learning such as wisdom, education, knowledge and common sense. Later we will consider some of these.

Chapter 2

THE BIBLE

The Bible is defined: 1.The Christian Scriptures. 2. The Jewish scriptures. 3. A copy of either the Old or New Testament. 4. Bible; a book regarded as authoritative.

The first five books of the bible tell how Israel became a nation, and came to possess the Promised Land. The Prophets describe the establishment and the development of the monarchy and relate the prophet's messages. The bible also includes poetry and teachings on good and evil and much history.

The New Testament contains early Christian literature. The Gospels tell of the life, person, and teachings of Jesus. The Acts of the Apostles gives us the earliest history of Christianity. The letters to the churches are written by the Apostles to give help to them. The Book of Revelation was written by John the Apostle, and he was instructed to write about the things that he has seen, the things which are, and the things which shall be hereafter.

There are those who do not believe the Bible is the word of God and others that go farther and criticize and ridicule it. Many of them have never read it and therefore know very little about it. For a while the Bible was almost put out of our schools but is coming back as more people are coming to realize its importance in education. Romans 15:4 says, for whatsoever things were written aforetime were written for our learning, that we through patience and comfort of the scriptures might have hope. It is those who have no hope who are against God and His word. They are to be pitied because they don't know what they are doing. Ephesians 2.12 says, 'At that time ye were without Christ, being aliens from the commonwealth of Israel and strangers from the covenants of promise, having no hope, and without God in the world." The truth of the matter is that liberalism is teaching people to throw away the only road map that can get them to heaven. The Bible has much to say in its own defense. Psalm 119.89 says, "Forever, O, Lord, thy word is settled in heaven." Matthew 24.35 says, "Heaven and earth shall pass away, but my words shall not pass away." Some church people are being hoodwinked into believing that the Bible is just old fashioned and out dated and in this modern age they think they need to believe science, so called, and evolution and other modern ideas. But be careful, true science is ok and some modern ideas and advancements are helpful. I am just trying to say we can't be too careful because the simple truth is that there is a lot of deceit out there.

Chapter 3

RELIGION

Religion is misunderstood by a large number of people and this is the cause of much confusion. Some-times we hear the expression they got religion, but what did they get? That depends on what ones understanding of religion is. It seems that originally religion meant belief in God or gods or something supernatural, but over time it has evolved to the point that today it can mean much more. It can be some-thing that has a controlling influence on a person. Archaeologists believe that religious beliefs have existed since the first humans.

Evolution is often referred to as a religion and more recently I have heard global warming called a religion. There are many more, such as communism which came into being to overthrow capitalism; and Nazism which started as a political party but came to be religious as well as political. Most of these were anti one thing or another, and many were anti God and anti church. Therefore it is not hard to understand that there are many and varied religions in the world today. The important thing is to know that contrary to popular opinion they do not all get you to heaven. It is often said that religions are like roads and they all lead to the same place; and if you are just sincere, that is what counts. I am reminded of the epithet on a mans tombstone; Here lies the body of William Jay who died maintaining his right of way, he was right, dead right as he sped along, but he is just as dead as if he were wrong. What concerns me is that so many may be on the wrong road and do not know it until it is too late. There is another common mistaken; which is the idea that we must wait until we arrive at the gates of heaven to find out if we are eligible to enter. The Bible says in Acts 16.31, "Believe on the Lord Jesus Christ and you shall be saved." In Romans 10.9 it says, "If thou shalt confess with thy mouth the Lord Jesus and shalt believe in thine heart that God has raised Him from the dead, thou shalt be saved." From these statements it is easy to see that salvation involves more than just being sorry for our sins. Keep these thoughts in mind for now and we will go into more detail later when we consider salvation more completely. I feel we should look at the truth of Christianity first.

Chapter 4

CHRISTIANITY

Christianity is a religion, but it is different from any other known religion. It came into being as the result of the teachings of Jesus in the first century A.D. The Bible gives us this account in Acts 11.25-26. "Then departed Barnabas to Tarsus to seek for Paul. And when he had found him he brought him to Antioch. And it came to pass, that a whole year they assembled themselves with the church, and taught much people. And the disciples were called Christians first in Antioch." The dictionary defines Christianity as the religion based on the belief that Christ is the incarnate Son of God, and on His teachings.

One thing that distinguishes Christianity is the emphasis that is put on love. First, "For God so loved the world that He gave His only begotten Son, that whosoever believes in Him should not perish, but have everlasting life."(John 3.16) Then Jesus told His followers that the greatest commandment is to love

God, and next is to love your fellow man. One time some observers remarked, "Behold how they love one another." Love is noticeably absent in most if not all other religions. Other things mentioned often along with love, are, joy and peace, longsuffering, goodness and kindness. At Jesus' birth the angels said, Glory to God in the highest, and on earth peace, good will toward men." (Luke 2.14) Those of us who read and study the teaching of Jesus realize that His emphasis is on the good.

Some thing to remember in our consideration of what is true; is that there are two forces operating in the world; they are good and evil. God is on the side of good; Satan is on the side of evil. For mankind the battle started in the Garden of Eden, where God told Adam and Eve they could eat of all the fruit in the garden except the fruit of the tree in the middle of the garden. God had told them. "You shall not eat of it, lest you die." (Genesis 2.17) The devil told the woman, "You shall not surely die." (Genesis 3.4) Adam and Eve ate the forbidden fruit and the human race has, suffered the consequences ever since that time. They didn't die physically but it was spiritual death, which they experienced.

Some people do not believe in God and some don't believe the devil is real but multitudes of people know that God is not dead and that the devil is still active. The proof is in the struggle between good and evil that is going on all around us today. It is going on in our public schools to a great extent. The story told about the boy whose dog followed him to school and was sitting outside the door when God came walking by. God reached down and patted the dog on the head and said, "That's alright boy they won't let me in there either." In our colleges and universities it is even worse; where many teachers are ultra liberal and anti God, and anti almost every thing that our country has stood for, for many years. In politics it is getting worse. Never have there been so much hatred and lies, and so many underhanded deals.

A study of history tells us of the great influence Christianity had and is still having in the United States. It is often said that we are a Christian nation but technically we are a nation with a multitude of Christians. Christianity and Christian principles had a great influence in the formation of our nation, its constitution, and its government. Sad to say; these principles are being undermined by those who think they are smarter than God. To them it is more important to be politically correct than to be scriptural. In a short time, compared to many nations, our nation has moved to number one, by following these principles. The big question is, why forsake them now? If it ain't broke don't fix it. It isn't broke yet but it may be cracked. That reminds me of the young lady who told her friend that she was going to marry a rather eccentric millionaire. But, her friend said, "Everyone thinks he's a little bit cracked." "He may be cracked," the young lady said, "but he certainly isn't broke." The simple truth is, some people have agendas of their own that do not make our nation better. They are more interested in personal things like fame, riches, and success. We are not in a war of ideas; we are in a war of beliefs.

Chapter 5

SALVATION

The dictionary says salvation is the saving of the soul from sin and its consequences. This is true but there is more to it. As we know salvation is necessary for us to get to heaven and most everyone wants to go there but many people do not seem to understand exactly how to go about it. We all seem to have a knack for making simple things complicated. Two or three years ago I was at a R.V. park in Arizona and one evening as I went for a walk I was going through a new part of the campground. There were three large motor homes parked together and three couples sitting around outside. While passing a few words with them the subject of heaven was mentioned and one of the ladies said, "I guess we will find out when we get there whether we have lived 'good' enough. I think many people have this mistaken idea. The truth is no one can live good enough because the Bible says, "it's not by works of righteousness which you have done." (Titus 2.5) And "by grace are you saved through faith." (Ephesians 2.8) Jesus said, "Except a man be born again he cannot see the kingdom of God." (John 3.3) Nicodemus, the man to whom Jesus said this, asks Jesus, "How can a man be born when he is old?"(John 3.4) This is something that many do not understand.

What Jesus was talking about was spiritual birth. When we are born in to this world, that is natural birth, and it takes more than that to go to heaven; so like the Philippian jailer we ask, "what must I do to be saved?" (Acts 16.30) The answer given to him was, "believe on the Lord Jesus Christ and thou shalt be saved."(Acts 16.31) The spiritual birth is not a reformation of the old nature but it is a creative act of the Holy Spirit. The important part is the believing on Jesus, this means to believe that He is the Son of God, that He came in to the world and died on a cross for the sins of the world, that He was buried and rose from the dead the third, day and ascended into heaven, there to be with His heavenly Father. It is necessary to believe this and in addition we have to admit we are a sinner in need of forgiveness and repent of our sins and ask for forgiveness. The Holy Spirit does a work of regeneration and the old sinful nature is taken away and a brand new nature takes its place. The old life is replaced with a new life that is eternal. It is all, free, because Jesus paid for it all on the cross when He died there for us. I guess it is hard to grasp because it is so simple and so easy. The scripture says;" for by grace ye are saved, through faith, it is the gift of God."(Ephesians 2.8) Through the new birth the believer becomes a partaker of the divine nature and of the life of Christ Himself. From here on there is freedom because sin no longer has dominion over us, and now we have the righteousness of Christ, so we don't have to get by on ours; but Jesus said in John 14.15, "if ye love me keep My commandments." The scripture sums it all up in John's gospel, chapter three verses sixteen thru eighteen; "For God so loved the world that He gave His only begotten Son, that whosoever believeth in Him should not perish but have everlasting life. For God sent not His Son into the world to condemn the world, but that the world might be saved, through Him. He that believeth on Him is not condemned, but He that believeth not is condemned already because he has not believed in the name of the only begotten Son of God." This is the simple truth about salvation and there is no other way. Jesus said. "I am the way, the truth and the life no one comes to the Father except through me." (John 14.6)

This statement of Jesus eliminates several things that some are depending on for their salvation; such as, I am a church member, or I have been baptized in water, along with, I am sincere in what I believe, and I do the best I can. Nothing else will do; there may be many doors but Jesus is the only way. There just isn't any do it yourself method. The Scripture says in Titus 3.5, "not by works of righteousness, which we have done but according to his (God's) mercy he saved us."

Chapter 6

THE CHURCH

I mentioned that the church cannot save you. Only belief in Jesus can accomplish that. However, after a person is converted the church is very important in their Christian life. There has been some confusion about the church, so we will try to get to the truth of the matter. First we need to understand that there are the local churches and there is, the church of Jesus Christ; which is made up of all born again believers in Jesus Christ. This latter is the church the new believer is baptized, or put into by the Holy Spirit. 1 Corinthians 12:13, "For by one Spirit are we all baptized in to one body, whether we be Jews or Gentiles, whether we be bond or free; and have all been made to drink into one Spirit." This is the true church which had its beginning on the Day of Pentecost, when God sent the Holy Spirit. You can read about it in Acts the second chapter. Jesus Christ is the head of the church, which is called the body of Christ, and later in scripture, is referred to as the Bride of Christ.

Another passage of scripture worth noting is Matthew chapter 16, verses 15-18 "He (Jesus), says unto them, But, whom say ye that I am? And Simon Peter answered and said: Thou art the Christ, the Son of the living God. And Jesus answered and said unto him, Blessed art thou, Simon Barjona for flesh and blood hath not revealed it unto you, but my Father in heaven: And I say, also, unto you, That thou art Peter, and upon this rock I will build my church: and the gates of hell shall not prevail against it." Another translation makes it easier to understand. This is the translation by Kenneth Wuest, who is a Greek scholar. "Spiritually prosperous are you: Simon Barjona, because flesh and blood did not reveal this to you but my Father who is in heaven. Moreover, as for myself, I also am saying to you, you are Rock [petros, masculine in gender, a detached but large fragment of rock], and upon this massive rock [petra, feminine in gender, feminine demonstrative pronoun cannot go back to masculine petros; petra, a rocky peak, a massive rock] I will build my church." All of that seems a bit involved but it is the best that I have found. The reason I went through all of that is that all through the New Testament we are told that Jesus is the head of the church and that He is the chief corner stone.

Chapter 7

THE HOLY SPIRIT

The Holy Spirit, referred to as the third person of the trinity, is sometimes not understood. Before Jesus left His followers to go back to heaven, He told them He would send them another comforter, which He did. The Holy Spirit came on the Day of Pentecost in a new and different capacity. In the Old Testament the Spirit of God was active, striving with men, enlightening, giving wisdom, and strength, and all kinds of help as it was needed. In the Old Testament the Spirit was with them; now in the New Testament, they were told 'He shall be in you.'

We noted previously that the believer is baptized, or put into the church by the Holy Spirit. This is salvation, and is sometimes confused with the baptism of the Holy Spirit, or baptism with the Holy Spirit, but there is another experience. Matthew chapter three and verse eleven explains. "I indeed baptize you with water unto repentance: but He that cometh after me is mightier than I, whose shoes I am not worthy to bear: He shall baptize you with the Holy Ghost with and fire." This is John the Baptist talking about Jesus. We have two different experiences because we have two different people doing the baptizing. In salvation the Holy Spirit does the baptizing, while with the baptism with the Holy Spirit Jesus does the baptizing. If you notice I use Holy Spirit in place of Holy Ghost; the word in Greek is pneuma, and can be translated either way; Spirit or Ghost. Spirit just sounds better to me. I do not believe I am any less spiritual because I say Holy Spirit instead of Holy Ghost, as used in the King James Version.

The importance of the Holy Spirit cannot be over emphasized. Jesus told His disciples that He had not told them certain things at the beginning because He was with them, but now the time had come for Him to go back to His Father who sent Him. John 16:7-11, "Nevertheless I tell you the truth; It is expedient for you that I go away; for if I go not away, the Comforter will not come unto you; but if I depart I will send Him unto you. And when He is come, He will reprove the world of sin, and righteousness, and of judgment: Of sin, because they believe not on me; of righteousness, because I go to My Father, and ye see Me no more; Of judgment, because the prince of this world is judged."

This portion of scripture tells us three important things the Holy Spirit came to do. He reproves the world of sin, but notice that Jesus specifies what the sin is. "Of sin, because they believe not on Me." This is so important because if they do not believe on Him they can't make it to heaven. This is one sin that is unpardonable. The second is in regard to righteousness, because Jesus was going back to heaven, where they could not see Him. He had been with them, as a guide and a helper and now the Holy Spirit would be their helper and their comforter. The third, is of judgment, because, the prince of this world is judged, and condemned. The prince of this world is the devil, or Satan himself. Satan was judged and condemned at the crucifixion of Jesus, but does not reach his final doom until much later. Revelation 20:10; "And the devil that deceived them was cast into the lake of fire and brimstone, where the beast and the false prophet are, and shall be tormented day and night for ever and ever. We shall try to get back to the devil later; and what else the Bible says about him.

For now we will look at what more the Bible says about the Holy Spirit in the New Testament. After Jesus was raised from the grave, and before He ascended into heaven, He, for forty days was seen by many, and spoke to the Apostles of things pertaining to the kingdom of God. "And, being assembled together with them, commanded them that they should not depart from Jerusalem, but wait for the promise of the Father, which, He says, ye have heard of me. For John truly baptized with water: but you shall be baptized with the Holy Ghost not many days hence." (Acts 1:4-5)

Of interest is the fact that Jesus used the phrase, "the promise of the Father." God made many promises but only one called the promise. Another place it is mentioned is in Galatians 3:14, "He redeemed us in order that the blessing given to Abraham might come to the Gentiles through Christ Jesus, so that by faith we might receive the promise of the Spirit" (N.I.V.) This shows to us the importance of the promise of the Holy Spirit. In fact how the Christian relates to the Holy Spirit determines the spiritual life of that person, because, an important work of the Holy Spirit is to teach us the things of Christ, and Jesus is the central focus of all believers. We should never put this experience of the infilling of the Spirit out of its proper place. The fundamental purpose of the baptism of the Spirit is to help Christians be effective witnesses of Christ, and the promise is to all believers; "For the promise is unto you, and to your children, and to all that are afar off, even as many as the Lord our God shall call." (Acts 2:39) The Holy Spirit is not the exclusive property of the Pentecostal churches. All Christians need all the help we can get to spread the gospel of Jesus Christ, and this is what the power of the Spirit can do. This is God's plan; He gave His Son that whosoever believes in Him can have eternal life. Our part is that they hear the good news of the gospel. The pattern is, repent, receive the new birth, take on the character of Christ, be endued with power from on high, and be His witnesses in action and in word.

When Jesus said, "I will send you another comforter," He was talking about more than a quilt. When a very young girl came home from Sunday School, her mother asked her what the lesson was about. Her daughter said, "Don't be scared you'll get your quilt. The mother was mystified and later in the day when she saw the teacher, she ask her what the lesson had been about. The teacher replied, "Fear not your comforter comes." Jesus was talking about things that would be extremely important to His followers. Jesus had been with them, teaching them, leading them, and helping them in many other ways; and now He was leaving and the Holy Spirit would be taking over these duties. Here are a few scriptures. Romans 8:16, "The Spirit itself bears witness with our spirit that we are the children of God." This is important because some think and some are teaching that we can't know that we are born again, but we just have to wait and find out. This would leave all believers in an extremely stressful situation, which it is very difficult to believe a loving and compassionate God would allow. Luke 12:11, "And when they bring you into the synagogues, and unto magistrates, and powers, take ye no thought how or what things you shall answer, or what you shall say: For the Holy Spirit shall teach you in the same hour what ye ought to say." John 14:26, "But the Comforter, which is the Holy Ghost, whom the Father will send in My name, He shall teach you all things, and bring all things to your remembrance, whatsoever I have said unto you." There are more scriptures that mention other characteristics of the Holy Spirit, and He can be rebelled against, lied to, vexed, and blasphemed. Matthew 12:31, "Wherefore I say unto you, all manner of sin and blasphemy shall be forgiven unto men; but the blasphemy against the Holy Ghost shall not be forgiven unto men." So the truth of the matter is that the Holy Spirit is very important. And it behooves all men to act accordingly.

Chapter 8

JESUS CHRIST

Probably the most misunderstood truth in the Bible is the truth about Jesus. As I have said before I don't claim to be an expert but I will try my best to explain this important truth. One thing to know is the fact that not everyone can understand all spiritual truth: This is true because there are two realms, the spiritual, and the natural realm. 1 Corinthians 2:14: But the natural man receives not the things of the Spirit of God; for they are foolishness unto him: neither can he know them, because they are spiritually discerned. The natural man is the person who has not been born again, which is the spiritual birth. For this reason the supernatural is not understood, which is the cause of much confusion, because so many things about Jesus are just that: He came to earth in a supernatural manner. Matthew 1:18, "Now the birth of Jesus Christ was on this wise: When as His mother Mary was espoused to Joseph, before they were come together, she was found with child of the Holy Ghost." Jesus was born; like the Christmas story tells us, in a manger in Bethlehem. Matthew 1:23: "Behold a virgin shall be with child, and shall bring forth a, son and they shall call his name Emmanuel, which being interpreted is, God with us." In John 14.9 Jesus said, "He that hath seen me hath seen the Father." This was one reason Jesus came into the world; to show mankind what the Heavenly Father is like. "God so loved the world that He gave His only begotten Son, that whosoever would believe on Him should not perish, but would have eternal life." Paul the Apostle said in 1 Timothy 1.15, "Christ Jesus came in the world to save Sinners; of whom I am chief." Jesus accomplished that by dying on the cross of Calvary.

There are several false ideas of who Jesus really is. It seems there is some special effort to make Him less than what He really is. Some say He was a good man, others that He was a Prophet; some claim He was an impostor, or a devil, and even that He is the half brother of Satan. If any of these were true all of mankind would be left as sinners on their way to hell. All of these are against the teachings of scripture concerning Jesus: So this is what the Bible refers to as antichrist.

Along with His supernatural birth, Jesus lived a supernatural life; healing multitudes of people, and performing many miracles. Jesus came to be a mediator. 1 Timothy 2:5 reads, "For there is one God, and one mediator between God and men, the man Christ Jesus." This means that we commune with

God through Jesus, and only Jesus; just like we are born again only by Jesus Christ, who said, "I am the way, the truth, and the life, no man can come to the Father but by Me." (John 14.6) Jesus was miraculously taken back to heaven to be with His Father. Acts 1:8-9 reads, "But you shall receive power, after the Holy Ghost is come upon you: and you shall be witnesses unto me both in Jerusalem, and in Judea, and in Samaria, and unto the uttermost parts of the earth. And when He had spoken these things, while they beheld, He was taken up; and a cloud received Him out of their sight." All of this makes it difficult for those who do not believe in the supernatural to come to know Jesus as their Savior and Lord.

In addition to showing us what God is like, and making a way of salvation for all mankind; Jesus also came to destroy the works of the devil; 1John, 3:8 says, He that committeth sin is of the devil: for the devil sinneth from the beginning. For this purpose the Son of God was manifested, that He might destroy the works of the devil. The devil has been busy deceiving, and still is deceiving people, and there is a great amount of lying and deceit going on all around us, which makes it necessary for us to search diligently for the truth. Another thing that Jesus came for was to show God's love for sinners. We read in 1 John, 4:8, 'He that loves not knows not God; for God is love. In this was manifested the love of God toward us, because God sent His only begotten Son into the world, that we might live, through Him." Jesus said in John 10.10, "I am come that they might have life, and that they might have it more abundantly,"

Some think that real Christians can't get any enjoyment out of life, but this is a mistaken idea, because many things are included in this abundant life. To mention a few, there is a clear conscience, which is very good to have: when I was in the service I would go to bed and almost instantly be asleep. One night when we were close enough to the front lines that we could hear our artillery shells going out and hear the enemy shells coming in, I had just hit the sack, but had not gone to sleep, one of my buddies said, "That's what a clear conscience will do for you." Along with a good conscience, the believer has peace and joy; 2 Corinthians: 9:8, says, "And God is able to make all grace abound toward you; that ye, always having all sufficiency in all things, may abound to every good work." Philippians 4.19, says, "But my God shall supply all your needs according to His riches in glory by Christ Jesus." One other thing is freedom; and it is a very good thing to be free. John, 8:32, "And ye shall know the truth, and the truth shall make you free."

Chapter 9

THE TRUTH ABOUT TRUTH

The question above all questions is what is truth? The dictionary that I have defines truth as, 1.The quality of being true. 2. Something that is true.

True is defined as 1.In accordance with fact. 2. In accordance with correct principles or an accepted standard, rightly so called, genuine and not false. 3. Exact, accurate.

I don't know who was first to ask the question, but it may have been Pilate. Jesus had been talking to Pilate; He said, "To this end was I born, and for this cause came I into the world, that I should bear witness to the truth. Every one that is of the truth hears my voice." Pilate said unto Him, "What is truth?" (John 18.37-38) After Pilate said this he went out and talked to the Jews and told them he could find no fault in Jesus at all. Pilate didn't give Jesus a chance to answer, but in John's gospel, chapter 14, verse 6, Jesus said to Thomas, "I am the way, the truth, and the life: no man cometh to the Father, but by me." Soon after this Jesus was praying to His Heavenly Father, in behalf of His followers, He prayed, "Sanctify them through thy truth: thy word is truth." Later the Apostle John in his first Epistle wrote, "it is the Spirit that beareth witness, because the Spirit is truth." (1 John 5.6) So we have the answer to the question: Jesus is the truth, God's word is truth, the Spirit is truth, and the Gospel is truth. The tragedy is that so many just do not want to accept the truth and some people will do most any thing too avoid obeying the truth.

While we are on the subject there is another verse of scripture we ought to take a look at, which has to do with truth. 2 Timothy 2:15 reads, "Study to show thyself approved unto God, a workman that needeth not to be ashamed, rightly dividing the word of truth." I think no other book is read like the Bible is read. People pick it up and open it up and read a little. The next time they open it at another place and read some more. That is better than not reading it at all, but it is no wonder that so many say they can't understand it. No one would read a letter that way, or most other books. Maybe they would read a book of poetry or a book of jokes that way.

This scripture mentioned study and there are a few guidelines for bible study. It is important to approach the Bible with an open mind, with the idea of learning what you can. To start with some preconceived idea, and try to prove it, is the wrong way to go about it. It can be made to say almost anything, by skipping around, just as you could with any other book: or like the politicians are doing today. It amuses me when the president or someone makes a speech. They tell us what their going to say, the speaker makes their speech, then they tell us what the speaker said, then they tell us what he really meant by what he said.

In bible study it is always a good idea to take what it says literally: However, this is not always possible because parts of the Bible are symbolical, or in parables, and scholars who are not literalists, can, and do make the Bible say almost any thing they want it to. We are warned against adding to or taking away from what the Bible says, and the consequences are quite severe, if we do. Another helpful thing to do is to compare scripture with scripture. For this it is helpful to have a concordance. It is important to pray for understanding; and remember that the Bible tells us that the Spirit of truth, the Holy Spirit, will guide us into truth, however, like an automobile, we have to be moving, in order to be guided.

I realize that most of us are busy, but it is like someone said to the Pastor who was explaining how busy he is; "we all have the same amount of time." The pastor acted a little embarrassed, as he admitted that it was true. Some times it would be nice if the days were longer but God knew what He was doing when He made them. The point is that as important as the Bible is, and as important as it is to our spiritual well being, we need to spend an adequate amount of time reading and studying it.

Chapter 10

FREEDOM

"Then said Jesus to those Jews who believed on Him, continue in my word, then are you my disciples indeed: And you shall know the truth and the truth shall make you free." John. 8: 31, 32. Free of what? We are Americans and we are told all the time that we are free. There is more than one kind of freedom; there is spiritual freedom and there are other freedoms, like mental freedom, social freedom and political freedom. The Jews told Jesus that they were Abraham's seed and were never in bondage to any man.(v.33) Jesus was talking about spiritual freedom.

The unconverted are in bondage because of the world, sin, and the devil. The Scripture tells us we were in bondage under the elements of the world, and in Romans 6.12-14 it says, "Let not sin therefore reign in your mortal body, that you should obey it in the lusts thereof. Neither yield your members as instruments of unrighteousness unto sin: but yield yourselves unto God as those that are alive from the dead, and your members as instruments of righteousness unto God. For sin shall not have dominion over you." Most unbelievers are like these Jews, in that they have no realization that they are in bondage; they think they are free and doing just what they want to do. Consequently they don't know that they need to be set free.

Paul in his Epistle to the Romans has the solution: chapter 6:17-18, "But God be thanked, that ye were the servants of sin, but ye have obeyed from the heart that form of doctrine which was delivered unto you. Being then made free from sin, you became the servants of righteousness." Notice a strange thing here, Paul is saying you were a servant of sin but now you are a servant of righteousness. The difference is, that in times past the yielding was to sin and the devil which leads to death, but now being free from sin, the yielding is to God and righteousness which leads to life: Therefore, stand fast in the liberty wherewith Christ has made us free, and be not entangled again with the yoke of bondage. (Galatians 5.1) According to the Bible the unconverted are spiritually dead. Here again in the same way that we had two types of freedom; we have physical death and spiritual death. It is extremely important in bible study that we keep this straight; otherwise we will find ourselves in much confusion. For example there is a man speaking on the radio, who is not a Preacher, but sets himself up as being more informed than all bible scholars. He teaches that because the sinner is spiritually dead he cannot do any thing, physically, to bring about his spiritual conversion, while the Bible says, believe on the Lord Jesus Christ and you shall be saved. What this man is doing is teaching a confusing falsehood because he is switching from one death to another.

He is saying that the spiritually dead person, who is alive, physically, cannot believe, which is physical activity. That may be a roundabout way of saying it, but with that kind of reasoning much false teaching comes forth, and people are deceived.

Although spiritual freedom is more important because it is eternal; there are other freedoms on the natural plane, which are important to all of us. I know some among us think they are too spiritual to be involved in politics and other mundane things in every day life. However in the Old Testament the spiritual things and the things of ever day life were all intermingled. We are inclined to departmentalize everything and this is not good, because people are inclined to live one way in church and any way they take a notion to the rest of the time. It seems that when Jesus was raised from the dead and ascended into heaven, He expected us to occupy until He came again; this being true we need to be involved and do what we can in whatever way we can. One thing we can all do is to vote every chance we get.

In my life time I have seen us lose some freedoms, and if the Liberals continue as they have been of late, things can get much worse. The truth of the matter is, that our rights do not come from the government, they come from God; However the government seems to be able to take them away; and if they could do away with the constitution and do something about God, which they are working on, things can become much worse.

What we needed are more people to accept the challenge as something worth doing and the feeling that something is expected of us. Too many people are like the old guy; they said he has just about had it; he never gets a new idea, and never gets rid of an old one. Insanity is when you keep doing the same thing and expect a different result. That reminds me of congress, here in 2007. And that in turn reminds me of the note on the hand drier; Push button for message from congress. Something to think about when voting: Someone said that Lawyers don't make good Politicians because they are taught to argue either side of the problem: consequently they are not good problem solvers. I don't know, but it is some thing to think about. Here is another bit of information that I just ran across, 20 million Christians do not vote, and if you don't vote, you are legalizing sin. That is putting it on the line, and it could be true. When you think about it, 20 million votes could determine the outcome in many elections in these days when we have so many very close elections. In these times, where so many issues are the difference between good and evil it becomes more serious, and the responsibility is much greater. It is not a mater of politics; it is a matter of morality. Jesus came into the world to destroy the works of the devil, and we are living in a time when the works of the devil are running rampant, and we need to make every effort to do all we can in the battle for the right. The spiritual way is to over come evil with good. History has proven that most times good people do nothing until it is too late, but it doesn't have to be that way.

In 1941 Franklin D. Roosevelt said he looked forward to a world founded upon four essential freedoms; Freedom of Speech, Freedom of Worship, Freedom from Want, and Freedom from Fear. After 66 years have passed it is hard to say how much we have gained or lost. It would make an interesting study, but I will leave that to someone more qualified than I am. We can look at a few of the most obvious changes. We still have freedom of speech, but it must be politically correct; the law hasn't changed much if any, but if you stop and think about it you must admit that it puts pressure on you to be careful what you say and who you say it about. One thing that causes concern is that it is lopsided; that means untrue, for example when it comes to religion, especially Christianity; which has been crowded out of our Public Schools in many places. In our institutions of higher learning it is even worse; there some religions are welcome, but not Christianity. They even have teachers of other cultures and religions that are opposed to our way of life, and our form of Government. That, they maintain, is tolerance, but at the same time there is extreme intolerance for God, Christianity and our way of life.

Chapter 11

THE U.S. CONSTITUTION

How much did you learn about our constitution during your years of education? Not much if your education was like mine; consequently, most of you can likely say with me, I am no expert. Nevertheless there are some things I have learned, that I believe to be true.

I heard to an Author being interviewed; who seemed well informed about many things: but he and the interviewer both spoke of the separation of Church and State, which is not in the constitution; what the constitution did was to prevent Congress from making a State Church such as existed in England where the framers of the constitution were from. Many countries have a mixture of religious and secular authority. The U.S.A. is different in one aspect; that it was founded on the one true God not on religion; a difference I attempted to explain earlier. I am not saying all of our founders were born again Christians, for some of them were Deists, who believed in Christian principles, such as creation, providence, and Jesus, in some respects, and in heaven. This is much different from a group of religious men. By putting this clause in the Constitution, Congress is prevented from forming a State Church. But it is not to be interpreted to mean that we take every thing Christian out of everything: like the Ten Commandments out of public places, God and Jesus out of schools, and changing traditional holidays. For many years God has blessed our nation so why try to kick Him out now. As we have considered before, there are two sides and only two: they are good, and evil, or putting it another way, godliness and ungodliness. Which do we want our nation to be? Anyone who wants to see what happens to ungodly nations needs only, to do a little research in the Old Testament of the Bible, where you will find that they came to destruction. The truth of the matter is that when good men do nothing, evil triumphs. Those of us, who are believers, know that in the end good will triumph. All through the Bible we are told that God will win, and the devil will lose. Those who don't believe will have to wait until later to be convinced. Proverbs 14:34, "Righteousness exalts a nation: but sin is a reproach to any people." I just now listened to someone read the Ten Commandments, which made me wonder, what would our nation be like if we did not have them? Think about it.

The second amendment, which guarantees the right of the people to keep and bear arms, is much debated. The simple truth is, as I see it, when the constitution was formed, they realized the need for the people to be armed in case of attack. Many things have changed since that time, and things can change much more rapidly today. During the previous administration our military was reduced to the point that at the present time our armed forces are spread so thin that it is working hardship on many people. If the wrong people get in power anything can happen, and it could happen rapidly. Some nations have been taken over by undesirable people; this happened because when the people rebelled they only had clubs and pitchforks for weapons: their guns had been taken from them.

It is interesting to read about how our constitution came into existence. It wasn't easy: there were several smart men working on it. They had differing opinions, which they debated over a period of time before coming up with, what is the oldest written national constitution in operation. Some of them gave credit to divine guidance; but I am certain they had no idea as to what they had accomplished. They came out with a balance between authority and liberty by limiting the power of the government and securing the liberty of citizens. It is a continual struggle to keep it in balance, for there are always those who want to change things. You have no doubt noticed that right now there is great pressure to have the government do more and more, which in turn takes away more and more of the freedom of the people. At the same time they are telling us, the people want this and the people want that, but let us remember that someone has to pay for it, and guess who that is. It is government of the people, by the people, and for the people, and it is paid for by the same people; and don't forget it. Someone recently came out with a poll that said a large percentage of the people said they wanted free health care, but I wonder if they ask them if they wanted their taxes raised.

We the people need to listen very carefully, because we are being told half truths, and many things with only an element of truth in them, and worse yet, out and out lies. If they could get God out of it completely they could do away with the truth altogether. However the formers of the constitution put in other safeguards when they put in the three branches of government, which give checks and balances against each other. They are, the legislative, the executive, and the judicial branches, and as they all work like they are intended to, they guarantee individual liberty and strike a balance between authority and liberty. As good citizens we need to keep informed on what is going on, and listen carefully and as the saying goes, only believe half of what you hear, and pray for wisdom to know which half.

Two Historians were discussing the history of the major nations, and telling how all but the United States had gone through a period of decline both in morality, and in power. They attributed this to the fact that the United States held to the principles spelled out in our constitution.

In a country where the U.S. has spent many dollars and shed blood, a recent case has turned perception on its head; Despite a host of trimmings and platitudes, this country's constitution promises freedom, tolerance, and human rights, But when it was recently learned that a man had, in 1990, converted to Christianity, he was arrested and condemned to die. People around the world were shocked, and after much outcry, and pressure, the President of this country put an end to this bizarre spectacle by allowing the condemned man to seek asylum in another country: but only after the man was declared unfit for trial, which meant that because he believed in Jesus Christ he was deemed mentally ill. This country assured the American public that this case was anomalous, which meant it was an irregularity. The truth of this matter is; instead of being justice; this was an object lesson in the reversal of Simple Truth.

Happenings like this are hard for us in America to grasp, for the simple reason that our country has its foundation on different principles, which are the principles of a different God: a God of love and mercy, the Bible is full of instances of His loving kindness and tender mercies. He is a God that has no pleasure in the death of the wicked. He requires righteousness from man but saves the unrighteous through sacrifice. In turn people of other nations which are founded on principles other than the principles of God, do not understand us, for the reason that the unconverted mind does not understand spiritual principles; and another thing that must be confusing to them is that they think we are a Christian nation, with every citizen being a Christian, when in reality many of us are Christian in name only, and do not act

like Christians, so as a result all of us are branded as
hypocrites.

Chapter 12

CIVILIZATION

It's not you and it's not me, it is us. Whoever thought that up was on the right track and it goes along with the following.

What ails civilization is too much jealousy and selfishness interfering with the minds of the people who order the world's work. They don't care for the ship as long as they get what they think they have coming to them; in rank, wages, shore leaves, and pensions. All the way down the line of human action, the machinery of progress is screechingly hot with the friction of personalities yelping for preferment. What civilization needs is a crew that understands the nature of the obligation to the ship.

I guess we have always had some of this kind of people, but it seems we have more of late; or maybe they are just more vocal. The news is flooded with criticism of our country to the point that it seems that these vocal people are more on the side of the enemy.

Instead of being concerned about the security of our country they are concerned about their own agendas. They want liberty but liberty can't stand alone. It hinges on other things. First, there is responsibility. Liberty without responsibility is only a façade. Real liberty can exist only through everyone having complete responsibility for the outcome of his own behavior. Man has freedom of choice and he must be responsible for his choices. Second is opportunity. Opportunity for everyone exists best where the State controls least. Supplied security is poison to opportunity and responsibility. When man has his security supplied he becomes less responsible for the results of his activities. Security makes man a drain upon society. If we seek security by giving up responsibility or opportunity we actually lose all three. Security exists only in prison, where all of ones needs are met. Of course, there isn't much liberty in one of those places. Third is belief in God. Without a belief in an, all powerful Supreme Being, civilizations decline and all elements of liberty disappear. Belief is the foundation upon which civilization is built. Belief in God is the most important element because without it responsibility and opportunity and liberty cannot exist. It seems some politicians want the government to do everything for as many people as they possibly can in order to get their votes. In order to do this they have to raise a tax, which usually has several unfavorable effects. There is a law that when profits increase unemployment decreases. Unearned security violated the law of production and works against liberty. If there is a lack of performance profits disappear and eventually there is no employment of the talents and abilities of the workers.

Here are some things that are having a great amount of influence on our civilization. We have worshiped other gods and called it multiculturalism. We have endorsed perversion and called it alternative life style. We have exploited the poor and called it the lottery. We have neglected the needy and called it self-preservation. We have rewarded laziness and called it welfare. We have killed the unborn and called it choice. We have shot abortionists and called it justifiable. We have neglected to discipline our children and called it building self esteem. We have abused power and called it political savvy. We have coveted our neighbors' possessions, and called it ambition. We have polluted the air with profanity and pornography and called it freedom of expression. We have ridiculed the time honored, values of our forefathers and called it enlightenment.

Then, there is what some Feminists say they believe and stand for.

1. No woman should be allowed to stay home and raise her children.
2. The end of the institution of marriage is a necessary condition for the liberation of women. The institution of marriage has failed and we must destroy it.
3. The care of children is infinitely better left to the trained practitioners. The fact that children are raised in families means that there is no equality. In order to raise children with

equality we must take them away from families and communally raise them.
4. Overthrowing capitalism is too small for us; we must overthrow the whole patriarchy.
5. To raise children to believe in human potential, not God.
6. We must go back to ancient female religion like witchcraft.
7. We must destroy love. Love promotes vulnerability, dependency, possessiveness, susceptibility to pain, and prevents the full development of women's human potential.

Someone hit the nail on the head with the following. The biggest guns of hell are zeroed in on the home and family, and the church, and anyone in them. The family pew is more important than the family purse.

Perhaps the deepest cause of moral confusion is the state of language itself; language that has been bleached of its moral distinctions, and turned neutral and value free and nonjudgmental. When that happens, moral discourse becomes difficult, moral distinction impossible and moral debate incomprehensible. If homosexuality is merely sexual preference then what is wrong with it, and all the things connected with it? But there is a fuss because there is a difference. But you can't understand either side with language that refuses to make distinctions. If abortion is simply termination of pregnancy, the moral equivalent of removing a tumor, how do you account for a movement of serious people dedicated to its abolition?

Thinking about these things I wonder how we came to be this kind of a nation in this comparatively short time? I don't know that I can answer that but here are a few things to consider. 1. As a nation we forsook our belief in any absolutes. 2. As a nation we threw over our belief in cause and effect. 3. As a nation we lost our belief in the need for personal restraint and discipline. 4. As a nation we emphasized the rights of our citizens rather than their responsibilities. 5. As a nation we decided to protect the deviant and deprecate the normal.

Along with these reasons there are two other things that come to mind. One is on our money. In God we trust. The other is. One nation under God; Of course there are efforts to change that. In fact I heard recently something about a proposal to put, In God we trust on the edge of the coins, or on the edge of some coins. There have always been those who are opposed to God, and in the end they are left behind. The winners are the ones on God's side.

Some times it looks like evil is winning, which causes some to feel helpless, and helplessness in turn can cause panic. That is when blazing determination is necessary. The end of helplessness is the beginning of success. And one of the principle aspects of the human species is the ability to feel deeply about things, and God gives us such a generous supply of beautiful emotions: love, hope, faith, the will to live, creativity, joyfulness, purpose, and determination: and it seems a shame to have them unexercised. We

are indeed fortunate to have more such people, than
is often realized. The United States has always had
more than its share of unsung heroes. Here is a poem
I found in my notes,

> Ah yes, it's easy to be a starter,
> But are you a sticker too?
> T'is fun sometimes to begin a thing.
> But hard to see it through;
> Yet sometimes failure is best,
> to keep you from being too sure.
> Success that is built on defeat you know,
> Will often times longest endure.
> T'is the sticker who wins in the battle of life:
> While the quitter is laid on the shelf.
> You are never defeated, remember this;
> Until you loose faith in your self.
>
> -author unknown

Chapter 13

CREATION

To accept creation you must first accept God. And to accept the existence of God takes faith. "But without faith it is impossible to please God: for he that comes to God must believe that He is, and that He is a rewarder of them that diligently seek Him." (Hebrews 11:6) In Exodus 3.14 God said, "I am, that I am." Thus showing the eternity of God, that is also mentioned in Psalms. 93:2, "Thy throne is established of old: Thou art from everlasting." And Psalms. 90:2, "Before the mountains were brought forth, or ever thou hadst formed the earth and the world, even from everlasting to everlasting, thou art God." The eternity of Jesus appears in Colossians 1:17: "And He (Jesus) is before all things, and by Him all things consist." Also in John 1:1, "In the beginning was the Word, (Jesus) and the Word was with God, and the Word was God. The same was in the beginning with God."

The eternity of the Holy Spirit is mentioned in Hebrews 9:14, "How much more shall the blood of Christ, who through the eternal Spirit offered Himself without spot to God, purge your conscience from dead works to serve the living God?" There is one thing more that existed in the beginning. Proverbs 8:12, 22-31, "I wisdom dwell with prudence, and find out knowledge of witty inventions... The Lord possessed me in the beginning of His way, before His works of old. I was set up from everlasting, from the beginning, or ever the earth was. When there were no depths, I was brought forth; when there were no fountains abounding with water. Before the mountains were settled, before the hills was I brought forth: While as yet He had not made the earth, or the fields, or the highest part of the dust of the world. When He prepared the heavens, I was there: when He set a compass upon the face of the depth: When He established the clouds above: when He strengthened the fountains of the deep: When He gave to the sea His decree, that the waters should not pass His commandment: when He appointed the foundations of the earth: Then I was by Him, as one brought up with Him: and I was daily his delight rejoicing always before him. Rejoicing in the habitable part of His earth; and my delights were with the sons of men." That is a lot of scripture, and you could have looked it up yourself: But I suspect that most of you would not.

Now let us look at the creation of the world, according to the Bible. "In the beginning God created the heavens and the earth. And the earth was without form, and void; and darkness was upon the face of the deep. And the Spirit of God moved upon the face of the waters. And God said, let there be light: and there was light. And God saw the light, that it was good: and God divided the light from the darkness. And God called the light day, and the darkness He called night. And the evening and the morning were the first day. And God said, Let there be a firmament in the midst of the waters. And let it divide the waters from the waters. And God made the firmament, and divided the waters which were under the firmament from the waters which were above the firmament: and it was so. And God called the firmament heaven. And the evening and the morning were the second day.

And every plant of the field before it was in the earth, and every herb of the field before it grew: for the Lord God had not caused it to rain upon the earth, and there was not a man to till the ground. But there went up a mist from the earth, and watered the whole face of the ground. And God said let the waters under the heaven be gathered together to one place, and let the dry land appear: and it was so. And God called the dry land earth; and the gathering together of the waters called He Seas: and God saw that it was good. And God said; Let the earth bring forth grass, the herb yielding seed, and the fruit tree yielding fruit after his kind, whose seed is in itself, upon the earth: and it was so. And the earth brought forth grass, and herb yielding seed after his kind, and the tree yielding fruit, whose seed was in its self, after his kind: and

God saw that it was good. And the evening and the morning were the third day.

And God said, Let there be lights in the firmament of the heaven to divide the day from the night; and let them be for signs, and for seasons, and for days, and years: And let them be for lights in the firmament of the heaven to give light upon the earth, and it was so. And God made two great lights; the greater light to rule the day, and the lesser light to rule the night: he made the stars also. And God set them in the firmament of the heaven to give light upon the earth, and to rule over the day and over the night, and to divide the light from the darkness: and God saw that it was good. And the evening and the morning were the fourth day.

And God said: Let the waters bring forth abundantly the moving creature that has life, and the fowl that may fly above the earth in the open firmament of heaven. And God created great whales, and every living creature that moves, which the waters brought forth abundantly, after their kind, and every winged fowl after his kind: and God saw that it was good. And God blessed them, saying, be fruitful, and multiply, and fill the waters of the seas, and let the fowl multiply in the earth. And the evening and the morning are the fifth day.

And God said, Let the earth bring forth the living creature after his kind, cattle, and creeping thing and beast of the earth after his kind; and it was so. And God made the beast of the earth after his kind and cattle after their kind, and every creeping thing that creeps upon the earth. And God saw that it was good.

And God said; let us make man in our image, after our likeness: and let them have dominion over the fish of the sea, and the fowl of the air, and over the cattle, and over the earth, and over every creeping thing that creeps upon the earth.

And the Lord God formed man of the dust of the ground, and breathed into his nostrils the breath of life; and man became a living soul. This is the book of the generations of Adam. In the day that God created man, in the likeness of God, made he him. And the Lord God said it is not good that man should be alone; I will make a help meet for him. And out of the ground the Lord God formed every beast of the field and every fowl of the air; and brought them to Adam to see what he would call them: and whatsoever Adam called every living creature that was the name thereof. And Adam gave names to all cattle, and to the fowl of the air and to every beast of the field; but for Adam there was not found an help meet for him. And the Lord caused a deep sleep to fall upon Adam, and he slept: and He took one of his ribs, and closed up the flesh thereof; and the rib, which the Lord God had taken from man, made He a woman, and brought her to the man. And Adam said this is now bone of my bones, and flesh of my flesh: she shall be called Woman, because she was taken out of man. And Adam called his wife's name Eve; because she was the mother of all living. So God created man in His own image, in the image of God created He him; male and female created He them. And God blessed them, and God said to them, be fruitful, and multiply, and replenish the earth, and subdue it: and have dominion over the fish of the sea, and over the fowl of the air, and over every living thing that moves upon the earth.

And on the seventh day God ended His work which He had made; and He rested on the seventh day from all His work which He had made. And God blessed the seventh day, and sanctified it: because that in it He had rested from all His work which God created and made.

I want to mention that this account of creation is taken from a chronological bible, which has taken the creation account from the first two chapters of Genesis, and arranged it in chronological order. In other bibles chapter 1, gives the account, and chapter 2, elaborates on it. The chronological arrangement makes it a little easier to understand.

Something to notice is that God had a plan. He didn't haphazardly throw things together. First He formed the earth, and then He filled it with plants and animals. After He divided the seas from the land He filled the seas with living creatures. God said, Let there be a firmament; and He called the firmament heaven, then He filled the heavens with stars and planets. God also did some dividing: He divided light from darkness, the dry land from the water, and the waters above from the water beneath the firmament. Seems a little more orderly than the theory of evolution; And a whole lot quicker.

After God created the world He didn't leave it to chance; He put man in charge. He blessed them and said to them, "be fruitful, multiply, and replenish the earth, and subdue it; and have dominion over it."

(Genesis 1.28) God finished His plan by making a wife for Adam, thereby establishing marriage and the family. Adam named his wife Eve; because she was the mother of all living. Verse 24 of Chapter 2, says, "Therefore: shall a man leave his father and mother, and shall cleave to his wife: And they shall be one flesh."

Chapter 14

THE THEORY OF EVOLUTION

I listened to a Bio Chemist talking about Intelligent Design, a subject that has been in the news of late. I don't know much about it, except what the name implies, but it seems to be sort of a compromise: But God doesn't compromise, and I do not think He wants His followers to. God is a God of love and peace, but He is a God of justice and right. To the repentant, God is forgiving, but to the rebellious He can be harsh.

We need to remember that until a theory has been disproved: no matter how fantastic it may appear in the light of our present knowledge: it should be given the respect due to a proposition that might be proved; sometime. The creation account is the statement of a fact, not a theory, but shouldn't it be given the same consideration? It is like the fellow said, when ask about the Bible account, "It is quite a story, but it hasn't ever been disproved," Basically it is just one sentence: "In the beginning God created the heaven and the earth."

This is the Bibles declaration of the origin of the material universe. The opposition says prove it, but it doesn't need to be proven: only believed. It takes faith, just like it takes faith to believe God when He says," I am." Some say I can't believe that, but they turn around and believe a theory that takes a lot more faith to believe. Many years a go when I first heard that someone thought we came from apes, as a child I thought they were crazy, and through all the years I haven't changed much. Now I might say they are badly misinformed.

Reason can rest in this statement: God created the heaven and the earth, as it cannot possibly do in any theory that leaves God out of the picture, and declares that the first cause was more or less the result of accident, or the existence of laws without mind, or of order without thought. It is much simpler to take at face value, the scripture that says: "He that comes to God; must believe that He is, and that He is a rewarder of them that diligently seek Him." (Hebrews 11.6) Another thing is that it is much quicker: It doesn't take millions of years. The creation story bridges the gulfs that have held up evolutionists for years and years; like the missing link, and many other problems that they have. This missing link problem is easily explained. God said, "Let the earth bring forth the living creatures after his kind,"_(Genesis 1.24). And they do not change from one species to another, and when He made man there was a change in the process; He said, "let us make man in our image, after our likeness and let them have dominion." (Genesis 1.26) "And the Lord God formed man of the dust of the ground and breathed into his nostrils the breath of life; and man became a living soul. (Genesis 2.7) If the evolutionists had read the Bible a little more closely they could have saved themselves a lot of trouble.

The simple truth is that evolution, like other false religions, started with an element of truth and added much theory and many false assumptions. Darwin began by studying evolution within certain species, which he found to be true then, and it continues to be true today. To this, through the years much has been added, until now many people are deceived, and believe much to be true; which is not true, or at best is only more theory. It has been said that Christianity resisted Evolution. But it seems it was the other way around. Evolution was, and is anti God and anti Christ and against Christianity and the Bible in general. Evolution is called a science; but in reality it is more like a religion. Science is defined as a branch of knowledge requiring systematic study and method. After about one hundred and fifty years what do they have? Evolution remains a theory; and remains further from the truth than Darwin was after his twenty years or more of study and writing. Darwinism hasn't done very well answering the age-old questions: Where did I come from? Why am I here? Where do I go from here?

The Bible answers these questions without difficulty. One of evolutions biggest arguments is that evolution is science and the Bible is not. The basic definition of science is that it is a branch of knowledge. The definition of knowledge is. 1. Knowing. 2. All that a person knows. 3. All that is known, an organized body of information.

Darwin's information concerning the altering of the species by various influences was probably correct. But when he, or later, some of his followers tried to carry it over to change from one species to another, they came in to conflict with what God had done in creation, which was to create each species after its kind, which prevents a monkey from turning into a man.

Another situation that the evolutionists created for themselves is brought out in, Romans 1:28, "And even as they did not like to retain God in their knowledge, God gave them over to a reprobate mind, to do things that are not convenient." Of course if they don't believe there is a God they don't believe that either, but I guess that is their problem. This scripture says that those who didn't like to retain God in their knowledge would do things that are not convenient, or not proper, which fits what Darwinism is doing with their lies and deceit. They have made their science, so called, their God, and denied the true and living God. True science is mans servant, but never his God.

The Bible says in Psalm 14.1, "The fool has said in his heart. There is no God. They are corrupt, they have done abominable works, there are none that doeth good." Evolution has made great inroads, and has promoted itself, until it has taken over our education system, and crowded Christianity out to a great extent. It can be taught as fact in our schools, while to teach creation is out. Our nation needs to wake up. As a nation we have gone down hill in some respects, and this is one of them. Our schools came into being so our citizens could read the Bible for themselves. Our first Colleges were founded as Christian institutions. Now there are efforts being made to exclude Christianity from our Public School System, and our institutions of, so called higher learning, are sometimes more like hot beds of immorality, and un-Americanism, along with anti God and anti Christ teaching.

John the Apostle writes about this in his second epistle, in the seventh and eighth verse, "For many deceivers are entered into the world, who confess not that Jesus Christ is come in the flesh. This is a deceiver and an antichrist. Look to yourselves, that we lose not those things which we have wrought, but that we receive a full reward." We know that if we are on Gods side, we are on the winning side, and will win in the end. In the mean time we ought to do what we can to stop the tide, so to speak. It is the same old battle, of good against evil; and we know good triumphs over evil in the end.

Chapter 15

WORLDLINESS

Here again we are up against an extremely large subject, and I do not claim to answer all the questions. I only hope to get to the simple truth of the matter. To begin we need to remember that, as Christians we are in the world, but not of the world. This presents many problems, because God has a plan and the world doesn't go along. Therefore; we have a conflict. The Bible tells us to not love the world; and, of course the world returns the favor; so to speak. The Apostle John, in the fifteenth chapter of his gospel records some things that Jesus said about the subject. "These things I command you, that ye love one another. If the world hates you, ye know it hated me before it hated you. If you were of the world, the world would love its own: but because ye are not of the world, but I have chosen you out of the world, therefore the world hateth you." (John 15.17-19) The dictionary definition makes this a little more understandable. Worldly: 1. of or belonging to life on earth, not spiritual. 2. devoted to the pursuit of pleasure or material gains or advantage. Christians, world wide, need to read that, and think seriously about it. One problem is that the world thinks it is not politically correct for Christians to take this attitude, and act accordingly: But they think it is alright for them to treat Christians just like the world treated Jesus when he was on earth.

The important thing for the followers of Christ to understand is that we can't live like the world: Because we don't want to go where the world is headed. We must set different goals. The world's goals, among others, are money, pleasure, and happiness. Jesus, however, said, "Seek ye first the kingdom of God, and his righteousness and all these other things shall be added unto you." (Matthew 6.33) It just makes good sense to do it God's way. I know the pressure is great to be like everyone else. That is what happened to God's people all through the Old Testament. The nations around then worshiped idols, so God's people worshiped idols: Then God's judgment came upon them; over and over this happen to them. But we ought to profit by their mistakes.

Many Christians have had the mistaken idea that worldliness was just a matter of doing some certain things that were considered to be sinful. But in reality it is having your life molded by the world: And controlled by the world. The Bible speaks of being in bondage to the world, and of being set free from the world, the flesh, and the devil at the time of salvation. It seems like some think it is too hard, but

Jesus didn't think that. Just before He went back to heaven He prayed to His Heavenly Father concerning His followers. "I have given them thy word; and the world hath hated them, because they are not of the world, even as I am not of the world. I pray not that thou shouldst take them out of the world, but that thou shouldest keep them from the evil. They are not of the world, even as I am not of the world. Sanctify them through thy truth: thy word is truth." (John 17.14-17)

Even though we are in a serious war between good and evil there is another angle to consider. "For God so loved the world; that He gave His only begotten Son; that whosoever believeth on Him, should not perish but have everlasting life. For God sent not His Son into the world to condemn the world: but that the world through Him might be saved." (John 3.16-17) Also we are told, "this gospel of the kingdom shall be preached in all the world for a witness to all nations: Then shall the end come." (Matthew 24.14)

Gods plan is quite extensive but at the same time it is simple. In the beginning God created man in His own image, with a will of his own, which means that man is free to make decisions of his own. Then God put the man and his wife in a beautiful place, with every thing they needed, and they had full freedom, except for one restriction. They were forbidden to eat the fruit of one tree in the middle of the garden. They disobeyed and ate it; and by doing so, they became sinners; and it doesn't stop with them; they passed it down to all mankind; so all are sinners; and all come short of the glory of God. Consequently, everyone is born with a sinful nature. The Bible calls it being in bondage to sin; that is why everyone must be born again to get to heaven. It is explained in John 3:18, "He that believeth on him (Jesus) is not condemned: but he that believeth not is condemned already, because he hath not believed in the name of the only begotten Son of God." The words; "condemned already," are very important; because they are central to the matter and many people do not know they are true; but they are, and there is only one remedy. It is impossible to get out from under this condemnation by going to church, being baptized, giving money to the church, being good, or any thing else, except, believing in Jesus Christ as your own personal Savior. This involves, believing Jesus came into the world to save sinners, that He died on the cross for our sins, that He was buried and rose again, then ascended into heaven, and is there praying for all those who have believed.

As Jesus was preparing to go back to heaven He told His followers, "It is expedient for you that I go away: for if I go not away, the comforter will not come unto you; but if I depart I will send him unto you. I have yet many things to say unto you, but ye cannot bear them now. Howbeit when He the Spirit of truth, is come, He will guide you into all truth: for He shall not speak of Himself; but whatsoever He shall hear, that shall He speak: and He will show you things to come. He shall glorify Me for, He shall receive of Mine, and shall shew it unto you. These things have I spoken unto you, that in Me you might have peace. In the world you shall have tribulation;

but be of good cheer; I have overcome the world."
(John 16.7, 12-14, 33) Jesus has overcome the world:
Our responsibility is to continue to follow Him. The
scripture further encourages and instructs followers
of Jesus: "Be not conformed to the world: but be ye
transformed by the renewing of your mind, that ye
may prove what is that good, and acceptable, and
perfect, will of God. For I say through the grace given
unto me, to every man that is among you, not to think
of himself more highly than he ought to think; but to
think soberly, according as God hath dealt to every
man the measure of faith." (Romans 12.2-3)

There is still a spiritual battle that Christians have
to fight, and the good thing about it is that Jesus has
left us well equipped. He has given us instructions,
and a measure of faith, and the Holy Spirit. Our job
is to believe that we can do the job. I am sure we can,
if we follow the leading of the Holy Spirit; and live
a Christian life, to the best of our ability. Someone
has said, it is not just dying for Christ, but it is living
for Him, and being willing to die if necessary. God
doesn't expect us to go out fighting with everyone
that we think is not a Christian. The scripture says:
"We wrestle: Not against flesh and blood, but against
principalities, against powers, against the rulers of
darkness of this world, against spiritual wickedness
in high places." (Ephesians 6.12) Then we are told
to put on the full armor of God, that we will be able
to stand in the evil day, and having done all to stand.
Stand, therefore having your loins girt about with
truth, and having on the breastplate of righteousness;
and your feet shod with the preparation of the gospel

of peace; Above all, taking the shield of faith, where-with ye shall be able to quench all the fiery darts of the devil. And take the helmet of salvation, and the sword of the Spirit, which is the word of God: Praying always with all supplication. (Ephesians 6.13-18) That is the formula for success. Here are a few other things to remember. As a little light dispenses much darkness, so a little good overcomes much evil. And even though they have the microphone we are still on the winning side in the battle.

Chapter 16

SATAN

You can find people who scoff at the mention of Satan. Some put him in the same category as Santa Clause and the Easter Bunny, but they are in for a dreadful surprise if they don't change their mind: Because the devil is headed for a place which has been prepared for him and his angels, and I expect that includes his followers.

Satan was created as an angel; he started out in heaven, but he decided to take over and become ruler, but there was war in heaven: And the Bible tells us in Revelation 12.7-12 "Michael and his angels fought against the dragon; and the dragon fought and his angels, And prevailed not; neither was their place found any more in heaven. And the great dragon was cast out, that old serpent, called the Devil, and Satan, which deceiveth the whole world: he was cast out into the earth, and his angels were cast out with him. And I heard a loud voice saying in heaven, now is come salvation and strength, and the kingdom of God, and the power of His Christ for the accuser of our brethren is cast down, which accused them before our God day and night. And they over came him by the blood of the Lamb, and by the word of their testimony; and they loved not their lives unto the death. Therefore rejoice ye heavens, and ye that dwell in them. Woe to the inhabitants of the earth and of the sea. For the devil has come down to you having great wrath, because he knowth that he has but a short time."

The devil made his appearance in the Garden of Eden, shortly after the creation of the universe. He appeared to Eve as a serpent; the craftiest of all the creatures the Lord God had made. He came asking Eve, "can't you eat of the fruit in the garden?" "Of course we may eat of it," the woman told him. "It is only the fruit from the tree at the center of the garden that we are not to eat. God says we mustn't eat or even touch it, or we will die. "That's a lie," the serpent hissed. "You'll not die. God knows very well that the instant that you eat it you will become like him, for your eyes will be opened and you will be able to distinguish between good and evil." The woman was convinced so she ate some of the fruit and gave some to her husband and he ate it too." This is from The Living - Bible, translation: Genesis 3:1-6

Jesus spoke of the devil one time when He was talking to the Scribes and Pharisees. (John. 8:44) "Ye are of your father the devil and the lusts of your father ye will do. He was a murderer from the beginning, and abode not in the truth, because there was no truth in him. When he speaketh a lie, he speaketh of his own: for he is a liar, and the father of it."

Lying is becoming more prominent in our society. In the news it seems someone is lying; or someone is being accused of lying. Have you noticed in several trials of late they couldn't convict the accused on the charges; so they convicted them for lying? It makes you wonder. It is not surprising when you think about what's being taught in our education systems. If it depends on the situation whether it is right or wrong: and if you can't know what is true or false maybe that is why there is so much lying.

The point is, that in the battle of good against evil, it is easy to see where the devil fits in. That should make us realize the seriousness of the fight. The Bible tells us that Jesus won the victory over Satan when He died on the cross but this is not final until Jesus comes again. In the meantime Satan will be one of our enemies. Sometimes some people try to paint the picture of being a Christian as a bed of roses without the thorns: But Jesus didn't do that. He gave us both sides. While here in this life on earth there will be both good and bad: But the blessings of eternity will more than make up for all suffering and hardship. Romans, 8:18:

"For I reckon that the sufferings of this present time are not worthy to be compared to the glory which shall be revealed in us.

Chapter 17

THE FLESH

As Christians we have three enemies working against us; we have considered two; the world and the devil. The third is the flesh and it may be the most troublesome of the three. Whether that is true or not the scripture has a lot to say about the flesh. When considering our battle against the devil we noted that we wrestle, not against flesh and blood, but against spiritual wickedness in high places. This was speaking of flesh and blood human beings. Flesh and blood means human nature, people with their emotions and human weaknesses, also called carnal nature as opposed to spiritual nature; fleshly, of the flesh, lascivious, sensual, worldly, not spiritual. Paul used the words, fleshly and carnal for the 'Adamic' nature, which was put upon the human race when Adam disobeyed in the Garden of Eden. When a person repents and believes on the Lord Jesus Christ as Savior the old nature is dealt with, and a spiritual nature is given to the believer. After this experience we are to live a life in the Spirit. (Romans 8:1-5) "There is therefore now no condemnation to them, which are in Christ Jesus, who walk not after the flesh, but after the Spirit. For the law of the spirit of life in Christ Jesus has made me free from the law of sin and death. For what the law could not do, in that it was weak through the flesh, God sending His own Son in the likeness of sinful flesh, and for sin, condemned sin in the flesh: That the righteousness of the law might be fulfilled in us, who walk not after the flesh but after the Spirit. For they that are after the flesh, do mind the things of the flesh; but they that are after the Spirit the things of the Spirit."

After salvation we continue to have a free will, and we can make choices. It is up to us as individual believers to make real sure that we are walking after the Spirit. Notice Galatians 5:19-25. "Now the works of the flesh are manifest, which are these; Adultery, fornication, uncleanness, lasciviousness, idolatry, witchcraft, hatred, variance, emulations, wrath, strife, seditions, heresies, envying, murders, drunkenness, reveling, and such like: of the which I tell you as I have also told you in time past that they which do such things shall not inherit the kingdom of God. But the fruit of the Spirit is love, joy, peace, longsuffering, gentleness, goodness, faith, meekness, temperance: against such there is no law. And they that are Christ's have crucified the flesh with the affections and the lusts. If we live in the Spirit, let us also walk in the Spirit." This shows us that being a true believer is serious business, and it is not for the faint of heart. But with the help of the Lord and the Holy Spirit we are well able to do it. In Romans 7.1-2, 11-14 there is some encouragement; "There is therefore now no condemnation to them which are in Christ Jesus, who walk not after the flesh, but after the Spirit. For the law of the Spirit of life in Christ Jesus has made me free from the law of sin and death." "But if the Spirit of Him that raised up Jesus from the dead dwell in you, He that raised up Christ from the dead shall also quicken your mortal bodies by his Spirit that dwelleth in you. Therefore, brethren, we are debtors, not to the flesh, to live after the flesh. For if ye live after the flesh, ye shall die: but if you through the Spirit do mortify the deeds of the body, (flesh) ye shall live. For as many as are lead by the Spirit of God, they are the Sons of God." What is needed is more dedicated Christians who are really concerned about the kingdom of God and pray like Jesus taught. "Our Father which art in heaven, hallowed be thy name, thy kingdom come, thy will be done on earth as it is in heaven." Matthew 6.9-10. God is building His kingdom and you and I can have a part in the building of it. At the same time God is concerned with what is taking place on earth, and Christians should be too.

Sometimes I think Christianity as a whole has a bad attitude, the believer in Christ Jesus should feel victorious. But too many are sitting around griping and complaining about how bad things are, when they should be doing what they can about the situations around them. It seems there is a defeatist attitude, with people throwing up their hands and saying it is no use. However there are many good things happening. I listened to a man who has been teaching at Harvard for forty years who said, that just a few years ago, the school wanted to add some classes on religion; which they did, then they wanted a class on Jesus, and he was designated to teach it. The class grew and grew, until one day the President of the college invited him to lunch and wanted to know what he was doing: passing out popcorn to get them to come to class? This Professor said, that there was much more interest in spiritual things, among the young people today than there was several years ago. That is encouraging to hear: And no doubt indicates that things are not as bad as we sometimes think they are. As the saying goes we need to concentrate on the opportunities instead of the problems. The worlds' reasoning, in some places, seems to be changing: Like; Jesus has been; "well influential". Another thing that we are hearing more about, is faith in healing, in the medical profession, often expressed as, it was a God thing. This indicates that Christians do not need to be hesitant when talking about spiritual things. You may be surprised, but most people are interested in, anything spiritual. This college teacher also reported that the younger generation, while cautious and cynical at times, their change toward religion is dramatic: And in that area of the country they are swarming into bible studies and church services.

Something else for Christians to consider is this matter of proselytizing. It is not politically correct if Christians do it but it seems to be all right for others. The sad thing is that Christians are falling for this, and it hinders their being a good witness for Jesus. Being a good witness has two sides to it. Being a follower of Jesus has many benefits and blessings. But on the other side rejecting His salvation leads to destruction. Telling people this is not a bad thing. It is like knowing that around the next curve is a deep canyon, the bridge has collapsed, if you don't warn people headed that way they will die. If we would warn one, we ought to warn the other.

Chapter 18

RIGHTEOUSNESS

"For they being ignorant of God's righteousness, and going about to establish their own righteousness, have not submitted themselves unto the righteousness of God. For Christ is the end of the law for righteousness to everyone that believeth." (Romans 10.3-4) Going about to establish their own righteousness, that's what many people are trying to do; many of them are good people, and they are sincere. The problem is they have wrong ideas, based on faulty information. What they need is the truth. Most people realize that they must be righteous to enter heaven. They don't realize that it can be as simple as it actually is to acquire the necessary righteousness. The scripture explains in Romans 10.8-11, 13: "The word is nigh thee, even in thy mouth, and in thy heart: That is the word of faith, which we preach; That, if thou shalt confess with thy mouth the Lord Jesus, and shall believe in your heart that God has raised Him from the dead, thou shalt be saved. For, with the heart man believeth unto righteousness; and with the mouth confession is made unto salvation. For the scripture saith, whoever believes on Him shall not be ashamed. For whosoever shall call upon the name of the Lord shall be saved." It goes way back to Abraham, who believed God, and it was counted to him for righteousness. The human nature has a tendency to say, I don't need any help, I can do it all by myself. The scripture goes on to say, if Abraham does it by his own effort he will have something to glory in; but by doing it God's way; Abraham just believed God, and the righteousness was added to his account.

Something to know is that after conversion is when good works are in order, but good works are worthless when going about trying to attain righteousness on your own. Some confusion comes from the Old Testament system under the Law of Moses; where to meet the requirement for the righteousness of the Law, they were required to keep all of the Law. When they failed in that, they had a system of sacrifices and offerings to help meet the requirements. When Jesus died on the cross, things changed. Romans 3.21-22 "But now the righteousness of God, without the law is manifested, being witnessed by the law and the prophets: Even the righteousness of God, which, is by faith of Jesus Christ unto all and upon all them that believe." Since the cross we are no longer under the Law, we are under a new covenant. Under the Law God demanded righteousness, but now under Grace He gives righteousness to everyone who believes. Law is connected with Moses and works. Grace is connected with Christ and faith. Law blesses the good: Grace saves the bad. Law demands that blessings be earned. Grace is a free gift. Grace begins with the death and resurrection of Christ. The point of testing is no longer legal obedience as the condition of salvation but acceptance or rejection of Christ, with good works as a fruit of salvation. Grace has a twofold manifestation; one in salvation and the other in the walk and service of the saved.

No one realizes it at the time; but every unconverted person is a servant of sin. They don't think so, because they think they are just doing their own thing. In reality they are very much under the control of the devil. The Bible speaks of being bound by sin and doing the works of the devil. One big change that takes place at the time of conversion is we stop serving sin and become a servant of righteousness. The rewards are much better.

Chapter 19

THE GOVERNMENT

This is one subject they tell us we shouldn't discuss; the other is religion. And maybe I shouldn't, because my island of knowledge is small and my shoreline of wonder is large. One reason for this is, that, like many Christians I didn't think it was very important or very spiritual either; so for much of my life I didn't pay much attention, but for several years now I have realized it is important. It is like someone said, "on these immoral issues, if you don't vote you are voting for it." I guess that is right; and if it is, it is serious.

One thing I have been able to do that has been interesting and I hope educational as well; was to listen to the confirmation hearings the past several years. I learned that the fellow that said, "Lawyers don't make good politicians, because they are taught to argue; they can take either side of an issue, and put up a good argument, but they are not so good at making decisions," was right. It was appalling, at times; even pathetic. It sounds like some of those guys were born on third base and think they hit a home run. In fact at times it is worse than that; it gets to the place that it is foolish. They ask the same question over and over, and keep getting the same answer. Someone said that to keep doing the same thing, and get the same result over and over, is stupidity.

Congress has been proving this statement to be true, by sending bills to the president, time and time again, when he has already said he would veto them. It is easy to see how congress can be so unpopular. It seems they are proving the statement: "Political parties every where, are merely crafts in which men are engaged for their own profit," made many years ago by Sen Ling. The goal for them is to make a good show on T.V. so they can get elected again. The problem is, there is so much jealousy and selfishness and hatred interfering with the minds of the people we voted in to run the government for us. It seems hatred is at the forefront with the present Congress.

You probably have noticed, as I have, that when any one in an elected position express their belief in God and spiritual things, that before long they have enemies. And from there on they are under attack. Dan Quail and James Watt are two in particular that I can remember in the recent past. However that shouldn't surprise us I suppose, because Jesus said, "In the world you will suffer persecution." And He also told us that there is victory ahead. Also we have the old saying: Be kind to your critics, they are using the only talent they have. That certainly does fit. On the other hand, many times it works the other way around: A number of folk show admiration and respect when they realize that a Christian is sincere.

Our education system does not teach people to think, but rather to have opinions. That is why we have many political ideas that have disturbed the world for the last sixty years or so. If there was more thinking and listening; and down to earth discussion and reasoning, instead of all the arguing and posturing more good governing could be accomplished. But it looks like we have a Kodak Generation: Over exposed and under developed. It must be terribly stressful on some politician, always trying to be a different person from who they are and doing it from one crowd to the other. They have to have many different costumes as they travel from crowd to crowd. I guess Shakespeare was right when he wrote 'all the world being a stage and the people merely actors.'

As U.S. citizens we need to do a lot of mental work. We ought to know, as much as possible, what is truly good for our country. Ask what do we want: A socialist society, or a capitalistic society? The liberals are going full bore for socialism; socialized medicine, socialized schools, government controlled businesses, higher taxes, more big spending to mention a few. I realize it is not easy for us ordinary citizens to understand exactly what is going on and I don't claim to have all the answers but here are a few things I have noticed. An elemental thing is where do we get our information? If we get it from the Newspaper and the T.V. news only, we come up short because it is slanted. It is never a good idea to do it because it seems that everyone is doing it. Some times it seems hopeless, but if we try then pray God will help us do what is right.

Some demonstrators wish to destroy what exists, rather than renew and correct. It looks like this is the goal of our present congress. What our government needs is a crew that understands the nature of its obligation to the ship. The truth of the matter is that Capitalism without God is hardly better than communism. I had a teacher once that told us the difference between socialism and communism is ten years. Maybe we ought to be more concerned about that than global warming: It is much closer. Here is a poem that speaks the truth.

'It Is The Veteran'
It is the Veteran, not the preacher:
Who gave us freedom of Religion.
It is the Veteran, not the reporter:
Who has given us freedom of the press,
It is the Veteran, not the campus organizer:
Who gave us freedom to assemble,
It is the Veteran, not the politician:
Who has given us the right to vote,
It is the Veteran, not the poet:
Who has given us the freedom of speech,
It is the Veteran, who salutes the flag:
Who serves under the flag: Whose coffin is
        draped with the flag.

Author Unknown.

Makes me wonder about those who make a big deal of supporting the troops while at the same time they make no secrete of the fact that they hate their Commander in Chief, and are doing all they can to counter act what is being accomplished by our armed services. A wise man said, "An idiot praises all countries but this one, and every country but his own." The Chinese are wise enough to know that a father cannot dignify himself by belittling his child, and we can't build up our prestige in the world by belittling our President and our Generals, and our country.

That is enough of that: As Christians we ought to not get hung up on the negative: But we do need to look at the facts and know what is going on around us. However we don't want to get so busy about the superficial things, and be dumb about the essentials. Let us have faith, and remember that faith; not only believes the truth, but submits to God, denies obstacles, calculates risks, vanquishes doubt, assumes success and releases energy for accomplishment. We know God is concerned about nations, and has certainly blessed ours. The best thing you and I can do is pray that God's will be done on earth, like Jesus taught His followers to pray. The Christians hope is not so much in social change, but in the second coming of Christ. But we must remember, Jesus said occupy until I come. Occupy means keep doing what we are supposed to be doing. Like the song says, "I'll work until Jesus comes." Some one asks, but how can we affect the destiny of the world? God's admonition was given to mankind, when He told Adam and Eve to be fruitful and multiply, and replenish the earth: That means to fill it, then He said subdue it, and have dominion over it. I guess we can say that gives us the fundamental principles: but where do we go from there?

First let us state the real problem: It is not just disagreements between Democrats and Republicans; it is a difference between right and wrong, the difference between good and evil which boils down to the simple truth of the war of the devil against God. Isaiah 28:15, describes some people, "Because ye have said, we have made a covenant with death, and with hell are we in agreement; when the overflowing scourge shall pass through, it shall not come unto us: for we have made lies our refuge, and under falsehood have we hid ourselves." Let's look at another scripture: 1John 3:8 "He that committeth sin is of the devil; for the devil sinneth from the beginning. For this purpose the Son of God was manifested, that He might destroy the works of the devil." That explains it: We must do all we can to accomplish the same things. It is well known that when good people do nothing sin abounds. We must be aware of the tricks of the devil: He has a bag full of them. He uses the news media and T.V. And he attacks the family, the church, the education system, the government, and everything important to our nation. One other verse of scripture in 2 Chronicles 7:14, which is addressed to the nation of Israel; but, applies to us I imagine. "If My people, which are called by My name, shall humble themselves, and pray, and seek My face, and turn from their wicked ways: Then will I hear from heaven, and will forgive their sin, and will heal their

land. The good ole U.S.A. could stand some healing.
When good people do nothing, evil triumphs.

Chapter 20

HELL

Everyone knows about hell, but how many know the truth about it? I will attempt to answer that with the help of the Bible. Hell is listed fifty three times in Strong's Concordance. It is mentioned other times by other names. Some people use it more times than that every day in conversation. In the end times the sheep are separated from the goats, with the sheep on the right and the goats on the left. Matthew 25:41 says, "Then shall He say also unto them on the left hand: Depart from me, you cursed, into ever lasting fire, prepared for the devil and his angels." Notice the key phrase: "Prepared for the devil and his angels." We often hear the comment, how could a loving God send anyone to hell? He doesn't, He gives everyone a choice, they are on the road to destruction, and God laid out a way of escape, believe on the Lord Jesus Christ and you shall be saved, and go into life eternal. There is no middle ground, it is one or the other, and the wonderful thing about it is it is our choice. The simple truth is that God did not prepare hell for mankind and technically He doesn't send anyone there.

Hell is a place of eternal punishment, a place of torment and it is called a lake of fire and in another place it is called a place of everlasting fire. Not a nice place. In addition to the devil and his angels, others will be there, including the antichrist, the false prophet and of course the multitudes that reject Christ Jesus as their Savior.

Chapter 21

THE ATHEIST

According to the dictionary an atheist is a person who does not believe in a god or gods. My Collegiate Encyclopedia elaborates by saying: "Unlike agnosticism which leaves open the question of whether there is a God, atheism is a positive denial." Psalms 53:1, says, "The fool hath said in his heart, there is no God." So putting it real simple, an atheist is a fool. The Bible says that the natural man receiveth not, the things of the Spirit of God, for they are foolishness to him, neither can he know them, for they are spiritually discerned."(1 Corinthians 2.14) I can understand how the preaching of the cross is difficult for some people to understand. They just can't believe the mighty power there is in the simple message of the cross of Christ. But we who are believers recognize the message as the very power of God.

For God says, "I will destroy all human plans of salvation no matter how wise they seem to be, and ignore the best ideas of men, even the most brilliant of them. So what about these wise men, these scholars; these brilliant debaters of the world's great affairs? God has made them all look foolish, and has shone their wisdom to be useless nonsense. For God in His wisdom saw to it that the world would never find God through human brilliance, and then He stepped in and saved all those who believed His message, which the world calls foolish and silly. It seems foolish to the Jews because they want a sign from heaven as proof that what is preached is true and it is foolish to the Gentiles because they believe only what agrees with their philosophy and seems wise to them. So when we preach about Christ dying to save them, the Jews are offended and the Gentiles say it is all foolishness. But God has opened the eyes of those called to salvation, both Jews and Gentiles, to see that Christ is the mighty power of God to save them; Christ Himself is the center of God's wise plan for their salvation. This so called foolish plan of God is far wiser than the wisest plan of the wisest man.(1 Corinthians 1.19-25 The Living Bible) Anyway it doesn't take a genius to figure out that anyone who calls them self an atheist isn't the brightest bulb in the chandelier.

A question that comes to mind: Why would anyone want to be an atheist? There must be some strong reason. I think the writer of Ecclesiastes 12:13 has the answer, "Let us hear the conclusion of the whole matter: Fear God, and keep His commandments; for this is the whole duty of man." Only two things: Fear God and keep His commandments. To fear God in the Bible means reverential trust, with hatred for evil. Why is it hard for mankind to obey? We do not want anyone or anything to have rule over us: We want to be free. The problem is complicated because of the failure to understand what true freedom actually is.

Chapter 22

FAITH

We need to take a look at faith and try to get at the simple truth concerning it. Basically faith is receiving and believing what God has revealed. Faith can be defined as trust in the God of scripture, and trust in Jesus Christ whom He has sent. In addition to trust we have belief, which carries the thought of confidence and conviction. Long ago Abraham believed God and it was counted to him for righteousness. Since then multitudes have become believers and many continue to believe today, all over the world. Missionaries went from the U.S. to other nations in the early 1900's and started Bible Schools to train pastors and others, and in many of those countries today there are multitudes of Christians. This doesn't often get out in today's news, however. Some times we get the mistaken idea that Christianity is in a diminishing condition, but we get very encouraging news when Missionaries return and give news of what is happening in their areas of the world. The Bible tells of the multitudes out of every kindred and tongue and people and nation, that will be in heaven.

Faith is essential for salvation: There must be a personal faith and trust completely apart from any work on our part. Paul's letter to the Romans explains it in chapter four verses one thru eight in The Living Bible. "Abraham was humanly, the founder of the Jewish nation. What were his experiences concerning this question of being saved by faith? Was it because of his good deeds that God accepted him? If so, then he would have something to boast about. But from God's point of view Abraham had no basis at all for pride. For the scripture tells us that Abraham believed God, and that is why God canceled his sin and declared him not guilty. But didn't he earn his right to heaven by all the good things he did? No, for being saved is a gift; if a person could earn it by being good, then it wouldn't be free; but it is free. It is given to those who do not work for it. For God, through salvation; declared sinners to be righteous in His sight, when they have faith in Christ to save them from God's wrath. King David spoke of this, describing the happiness of an undeserving sinner who is declared not guilty by God. Blessed, and to be envied, he said, are those whose sins are forgiven and put out of sight. Yes what joy there is for anyone whose sins are no longer counted against him by the Lord."

"But without faith it is impossible to please Him; for he that comes to God must believe that He is, and that He is a rewarder of them that diligently seek Him." Hebrews 11:6. It takes faith to believe that God exists, and this is the first step. No spiritual progress can be made in any other way. It is also necessary to believe that He rewards those who come for salvation.

Salvation is a free gift. This is hard for mankind to understand, and I think I know part of the reason. It is the fault of grandparents along with parents who tell kids, "if you are good Grandma will bring you something when she comes, or maybe it is if you are good you will get an ice cream when we get to the store," It is the same thing with allowances, you have to earn them. And even at Christmas time if someone gives you a gift you have to be sure to give one in return. Later we learn you are supposed to give a days work for a days pay. The Bible says you are saved by grace through faith. A free gift is free. There is no way you can earn it. Grace means, granted as a favor, not as a right.

Communion with God is one of the privileges Christians have, and a part of that communion is prayer. For prayer to be effective faith must be involved. Otherwise prayer becomes just idle words. The Apostle John, in 1 John 5:13-15 writes, "These things have I written unto you that believe on the Son of God; that you may know that you have eternal life, and that you may believe on the name of the Son of God. And this is the confidence that we have in Him, that if we ask anything according to His will, He heareth us. And if we know He hears us, whatsoever we ask, we know that we have the petitions that we desired of Him." The "According to His will" is important, because this is at the root of many unanswered prayers. Many prayers are based on our will, instead of God's. When Jesus taught His disciples to pray, a part of that prayer is: "Thy kingdom come, thy will be done in earth as it is in heaven." (Matthew 6.10) This should be the goal of every one of us: To get our will lined up with His will.

The thought just came to me that I should explain why I am typing out as much scripture as I am. First off I don't like to read a book with a lot of scripture references that I have to stop and look up, or just keep reading and wonder what a lot of them say. The other reason is that I think most of you would do the same thing. This way you get more of God's word, and that is more important than what I can give you anyway. So here we go again, this is one you may know. Hebrews 11:1-3, "Now faith is the substance of things hoped for, the evidence of things not seen. For by it the Elders obtained a good report. Through faith we understand that the worlds were framed by the word of God. So that things which are seen, were not made of things which do appear."

Previously the scripture told us that we must, by faith know that God is real. Now this last scripture points out that the way we understand how the world came into existence, is by faith. Evolutionists can't believe the Bible account of creation because they don't have the right kind of faith. They have a worldly faith that enables them to believe, an unbelievable bunch of lies.

Faith is the working principle in every-day life. Faith works in all things: The small things as well as the big serious things that come our way. The eleventh chapter of Hebrews tells of the great accomplishment of people down through the ages of history. Read it, it will do you good.

One of our biggest problems is the world with all of its evils and pressures, which work against every thing that Christianity stands for. 1 John 5:3-5: "For this is the love of God, that we keep His commandments; and His commandments are not grievous. For whatsoever is born of God overcometh the world; and this is the victory that overcometh the world, even our faith. Who is he that overcometh the world, but he that that believeth that Jesus is the Son of God." Christians should not be allowing themselves to be conformed to the world, for the scriptures tell us to "love not the world, neither, the things that are in the world." (1 John 2.15) This scripture tells us that our faith is what gives us victory over the world.

One time when Jesus was teaching His Apostles concerning forgiving those that trespassed against them; they said to Jesus: "Increase our faith." (Luke 17.5) Jesus was giving them something very hard to do, and they must have realized they needed help. That is how it is with us when we face the problems of this life; and we need to pray the same prayer, Lord Jesus increase our faith. The first four verses of the twelfth chapter of Hebrews give us an example. "Wherefore seeing we also are compassed about with so great a cloud of witnesses, let us lay aside every weight, and the sin which does so easily beset us, and let us run with patience the race which is set before us; Looking unto Jesus the author and finisher of our faith; who for the joy that was set before Him endured the cross, despising the shame, and is set down at the right hand of the throne of God. For consider Him that endured such contradiction of sinners against Himself, lest you be wearied in your minds. You have not yet resisted unto blood, striving against sin."

Chapter 23

ENVIRONMENT

Environmentalism is the defender of the preservation and improvement of the natural environment, especially the social movement to control environmental pollution. Other specific goals include 1.Population growth. 2. The conservation of natural resources. 3. The restriction of the negative effects of modern technology. This was the definition in 2000.

These are legitimate goals, with the possible exception of control of population growth, but since then a number of things have been added, which are objectionable to thinking people. One big danger lies in the possibility of exaggeration, which some Politicians and most of the News Media, are getting quite adept at. Another danger is the possibility of government getting too big and controlling, which can result in the loss of more freedoms of the citizens.

Most citizens are concerned about the environment, especially hunters, hikers, fishermen, loggers, and others who work and live outdoors. Others that are concerned are Timber Companies, Fish and Game Commissions, which have been studying and spending money to preserve the environment. On the other hand we have some other groups out there that are extremists. They aren't well informed but they can keep things riled up with half- truths, exaggerations, and lies.

Let us remember that God created animals and vegetation for man, not for the earth. There is some modern thinking that tends to turn it around, and make the earth the main thing. It is important to keep the main thing, the main thing, or we get into trouble. God said to Adam and Eve, "Be fruitful, and multiply, and replenish the earth and subdue it: And have dominion over the fish of the sea, and over the fowl of the air, and over every creeping thing that creepeth upon the earth." (Genesis 1.26) Some today want to make man accountable for every thing that goes wrong, or sometimes it is just something they don't like. If the sun gets to hot, it is mans fault: And if it is to cold, that is mans fault. I am inclined to believe that the same God who created the earth is in control of it. "While the earth remaineth, seedtime and harvest, and cold and heat, and summer and winter, and day and night shall not cease." (Genesis 8:22) "And God said, "Let there be lights in the firmament of the heaven to divide the night from the day: And let them be for signs, and for seasons, and for days, and for years: And let them be for lights in the firmament of the heavens to give light upon the earth: And it was so." (Genesis 1:14-15) It seems to me that God put things into motion that are still operating many years later, and I am confident will continue until the end, and God is able to see us through to a happy ending. The most comforting thing about the riddle of the universe is that no one is required to solve it, or understand it completely.

The same people who say there is no God are the most prominent in endeavors to control and improve what God has created. The reason they have so many failures, is their neglect of three important things; wisdom—knowing what to do; skill—knowing how to do it; virtue—doing it.

"Wisdom is the principle thing; therefore get wisdom; and with all your getting get understanding." (Proverbs 4:7) However, like many other things, there are two kinds of wisdom, as mentioned in, 1Corinthians 3:19: "For the wisdom of this world is foolishness with God: For it is written, "He taketh the wise in their own craftiness." The two kinds of wisdom; are the wisdom of this world, also called fleshly wisdom in the Bible, and the wisdom of God. We are seeing some of the results of worldly wisdom, which is foolishness, in operation all around in many areas. We see it in extreme environmentalism, in global warming, in government, and in the many destructive ideas that are being pushed by some people. Serious thinking people need to sit up and pay attention to what is happening. Don't be brainwashed by what you see, hear, and read: Much repetition doesn't make it true. Here is something else to consider. The scripture says, "because they received not the love of the truth, that they might be saved, for this cause God shall send them strong delusion, that they should believe a lie." (2 Thessalonians 2:10)

The second important thing is skill: It seems we have too many people, elected, and appointed, to very important positions, who, along with their shortage of wisdom, come up short on skill. But they are telling others what to do and how to do it. If they would mind their own business, they wouldn't have time to be minding anyone else's. An example would be congress, even if some have been there forty years, they are not likely to be qualified to tell four star Generals how to run their business: And to criticize and ridicule them is sheer stupidity.

I want to point out that I know we have some good people in leadership: And I appreciate them, and I am thankful for what they do, and I am thankful for America and the privilege to live here. However I am concerned with the downward trend of our nation. The Bible says righteousness exalts a nation. If you remember what the Old Testament tells us about the history of the nations, you know that good nations had good things happen to them, and evil nations had some very bad things happen to them. The nation of Israel was blessed when they obeyed God: But when they worshiped idols and lived in immorality like their neighboring nations, God punished them severely to bring them to a place of repentance.

Chapter 24

POSITIVE THINKING

Somewhere I read that a book is less important for what it says than for what it makes you think. I trust this one is doing that. It has been said that the reason so many people get lost in thought is that it is unfamiliar territory. Since you are reading this you probably are not in that category, because readers are thinkers.

There are two ways of thinking: Positive and Negative. And an empty mind will automatically fill up with negative thoughts. I don't know why; but I suppose they have a law named for it. It works like having a good garden spot and not planting it one year. What happens? With you doing nothing it will grow a good crop of weeds. This is the reason we live in a world that is so full of negative thinking, which in turn results in negative activity.

You can easily test to see that this is true. Every morning, for a few days, when you get up, say I feel great, I'm glad to be alive. You will begin to see a difference. No person who takes possession of their own mind and directs it to definite ends needs to remain the victim of poverty or anything else they do not desire. A person who is not master of himself may never become master of anything outside of himself.

There is a connection between faith and positive thinking. Faith is positive, while doubt and fear are negative. Faith is not a mere sentiment, but a substantial reality. Faith is always in the present, it is not a future hope, but it is a present fact. The Bible describes it as the substance of things once hoped for, but now, not hoped for, but believed. Perhaps the most vital and supernatural feature about faith; is it's supernatural power to anticipate the future and call the things that are not as though they are. Faith is the connection between helpless man and the infinite resources of God. Faith is the principle by which our very life is sustained. The just shall live by faith. In Abraham we see faith not trying to get something from God but faith doing something to please God. If we stop and think we may find that the reason we don't get more from God is because God has been waiting to get some thing from us. THE QUESTION IS HAVE WE LEARNED THE OBEDIENCE OF FAITH?

Faith is a state of mind. Hope is the forerunner of the greatest of all states of mind, faith. Hope sustains one in times of emergency when without it fear would take over. Hope keeps the soul of man alert and active in his behalf, and clears the line of communication by which faith connects one with God. Faith is the means of communication between the conscious mind of man and God who is the great universal reservoir of Infinite Intelligence. Faith gives creative power and action to the impulse of thought. Live on God's schedule and you will always have His help.

The power of the will is boss of all departments of the mind. It is the power that puts the emotions under control; and it is subject to direction only by self-discipline. It takes orders from the conscious mind, but recognizes no other authority. Therefore it is up to us, because we are in control. There are three important things. 1. If you do nothing with your garden it will grow weeds and grass. 2. If you do nothing with your mind it will produce negative thoughts. 3. If you do nothing with your soul it will be lost.

All around us we have positive and negative. I have had a few people say to me I don't believe in all that positive stuff. In reality their problem is they are not aware of all that negative stuff. There is good and evil, cold and hot, wet and dry, and light and dark. A person who doesn't like the dark, and is even afraid of it, can talk about it and complain about it, but no matter how they feel or how they think; it only gets worse. The truth is; if you don't try to be good you will be bad, if you don't put forth effort you will be poor, if you don't turn on the light you are in the dark and if you don't concentrate on being positive you will be negative.

It is depressing to be around negative thinking people, they are sad and disagreeable. On the other hand positive people are uplifting, because they are expecting things to be better: They are happier and more content. When you leave their presence you feel encouraged and uplifted. The problem is that statistics tell us that only five percent of people are positive, I hope there is more than that, but they may be right.

The creative mind; also called the subconscious mind does its best work while the conscious mind is inactive or pleasantly occupied. This gives you the happy news that to be successful, it is a good idea to take time for enjoyable diversion, instead of working harder and longer. This is true because it gives the subconscious mind a chance to work and solve problems, and to do your constructive thinking and planning. After which your conscious mind can put into action the results of your creative mind.

The creative mind works twenty-four hours a day. If it is not directed in positive channels it will be working against you by working on the negative all the time. It is bad memories of the past and fear of the future that make the present so difficult. Recalling unpleasant situations of the past may tend to neutralize the success pictures of your future. You are what you think you are.

The impression you have of yourself represents an accumulation of mental pictures throughout your lifetime. Since ninety five percent of all people incline toward the negative side it is likely that you have a negative impression of yourself, unless you are one of the fortunate five percent. In other words you probably think of yourself as being destined by fate to live a hard life, and as a rule you do. We must first think in terms of success before we manifest success. A success consciousness is that state of mind in which you cannot think of yourself as anything but a success. The normal view should be the positive view.

Chapter 25

PROSELYTING

The dictionary definition is: To try to convert people to one's belief or opinions. Christians are accused of this, and consequently in many places they are suffering persecution because of it. Being a proselyte is permissible for everyone; except, for Christians, for them it is a no, no. Where do we go for the truth concerning this practice? How about the Bible? In Matthew 24:14 we read, "This gospel of the kingdom shall be preached in the whole world as a testimony to all nations, and then shall the end come." Jesus told His Disciples, "But ye shall receive power after that the Holy Ghost is come upon you; and ye shall be witnesses unto me both in Jerusalem, and in all Judea and in Samaria, and to the uttermost part of the earth." (Acts 1:8)

In Matthew's Gospel 10:32; Jesus approaches the matter from a different angle. He says, "Whosoever therefore shall confess me before men, him will I confess also before My Father which is in heaven. But whosoever shall deny me before men, him will I also deny before My Father which is in heaven." This shows there is a consequence involved in doing or not doing what God wants.

The Bible is a progressive unfolding of truth, and truth must not be hoarded, and hidden away from those who need it. That would be cruel and inhumane treatment. Truth must be shared, so that those who are on their way to the punishment of hell can be rescued.

The Gospel is good news; it is not a bad thing to give out good news. The gospel is also a warning and it is not a bad thing to warn people of danger. Multitudes are slaves to sin and Satan; they need to be set free and the sure way is through the gospel of Jesus Christ. The battle goes on between God and Satan, who has a vast army of helpers. Many people do not realize which side they are on. For example it is not politically correct to try to make Christians out of sinners. Now how does that come about? It is a brainwashing process with a lot of people involved: Like the News Media, especially T.V. and the education system and liberal government agencies all working together and saying the same thing; soon good people, who ought to know better, believe a lie. Consequently many people around the world are giving their lives for the cause of Christ. Therefore in some Countries, Christianity is growing at a very rapid rate. It is like in the New Testament Church, when the Church was persecuted, the Church grew. Jesus told His followers, "if the world hates you,

you know that it hated me before it hated you." One of the beatitudes says, "Blessed are they which are persecuted for righteousness sake: For, theirs is the kingdom of Heaven." (Matthew 5.10)

Chapter 26

THE RESURECTION

1 Peter 2:19 NIV "For it is commendable if a man bears up under the pain of unjust suffering because he is conscious of God. But how is it to your credit if you receive a beating for doing wrong and endure it? But if you suffer for doing good and endure it, this is commendable before God. To this were you called, because Christ suffered for you, leaving an example that; you should follow in His steps." He did not reply when accused. He did not retaliate when abused. He did not accept the cup (narcotic). He did not come down from the cross. If you leave out the cross you kill the religion of Jesus.

However, the resurrection of Jesus Christ is also a vital part of the gospel message, for a dead Christ can save no one. Paul said to the church at Corinth: (1Corinthians 15:1-8, 16-22 NIV) "Now brothers, I want to remind you of the gospel I preached to you, which you have received and on which you have taken your stand. By this gospel are you saved, if you hold firmly to the word I have preached to you: Otherwise you have believed in vain. For what I received I passed on to you as of first importance: That Christ died for our sins according to the scriptures, that He was buried, that He was raised on the third day according to the scriptures, and that he appeared to Peter, and then to the twelve. After that He appeared to more than five thousand of the brothers at the same time. Then He appeared to James, then to all of the Apostles, and last of all He appeared to me (Paul) also…. If Christ has not been raised, our preaching is useless and so is your faith. More than that, we are found to be false witnesses about God. And if Christ has not been raised your faith is useless. For since death came through a man (Adam) the resurrection of the dead comes also through a man (Jesus). For as in Adam all die, so in Christ all will be made alive."

The empty tomb is proof that He is the Son of God. "Christ Jesus, who through the Spirit of holiness was declared with power to be the Son of God by His resurrection from the dead." (Romans, 1:4. NIV)

The empty tomb is proof that believers have a future inheritance. "Praise be to the God and Father of our Lord Jesus Christ! In His great mercy He has given us new birth into a living hope through the resurrection of Jesus Christ from the dead, and into an inheritance that can never perish, spoil or fade; kept in heaven for you, who through faith are shielded by God's power until the coming of the salvation that is ready to be revealed in the last time." (1 Peter 1:3 NIV)

Some churches that are proud to be progressive are leaving out the cross because it is too bloody, and they aren't preaching the Resurrection of Jesus from the dead, because they don't believe in anything supernatural. When they do that they cease to be Christian because these two things are the foundation of the gospel of Jesus Christ.

Chapter 27

SIN

Misunderstandings are quite numerous concerning sin and at a glance it doesn't seem complicated, consequently, it isn't considered to be very important. We shall attempt to examine it as thoroughly as we can. First off it is universal, "For all have sinned, and come short of the glory of God." (Romans 3:23) This means everyone, no exceptions. The reason for that is all have a sinful nature that came about when Adam and Eve disobeyed in the garden. Romans 5:12, explains, "Wherefore, as by one man sin entered into the world, and death by sin; and so death passed upon all men, for all have sinned." So we need to think in terms of both sins and sin. Sin means a sinful nature, a tendency to commit sins: Sins are the actions of committing the sinful acts. So salvation involves more than just having sins forgiven: It includes having the sinful nature changed to a sinless nature. The scripture speaks of becoming a new creature in Christ.

Sin may be summarized as threefold. 1. An act: the violation or lack of obedience to the revealed will of God. 2. A state: The absence of righteousness. 3. A nature: Enmity toward God.

Several other words are used in Scripture to define different aspects of sin. Basically sin is transgression, an overstepping of the divine boundary between good and evil. Iniquity is an act, which is inherently wrong, whether forbidden or not. Error: A departure from right. Missing the mark: A failure to meet the divine standard. Trespass: The intrusion of self-will into the sphere of divine authority. Lawlessness: Or spiritual anarchy. Unbelief: Or an insult to God.

Sin is a serious matter; it has affected all mankind. We find it difficult to even think what the world would be like if it was free from sin. And it is difficult to realize how there could be a solution for such an immense problem. However, God had a plan, He so loved the world that He gave His only begotten Son, on the cross of Calvary to pay the penalty. The penalty for sin is death, and Jesus willingly paid the penalty for whoever will accept the gift of salvation. It cannot be bought, earned, or deserved in any way whatsoever. It is absolutely a gift, and everyone knows that all you have to do is just accept a gift, no work, no money and no being good enough; just come as you are and accept it.

There are two things that are hard for most people when it comes to Salvation. The first thing is admitting that they need it, then after they do come to the realization that they are a lost sinner in need of Salvation; they have a problem of accepting the fact that Jesus did everything, and there is nothing else to do, and that it is all free, and all they have to do is accept it. I believe no one, is disappointed after they accept salvation; because being free from sin is just the beginning. "But now being made free from sin, and become servants of God, you have your fruit unto holiness, and the end eternal life. For the wages of sin is death; but the gift of God is eternal life through Jesus Christ our Lord." (Romans 6:23) Also, at the time of salvation the believer not only gets rid of sins and the tendency to sin: they receive righteousness. They exchanged their old sinful nature for a righteous nature. "For, as by one man's disobedience, many were made sinners, so by the obedience of one, shall many be made righteous." (Romans 5:19)

Among the many benefits of believing on Jesus Christ is the peace of mind of knowing that you have the righteousness that is needed to enter heaven. But the critic says, "What if all this religious stuff turns out to be false?" Then nothing is lost, in the sense that the Christian, will be no worse off than the heathen. If that happens, we will all die like dogs and that will be the end.

Chapter 28

GOOD WORKS

The reason good works are misunderstood is that it makes a difference as to where they are accomplished. The good works themselves are basically the same: The dividing point is the cross on which Jesus died. The Jews, living before the cross, and under the law, were commanded to do good works in order to keep in right relation with God: But after the cross all of that changed as we can see in (Galatians 2:16) "Knowing that a man is not justified by the works of the Law, but by the faith of (in) Jesus Christ, even we have believed in Jesus Christ, that we might be justified by the faith of (in) Jesus Christ, and not by the works of the law, for by the works of the law shall no flesh be justified." "Not by works of righteousness, which we have done, but according to His mercy He saved us, by the washing of regeneration, and renewing of the Holy Ghost: Which He shed on us abundantly through Jesus Christ our Savior." (Titus

3:5-6) This side of the cross, salvation is by faith, and not by works.

After a person becomes a believer there is something else to know. (James 2:17-20 NKJV) "Thus also faith by itself, if it does not have works, is dead. But someone will say, "You have faith, and I have works." Show me your faith without your works, and I will show you my faith by my works. You believe that there is one God. You do well. Even the demons believe—and tremble! But do you want to know, O foolish man, that faith without works is dead?" That explains it; if a person says they are a believer and they do nothing; that is they do no good works their salvation is not genuine.

To sum it up: The simple truth is this. In order to become a believer, faith and faith alone is all that God requires, and all that He accepts. After becoming a believer, good works added to faith is necessary. The works are the visible evidence that the faith exists. If someone claims to be a believer, it is necessary to take their word for it, until we see the proper actions, after which we are sure.

Chapter 29

GLOBAL WARMING

The definition of global warming is the potential increase in average global atmospheric temperature resulting from the enhancement of the greenhouse effect by air pollution. Many scientist predict that this increase will significantly altar climate patterns, increasing global average temperatures by as much as 9 degrees by the middle of the this century. Such global warming would cause the polar ice caps and mountain glaciers to melt rapidly; significantly raising the levels of coastal waters, and would produce new patterns and extremes of drought and rainfall, seriously disrupting food production in certain regions. Other scientists maintain that such predictions are overstated.

Let us look at a few words in this definition: The word, "potential" if left out would change the meaning. "Many scientists," in the third line, and, "other scientist," in the last line can be emphasized in a way to change the meaning. "By as much as," is almost meaningless. If some guy tells me, this gadget will increase your gas mileage as much as ten miles per gallon, my brain tells me, maybe zero, or at best two or three.

The big question to me in the whole thing is, what kind of scientist? In my dictionary the definition of science is a branch of knowledge requiring systematic study and method. Just below that science fiction was defined as, stories based on imaginary future scientific discoveries or, "changes of the environment," or space travel or life on other planets. I was surprised to see changes of the environment listed in science fiction but I think they got it right.

As I said before I'm no expert, and I certainly am not up on this subject: But I will attempt to give you the truth as I see it. I am an environmentalist; Not one of those wacko environmentalist that thinks that animals are more important than humans. I love the outdoors and I am thankful for it for the opportunity we have to enjoy it, and I believe we should take good care of it. However I think God expects us to use it and enjoy it. I believe that most of our population feels the same way.

Back to global warming: A couple days ago I heard John Coleman being interviewed on the radio. As I understand it he is the founder of the weather channel and works for KUSI Weather Channel at the present. Among other things he said the basic research on global warming is flawed. He said most of the scientists fear telling the truth because of the powers that be. There is so much money involved that people are loosing their jobs if they don't go along. The science is corrupt, what they say about carbon is not scientific and there is corruption of science. From 1940 to 1946 the climate cooled. The reason Coleman is talking freely is because he is retiring and they can't fire him.

The solutions to solving global warming are drive less, tax more, cut back on everything, and cut freedoms by making more and more regulations. What does that make you think of? Makes me think it sounds exactly like the liberal policies for the last thirty years. I almost forgot the biggest hoax to come along for a while: THE CARBON CREDIT HOAX. The rich can live like they want, to live, in their big houses, and drive their big cars and just buy a few carbon credits; but more than that that; more million-aires will be made by selling carbon credits to the uninformed and the gullible. As the saying goes, follow the money. That always explains most things. The other big thing to watch is, control of the people, which means taking away freedoms. Government is too big and getting larger very rapidly, which means more regulations, which in turn means less freedom for the people, and no doubt more taxes.

Instead of being true science, global warming is a mixture, some true, some exaggerated, and some out and out false. It seems it is more accurate to call it a religion: which is defined as the existence of a superhuman controlling power, especially of God or gods. Global warming doesn't exactly fit this defini-tion, because basically they are denying, or at least replacing God. They are saying in so many words, man is wiser than God. Maybe it is more like a cult.

Maybe the climate has warmed a degree, or cooled a degree and in certain areas the snow and ice melt is on the increase, but not in others. What we are not told is that in the late nineteen seventies it was cooling and the concern was that it was to get colder and everything was going to freeze up, but it didn't. The truth evidently is that we have cycles of twenty or thirty year spans, where it warms up for a few years and then cool down for a few years and probably the temperature of the sun changes or some other natural cause is responsible, and not man at all. It is evident that we have too much pollution, especially around the cities, and we need to work on that. But there is no need to bankrupt our nation, and strip away the freedoms of the people to the point that they begin to rebel and demonstrate like the people in several other countries are doing at this present time. In my opinion this is not a time to go off halfcocked. Why not get the facts first, instead of acting on speculations and uneducated guesses, and on inadequate measurements. A few years ago the state of Washington had a lady Governor. I heard her say that it is impossible to get accurate measurements because they fluctuated so much, and there are so many variables.

Another point to think about is this: Even if the temperature should warm several degrees all is not lost, because some areas will be better, while other areas may be worse in some respects. No doubt there would be many changes, but we should be used to change, because we have it going on all around us, and we seem to be coping with it without having a panic attack. Why not take the money that will likely be wasted and hoarded, and put it, and the needed effort into solving some of the "close" up problems facing our nation at the present? A few minutes ago on the radio I heard that there are seven big issues facing congress now, and nothing is being done about them. At the same time they are hassling and going to court over gasoline mileage and pollution standards for automobiles and trucks. This is just one example, but no doubt much tax money is being spent in this manner. Here is a fact of life: If giving advice worked there wouldn't be many problems left in the world.

Chapter 30

THE FLOOD

And the Lord said, "My spirit shall not always strive with man, for he is also flesh; yet his days shall be one hundred and twenty years...And God saw that the wickedness was great in the earth, and every imagination of the thoughts of his heart is only evil continually. And it repented the Lord that He had made man on the earth, and it grieved Him at his heart. And the Lord said, "I will destroy man whom I have created, from the face of the earth; both man, and beast, and the creeping thing, and the fowls of the air; for it repenteth me that I have made them. But Noah found grace in the eyes of the Lord." (Gen. 6:3, 5-8)

Wickedness was the cause of the flood: It was terrible wickedness. Noah and his family were the only ones who were not caught up in the wickedness. Noah was a just man and perfect in his generations, and he walked with God. He preached to the people while he was building the ark but he had no converts.

The account of the flood is found in the history of many ancient people, and the results of the flood are seen in many places on the earth. Jesus spoke of the flood, Matthew 24:37-39, "But as the days of Noah were, so shall the coming of the Son of man be. For as in the days that were before the flood they were eating and drinking, marrying and giving in marriage, until the day that Noah entered the ark, And knew not until the flood came and took them all away; so shall also the coming of the Son of man be. "Peter also believed in the flood. (1Peter, 3:20) "When once the long suffering of God waited in the days of Noah, while the ark was a preparing, wherein few, that is eight souls were saved by water." God was long suffering then and is long suffering toward us, not willing that any should perish but that all should come to repentance.

It took about ten generations for the world to reach the point of no return. The whole population of the world was inwardly corrupt, outwardly violent, and completely rebellious. The world is becoming more wicked every day; and when it becomes as wicked as it was in Noah's day, watch for the Lord to return. Noah was saved by grace through faith. He heard God's word, believed God's promise of protection, and proved his faith by his works. There was only one way to be saved from destruction, and that was by entering the ark; and the ark had only one door. It is a picture of our salvation through Christ.

"By faith Noah, when warned about things not yet seen, in holy fear built an ark to save his family. By his faith he condemned the world and became heir of the righteousness that comes by faith. Without faith it is impossible to please God, because he that cometh to God must believe that He is and that he is a rewarder of those who diligently seek Him." (Hebrews, 11:6)

When Noah and his family, and all the animals walked out of the ark after the flood: Noah built an altar to the Lord and, taking some of all the clean animals and birds, he sacrificed burnt offerings, on it. "And the LORD smelled a sweet savour; and the LORD said in his heart, I will not again curse the ground any more for man's sake; for the imagination of man's heart *is* evil from his youth; neither will I again smite any more every thing living, as I have done. While earth remaineth, seedtime and harvest, cold and heat, summer and winter, day and night will never cease." (Genesis 8.21-22)

Then God blessed them and told them to be fruitful and fill the earth. God told them that all living creatures would fear them, and that they are given to them for food: Whereas, after the creation, He had given them only the green plants for food; which means that for that period of time they had not been told that they could eat the animals. After this God made a covenant with Noah and his sons to the effect that He would not destroy all the earth with a flood again; and He gave them the rainbow as a sign of the covenant.

Now Noah and his family were the only people on the earth, and God gave them new rules for life on the cleansed earth and from Noah's three sons He made a new beginning. From these three sons the nations of the world came into being. From Shem came the godly line of Abraham and God's chosen people, the Jews. The rest of the numerous nations are Gentile nations. This is the true beginning of modern world history. Archaeological findings are harmonizing with, and proving much of what is recorded in the Bible. We need to realize that the Bible is not a history book, the Old Testament is a history, primarily, of the nation of Israel, it is true, and the New Testament is primarily a history of the Church of Jesus Christ, and an account of the end times, and the setting up of the everlasting Kingdom of God.

The battle, which has been in process since Satan was thrown out of heaven, will continue and become more intense right up to the end. Satan will gather all of the ungodly nations together against God's people. Jesus Christ shall come from heaven with His Saints and defeat Satan and his hosts. Satan will be cast in to the lake of fire where the beast and the false prophet are, while the followers of Jesus enter eternity to live forever. The mention of eternity brings up the question: What is eternal life? It is one of those things that is often talked about, but is difficult to define.

Chapter 31

ETERNAL LIFE

I thought the dictionary would be a good place to start, and was amused at what it said. Eternity.1. Infinite time, past or future. 2. The endless time of life after death. 3. A very long time."

It is called eternal life because it was from the eternity which is past unto the eternity which is to come. It is the life of God, which is revealed in Jesus Christ, and it is the gift that is given when a person is born again, as explained by Jesus in John 3:1-7, "There was a man of the Pharisees, named Nicodemus, a ruler of the Jews: The same came to Jesus by night, and said unto Him, Rabbi, we know that thou art a teacher come from God: For no man can do these miracles that thou doest, except God be with Him. Jesus answered and said unto him, verily, verily, I say unto thee, except a man be born again, he cannot see the kingdom of God. Nicodemus saith unto Him, how can a man be born when he is old? Can he, enter the second time, into his mother's womb, and be born? Jesus answered, verily, verily, I say unto thee, except a man be born of water and of the Spirit, he cannot enter into the kingdom of God. That which is born of the flesh is flesh; and that which is born of the Spirit is Spirit. Marvel not that I said unto thee, ye must be born again."

In our first birth we are born of the flesh, natural birth, but in our second birth we are born from above, born of the Spirit. The first birth leads to death, but the second birth gives eternal life and a new beginning, the scripture says that all things are new. The old sinful nature is dead and a new spiritual nature takes control. The desire to sin is replaced with the desire to please God. Jesus said, "I am come that they might have life, and that they might have it more abundantly." (John 10.10) Here is another passage that explains a little more what this eternal life is. 1Corinthians 2:9, "But it is written: Eye hath not seen, nor ear heard, neither have entered into the heart of man, the things, which God hath prepared for them that love Him."

For those who believe in Jesus Christ, eternity means all things new. Life for mankind began in a garden and ends with a city that is like a garden. The most important thing about the heavenly city is the presence of God in all of His glory. Everything is so wonderful and the only way John can describe it is to tell what is not there. Its beauties and blessings are beyond human words to describe or explain. There is no sin, no darkness, pain, death, sorrow, or crying, and no more curse. John gives this preview of eternal glory to encourage believers who were going through trials and persecution. Jesus comforted His followers: "Let not your hearts be troubled; ye believe in God, believe also in me. In my Father's house are many mansions; if it were not so, I would have told you. I go to prepare a place for you. And if I go and prepare a place for you, I will come again, and receive you unto myself; that where I am there ye may be also." (John 14.1-3)

CHAPTER 32

SECOND COMING

The second coming of the Lord Jesus Christ back to earth from heaven where He is now, after ascending there, almost 2000 years ago, is also referred to as the second advent of Christ. Advent is defined as the arrival of an important person, event, or development. The reason that it is the second coming is that there was a first coming, when He came as a baby in a manger.

The very important question is why? Why would Jesus leave heaven with all its glories? Why, when most of the world is struggling to attain more status and glory, would Jesus lay aside all of His; and become a man? There are about ten reasons mentioned in the Bible. Probably the reason most mentioned is, to save sinners. Jesus Himself said, "I am come, not to call the righteous, but sinners to repentance." (Matthew 9.13) He said in Matthew 5:17-18, "Think not that I am come to destroy the Law, or the Prophets: I am not come to destroy but to fulfill. For verily I say unto you: Till heaven and earth pass, one jot or one tittle shall in no wise pass from the Law, till all shall be fulfilled." Also in Matthew 20:28 it says "Even as the Son of man came not to be ministered unto, but to minister, and to give His life a ransom for many." Here again Jesus does the opposite, because the natural trend is that most want to be served. "And He said unto them, I must preach the kingdom of God to other cities also; for therefore am I sent. And He preached in the synagogues of Galilee." (Luke 4:43-44) Note that much of the ministry of Jesus was to the Jews. He was their Messiah. The scripture says, "He came unto His own, and His own, received him not."(John 1.11) The thirty or so years that Jesus was here on earth was a period of transition from the Old Testament to the New Testament. There was no church until after Pentecost so the place the people gathered was at the synagogue. So Jesus and the Apostles did much of their preaching and teaching there.

In John 18:37-38, Jesus said, "To this end was I born, and for this cause came I into the world, that I might bear witness to the truth. Everyone that is of the truth heareth my voice. Pilate says unto Him: What is truth?"

John 1:14 reads, "And the Word (Jesus) was made flesh and dwelt among us, (and we beheld his glory, the glory as of the only begotten of the Father), full of grace and truth." Jesus came to show us the Father and He came to do the will of the Father.

John 14:5 "Thomas says unto Him, Lord, we know not whither thou goest and how can we know the way? Jesus saith unto Him, I am the way, the truth, and the life; no man cometh unto the Father but by Me." This verse sums it up: Jesus came to give us the truth, to show us the way, so that we can have eternal life.

Well, we spent a bit of time on the first advent, because it was the most important event that the world had experienced up to that point. I know that some people do not believe this; or at least they don't want to believe it, because they do not want to admit they are not in complete control.

The next important event to happen will be the second coming of the Lord Jesus Christ. After Jesus was raised from the dead; He walked, for forty days, among the people to show himself alive as proof of His resurrection. And He gave commandments to His Apostles, and spoke to them of things pertaining to the kingdom of God. Acts 1:7-11 reads "And he (Jesus) said unto them: "It is not for you to know the times or the seasons, which the Father has put in His own power. But you shall receive power, after that the Holy Ghost is come upon you: And you shall be witnesses unto me both in Jerusalem, and in all Judea, and in Samaria, and unto the uttermost part of the earth. And when He had spoken these things, while they beheld, He was taken up; and a cloud took Him out of their sight. And while they looked steadfastly toward heaven as He went up, behold two men stood beside them in white apparel: Which also said, ye men of Galilee, why stand ye gazing up into heaven? This same Jesus, which is taken up from you into heaven, shall so come in like manner as ye have seen Him go into heaven."

While the main question about the first advent of Jesus, was why? The question concerning the second advent of Jesus is, when? The answer to this question is simple. No one knows, except God Himself. Jesus tells us this in Matthew 24:36, "Of that day and hour knoweth no man, no not the angels of heaven but my Father only." Down through the years people have been setting dates for when Jesus is coming back, but they are consistently wrong.

Throughout the Bible we find phrases like, He is coming soon, the time draws near, and many others, so people expect it to be sooner than it is. From the way the writers of the Bible wrote it seems that they thought it would happen in their life-time: I have heard people from time to time, who say the same thing. God in His infinite wisdom doesn't view time as we do. To Him a thousand years is as a day, we are told this in the Bible. To put that in perspective we have to think of it as God seeing the whole picture and us seeing a very small part. God sees time from eternity past to eternity future, while we think fifty years is a long tine.

Why is it taking so long? God has a plan, briefly; it started with the creation of Adam and Eve who did as they were instructed and multiplied and replenished the earth: But in about sixteen or seventeen hundred years "God saw that the wickedness of man was great in the earth, and that every imagination of the thoughts of men's hearts were only evil continually. And it repented the Lord that He had made man on the earth, and it grieved Him at his heart. And the Lord said, I will destroy man whom I have created from the face of the earth." (Genesis 6:5-7) Only eight people were saved from the flood And God said the same thing to them that He had said to Adam and Eve. "And God blessed Noah and his sons, and said unto them, be fruitful, and multiply, and replenish the earth." (Genesis 9:1) God made a covenant with Noah and his offspring and then approximately two hundred and fifty years later God talked to Abraham and he believed God and it was counted to him for righteousness. God made a covenant with Abraham and promising to make a great nation of him, (Genesis 12:1-3) "Now the Lord had said unto Abram, get thee out of thy country, and from thy kindred, and from thy father's house, unto a land that I will show you. And I will make of thee a great nation. And I will bless thee, and make thy name great; and thou shalt be a blessing. And I will bless them that bless thee, and curse him that curseth thee, and in thee shall all of the families of the earth be blessed."

What God promised came true and from Abraham came the Nation of Israel, which became God's chosen people. Out of which came Jesus Christ who came to be the Savior of the world. After the death of Jesus on the cross, and after the day of Pentecost: The Jews having rejected Jesus, their Messiah; Peter and Paul began ministering to the Gentiles many of whom became believers. God's plan included building a church, which was to be made up of those who believe in His Son: Believing Jews and believing

Gentiles were blended together to form one group, called the Body of Christ, the Church, with Christ as the head. God set the unbelieving Jews aside: But they continue to be the nation of Israel, and they are still God's chosen people. God's plan is to continue to build the true church, primarily with converts from the unconverted Gentiles throughout the whole world. This plan is being accomplished during this present age, at a rapid rate, as missionaries are going all over the world with the message of Salvation. What does all of this have to do with the Second Coming of the Lord? It is important because when the last person is converted and thus completes the Body of Christ, the Church, then the Lord will come.

Just as God was long suffering before He destroyed the world by flood; He is longsuffering before the coming of the Lord. Two portions of scripture make this plain. (1 Peter 3:20) "When once the longsuffering of God waited in the days of Noah, while the Ark was being prepared, wherein few, that is, eight souls were saved by water." Noah preached all the time he was building the Ark, with no results. (2 Peter 3:9) "The Lord is not slack concerning His promise, as some men count slackness; but is longsuffering toward us, not willing that any should perish, but that all should come to repentance."

"For God so loved the world that He gave His only begotten Son, that whosoever believeth in Him should not perish, but have everlasting life:" John 3:16."It is difficult to understand why anyone would refuse the free gift of Salvation, and in turn, not be ready when Jesus returns to earth again.

It is interesting that each chapter of First Thessalonians ends with a reference to the coming of the Lord. (1.9-10) "How ye turned to God from idols to serve the living and true God: And to wait for His Son from heaven, whom He raised from the dead, even Jesus, which delivered us from the wrath to come" (2.19-20) "For what is our hope, or joy, or crown of rejoicing? Are not even ye in the presence of our Lord Jesus Christ at His coming? For ye are our glory and joy". (3.19) "To the end that He may stablish your hearts unblamable in holiness before God, even our Father, at the coming of our Lord Jesus Christ with all His saints". (4.16-18) "For the Lord Himself shall descend from heaven with a shout, with the voice of the archangel, and with the trump of God; and the dead in Christ shall rise first: Then we which are alive and remain shall be caught up together with them in the clouds, to meet the Lord in the air; and so shall we ever be with the Lord. Wherefore comfort one another with these words." (5.23) "And the very God of peace sanctify you wholly; and I pray God your whole soul and spirit and body be preserved blameless unto the coming of our Lord Jesus Christ."

While the first question concerning the second advent of our Lord is when, there are other questions like how and why. The question of how is easy because the book of The Acts tells us in chapter one verse nine thru eleven: "And when He had spoken these things, while they beheld, He was taken up; and a cloud received Him out of their sight. And as they looked steadfastly toward heaven as He went up, behold, two men stood by them in white apparel: Which also said, Ye men of Galilee, why stand you gazing up into heaven? This same Jesus, which is taken up from you into heaven, shall so come in like manner as ye have seen Him go into heaven." This is the main characteristic of the coming of Jesus back to earth again: coming in the clouds of heaven, and in another place coming in a cloud with power and great glory.

Another question is why is he coming back again? For starters let us look at 1Corinthians 4:5 (NIV): "Therefore judge nothing before the appointed time; wait till the Lord comes, He will bring to light what is hidden in darkness and will expose the motives of men's hearts. At that time each will receive his praise from God." We desire to understand everything, but the truth is we do not. We would like to know, but there are many things that are hidden. In the scriptures there are many mysteries, some have been revealed from time to time, but some will remain hidden until the coming of the Lord. When He comes He will bring understanding. In the, mean time, the next verse (6) tells us, "Do not go beyond what is written." When we do we can get into a lot of confusion. Then everyone comes up with different ideas.

"For the Son of man (Jesus) will come in the glory of his Father with His angels, and then He will reward every man according to his works." (Matthew 16:27) Giving rewards and praise where it is due is part of what takes place at the second coming of the Lord Jesus.

We are inclined to think of the happenings in scripture as events, when in reality, most times they are extended over a period of time; this is especially true of the second coming, which includes judgments of the unbelieving individuals, the judgment of nations, the setting up of a kingdom, among others. The second coming of Christ includes the rapture of the saints which is our blessed hope, followed by the visible return of Christ with His saints to reign on the earth for a thousand years.

"For as the lightning comes from the east and flashes to the west, so will be the coming of the Son of man. Wherever there is a carcass, there the vultures will gather. Immediately after the distress of those days the sun will be darkened, and the moon will not give its light; the stars will fall from the sky, and the heavenly bodies will be shaken. At that time the sign of the Son of Man will appear in the sky. And all of the nations of the earth will mourn. They will see the Son of Man coming on the clouds of the sky, with power and great glory." (Matt. 24:27 NIV)

"I saw heaven standing open and there before me was a white horse, whose rider is called Faithful and True. With justice He judges and makes war. His eyes are like blazing fire, and on His head are many crowns, He has a name written on Him that no one but Himself knows. He is dressed in a robe dipped in blood, and His name is the Word of God. The armies of heaven were following Him, riding on white horses and dressed in fine linen, white and clean." (Rev. 19:11 NIV)

"And I saw an angel coming down out of heaven, having the key to the Abyss and holding in his hand a giant chain. He seized the dragon, that ancient serpent, which is the devil, or Satan, and bound him for a thousand years. He threw him in the Abyss, and locked and sealed it over him, to keep him from deceiving the nations any more until the thousand years were ended. After that, he must be set free for a short time. I saw thrones on which were seated those who had been given authority to judge. And I saw the souls of those who had been beheaded because of their testimony for Jesus and because of the word of God. They had not worshiped the beast or his image and had not received his mark on their foreheads or their hands. They came to life and reigned with Christ a thousand years. (The rest of the dead did not come to life until the thousand years were ended.) This is the first resurrection. Blessed and holy are those who have part in the first resurrection. The second death has no power over them, but they will be priests of God and of Christ and will reign with Him a thousand years." (Rev. 20:1-4 NIV)

The thousand year reign will bring the salvation of national Israel and the establishment of universal peace. (Rom. 11:25-26) "For I would not, brethren, that ye should be ignorant of this mystery, lest ye should be wise in your own conceits; that blindness in part is happened to Israel, until the fullness of the Gentiles be come in. And so all Israel shall be saved, as it is written, there shall come out of Sion the deliverer, and shall turn away ungodliness from Jacob. For this is my covenant unto them when I shall take away their sins." That is a lot of scripture and it gives us some things to think about. The problem is that it is difficult to put it all together in proper order, which is what most of us would like to do. However the purpose of scripture is to save sinners and sanctify character, not satisfy curiosity. There is much in scripture about the coming of the Lord and the end times, but there are many mysteries, which are not revealed; and at this time we are left in the dark, so to speak. As time goes on, and we get closer to the end we will be able to understand more. Jesus said, "And when these things begin to come to pass, then look up and lift up your heads for your redemption draweth nigh." (Luke 21.28)

Since there are several schools of thought I won't be dogmatic. When I started this book, my purpose was to write the simple truth about some truths which are quite plain in scripture, but about which there is confusion, in the mind of some. The point being this subject doesn't fit; so I will give you a few thoughts that may be of benefit.

Many believe that the next event will be the rapture, which is explained in 1 Thessalonians. 4:16: "For the Lord Himself shall descend from heaven with a shout, with the voice of the archangel, and with the trump of God; and the dead in Christ shall rise first: Then we which are alive and remain shall be caught up together with them in the clouds, to meet the Lord in the air; and so shall we ever be with the Lord. Wherefore comfort one another with these words." This is referred to as the blessed hope of the

Church; it is a source of strength in time of persecution and trouble.

The rapture is followed by the visible return of Christ with His saints to reign on earth for one thousand years. This millennial reign will bring the salvation of Israel and the establishment of universal peace.

There is the Great Tribulation, which is a period of seven years in which the Antichrist, also called the beast, gets control. This seven- year period is believed to come after the rapture and before the second coming of the Lord. If this is true the true Church will be taken out before the Tribulation and return with the Lord at His second coming. Then the Lord will defeat the Antichrist and all the armies assembled with him. After that will be the thousand year millennial reign of Christ. There will be a final judgment in which the wicked dead will be raised and judged according to their works. Whosoever is not found in the book of life, together with the devil and his angels, the beast and the false prophet, will be assigned to everlasting punishment in the lake which burns with fire and brimstone, which is the second death.

2 Peter 3:10: "But the day of the Lord will come as a thief in the night; in the which the heavens shall pass away with a great noise and the elements shall melt with fervent heat, the earth also and the works that are therein shall be burned up. Seeing then that all these things shall be dissolved, what manner of persons ought ye to be in all conversation and godliness: Looking for and hasting unto the coming of the

day of God, wherein the heavens being on fire shall be dissolved, and the elements shall melt with fervent heat? Nevertheless we, according to His promise, look for new heavens and a new earth, wherein dwelleth righteousness. Wherefore, beloved, seeing that ye look for such things, be diligent that you might be found of him in peace, without spot, and blameless. And account that the longsuffering of our Lord is salvation; even as our beloved Paul also according to the wisdom given unto him has written unto you: As also in all his epistles, speaking in them of these things; in which are some things hard to be understood, which they that are unlearned and unstable wrest, as they do also the other scriptures, unto their own destruction. Ye therefore beloved, seeing you know these things before, beware lest ye also, being led away with the error of the wicked, fall from your own steadfastness. But grow in grace and in the knowledge of our Lord and Savior Jesus Christ: To Him be glory both now and forever. Amen."

The Bible gives us an abundance of information about the coming of our Lord but it doesn't spell every thing out and line it all up for us, and although, as Peter says, some things are hard to understand, much of the Bible is very plain, especially on the basics of the gospel of Jesus Christ. We are told the Lord is coming, and we are told again and again that we ought to be ready.

The important thing is to get the important things right. Peter uses the word wrest, which means, to twist or distort. One rule of Bible interpretation is to take it literal whenever possible. That means, it means, what it says, unless there is good reason to think otherwise. Another rule is compare scripture with the rest of scripture, and if it isn't in harmony, further study is necessary. Peter is warning against listening to those who are in error, and twisting the scripture. Sometimes good people get led away from the truth. However bible scholars do disagree on some points at times but that cannot be avoided, considering the differences in humans; but let us disagree peaceably. One problem is those three words that are so hard to say; "I don't know."

CHAPTER 33

PARABLES

There is some confusion concerning parables, as Jesus used them in His ministry. The definition of parable is, a story told to illustrate a moral or a spiritual truth. In the thirteenth chapter of the gospel of Matthew Jesus uses seven parables to illustrate what the Kingdom of Heaven is like. Each of these parables deals with a mystery of the Kingdom of Heaven. A mystery is a previously hidden truth, now divinely revealed, but in which a super natural element still remains. These seven mysteries together describe the presence of the Gospel in the world during this present age; starting with the ministry of Jesus and ending with the harvest of redeemed souls at the end of the age.

Jesus used parables in this instance because He wanted His followers, the believers, to understand the mysteries of the Kingdom of Heaven, but it wasn't for the unbelievers. After Jesus finished speaking to the great multitude that had gathered on the sea shore the Disciples said to Him, "Why speakest thou to them in parables? He answered and said unto them, because it is given unto you to know the mysteries of the Kingdom of Heaven, but unto them it is not given." (Matthew 13:10) Then verse thirty-four says; "All these things Jesus spake unto the multitude in parables; and without a parable spake he not unto them, (the multitude).

This phrase; "without a parable spoke He not unto them," has been twisted by some to mean that this applies to the whole scripture, In other words, in all scripture, God is speaking in parables; consequently it can be interpreted as a parable. But Jesus spoke to the multitude in parables, so the unbelievers in the multitude would not understand. The point being, that if you interpret the Bible as a parable you can make it mean most any thing you want it to mean.

Much of the Bible is History, telling of events that happened, and telling what people accomplished, and what they did right, and many times what they did wrong. However the scripture tells us: "All scripture is give by inspiration of God, and is profitable for doctrine, for reproof, for correction, for instruction in righteousness:" (2 Timothy 3:16) So we can see that much of the Bible cannot be rightly interpreted by treating it as a parable. Another point to notice is that Jesus didn't always talk to the multitudes in parables. (Matthew 22:31-33) "But as touching the resurrection of the dead, have ye not read that which was spoken unto you by God saying, I am the God of Abraham, and the God of Isaac, and the God of

Jacob? God is not the God of the dead, but of the living. And when the multitude heard this, they were astonished at His doctrine." It is important to not take other people's interpretation without checking it out. Be like the people of Berea who were said to be "more, noble than those in Thessalonica, in that they received the word with all readiness of mind, and searched the scriptures daily, whether those things were true. Therefore many of them believed: Also of honorable women which were Greeks, and of men not a few." (Acts 17:11-12)

Jesus also used parables extensively in His teaching, by comparing everyday stories to spiritual truths. (Matthew 24:32-33) "Now learn a parable of the fig tree; when his branch is yet tender, and putteth forth leaves, ye know that Summer is nigh: So likewise ye, when ye shall see all these things, know that it is near, even at the doors." Jesus is telling them of His return to earth, and is referring to the things He had just mentioned to them; the sun and moon becoming dark, the stars falling, and the powers of heaven shaken.

Some people want to interpret the parable by giving meaning to the falling stars and each of the other items of the parable. It is easy to see how you can end up with almost any interpretation. However, there are some portions of scripture that require this kind of interpretation. The book of Revelation, for example has some symbolism that requires it. When this is necessary it is important to compare scripture with scripture and be sure our interpretation does not depart from the over all teaching of the whole Bible.

It is very necessary to approach Bible study with an open mind but it seems that it is exceedingly difficult for many people to do that. I am fearful that to many times the scripture is approached, whether consciously or not, with the purpose of proving what is already thought to be true or what is desired to be true. It is possible to make the Bible say almost anything, but it should always be our goal to strive for its true meaning.

CHAPTER 34

THE GODHEAD

Jesus said, "If ye love Me, keep My command-ments. And I will pray the Father and He shall give you another Comforter, that He may abide with you forever: Even the Spirit of truth; whom the world cannot receive, because it seeth him not, neither knoweth Him; but ye know Him; for He dwelleth with you, and shall be in you." (John 14:15-17) Here, Jesus is speaking, and He is talking about the Father and the Holy Spirit, who He refers to as, both another Comforter and as the Spirit of truth. These verses show us that the Godhead is composed of three persons, Father, Son and Holy Spirit. Throughout scripture we find distinctions and relationships in the Godhead. There is a unity in the Godhead. There is that in the Father which makes Him the Father and not the Son; there is that in the Son which makes Him the Son and not the Father; and there is that in the Holy Spirit which makes Him the Holy Spirit and not either the Father or the Son. The Father is the Begetter; the Son is the Begotten; the Holy Spirit is the one proceeding from the Father and the Son. Because these three persons in the Godhead are in a state of unity there is but one Lord God Almighty and His name one as compared to many gods.

The Father, the Son, and the Holy Spirit are never identical as to person; nor confused as to relation; nor divided in respect as to the Godhead; nor opposed as to cooperation. The Son is in the Father and the Father in the Son as to relationship. The Son is with the Father and the Father is with the Son as to fellowship. The Father is not from the Son, but the Son, is from the Father, as to, authority. The Holy Spirit is from the Father and from the Son proceeding, as to nature, relation, cooperation, and authority. Hence no person in the Godhead, either exists or works separately or independently of the others.

The Lord Jesus Christ is a proper name and it is never applied, in the New Testament, either to the Father or the Holy Spirit. It therefore belongs exclusively to the Son of God. The Lord Jesus Christ, as to His divine and eternal nature, is the proper and only Begotten of the Father, but as to His human nature, He is the proper Son of man. He is, therefore, acknowledged to be both God and man; who because He is God and man, is Immanuel, which means God with us. Since the name Immanuel embraces both God and man, in the one person, our Lord Jesus Christ, it follows that the title Son of God describes His proper deity, and the title Son of man, His proper humanity. Therefore the title Son of God belongs to the order of eternity, and the title of Son of man to the order of time.

"I have not written unto you because you know not the truth, but because ye know it, and that no lie is of the truth. Who is a liar but he that denieth that Jesus is the Christ? He is antichrist that denieth the Father and the Son. Whosoever denieth the Son, the same hath not the Father: But he that acknowledgeth the Son hath the Father also." (1John 2:21-23)

"Beloved, believe not every spirit, but tries the spirits whether they are of God: because many false prophets are gone out into the world. Hereby know ye the Spirit of God: Every spirit that confesseth that Jesus Christ is come in the flesh is of God: And every spirit that confesseth not that Jesus Christ is come in the flesh is not of God: and this is that spirit of antichrist, whereof ye have heard that it should come; and even now already is it in the world. Ye are of God, little children, and have overcome them: because greater is he that is in you, than he that is in the world. They are of the world: therefore speak they of the world, and the world heareth them." (1John 4:1-5)

From these scriptures it can be seen that to deny that the Father as a real and eternal Father, and the Son as a real and eternal Son, is a denial of the distinction and relationship in the being of God; and the denial of the Father and the Son and a displacement of the truth that Jesus Christ is come in the flesh.

"Whosoever transgresseth, and abideth not in the doctrine of Christ, hath not God. He that abideth in the doctrine of Christ, he hath both the Father and the

Son.If there come any unto you, and bring not this doctrine, receive him not Into your house, neither bid him God speed:" (2John 1.9-10)

The Son of God, our Lord Jesus Christ, having by Himself purged our sins, sat down on the right hand of the Majesty on high; angels and principalities and powers having been made subject unto Him, and having been made both Lord and Christ. He sent the Holy Spirit, that we, in the name of Jesus, might bow our knees and confess that Jesus Christ is Lord to the glory of God the Father until the end, when the Son shall become subject to the Father in order that God may be all in all.

Since the Father has delivered all judgment unto the Son, it is not only the express duty of all in heaven and all on earth to bow the knee, but it is an unspeakable joy in the Holy Spirit to ascribe unto the Son all the attributes of deity, and to give Him all the glory and honor due to His name.

"Let this mind be in you, which was also in Christ Jesus: Who, being in the form of God, thought it not robbery to be equal with God: But made himself of no reputation, and took upon him the form of a servant, and was made in the likeness of men: And being found in fashion as a man, he humbled himself, and became obedient unto death, even the death of the cross. Wherefore God also hath highly exalted him, and given him a name which is above every name: That at the name of Jesus every knee should bow, of things in heaven, and things in earth, and things under the earth; And that every tongue should confess that Jesus Christ is Lord, to the glory of God the Father." (Philippians 2:5-11)

We are assured that Jesus is divine because of several things: 1. He is the only begotten Son of God.2. His virgin birth. 3. His sinless life 4. His miracles 5. His death on the cross 6. His resurrection 7. His exaltation to the right hand of God, in heaven

There is opposition to the Lord and Savior Jesus Christ, with many religions refusing to accept that He is divine. Many say He was a good man, and others say He was a Prophet, while others are hostile toward Him.

Paul the Apostle in his letter to the Colossians 2:8-10 has this to say, "Beware lest any man spoil you through philosophy and vain deceit, after the tradition of men, after the rudiments of the world, and not after Christ. For in him dwelleth all the fulness of the Godhead bodily. And ye are complete in him, which is the head of all principality and power:" Notice that he is stating that in Christ exists, all the fullness of the Godhead: And that He is head of all principality and power: And in verse three, in Him are hid all the treasure of wisdom and knowledge. When you put all of that together it gives you something to think about, especially when we think of everything else He has done for us.

"Giving thanks unto the Father, which hath made us meet to be partakers of the inheritance of the saints in light: Who hath delivered us from the power of darkness, and hath translated us into the kingdom of his dear Son: In whom we have redemption through his blood, even the forgiveness of sins:

Who is the image of the invisible God, the firstborn of every creature: For by him were all things created, that are in heaven, and that are in earth, visible and invisible, whether they be thrones, or dominions, or principalities, or powers: all things were created by him, and for him: And he is before all things, and by him all things consist. And he is the head of the body, the church: who is the beginning, the firstborn from the dead; that in all things he might have the preeminence. For it pleased the father that in him should all fullness dwell;" (Colossians 1:12-19)

Ephesians 1:20-23 tells us about God's mighty power. "Which he wrought in Christ, when he raised him from the dead, and set him at his own right hand in the heavenly places, Far above all principality, and power, and might, and dominion, and every name that is named, not only in this world, but also in that which is to come: And hath put all things under his feet, and gave him to be the head over all things to the church, Which is his body, the fullness of him that filleth all in all."1Peter 3:22 adds, "Who (Jesus) is gone into heaven, and is on the right hand of God; angels and authorities and powers being made subject unto him."

Many have denied, and many still are denying Jesus, while others attempt to diminish Him to a position of a much lesser importance; however these portions of scripture, and many others, prove without a doubt that God has put His Son in control of much of what is taking place today, and will take place in the future. All, of the world needs to know; most of all, that Jesus is the only way to heaven, and eternal life.

CHAPTER 35

GRACE

The law came through Moses, while grace and truth came by Jesus Christ. This was undoubtedly the greatest change in Christianity. The big difference is that law is connected with Moses and works, and grace is connected with Christ and faith. Grace is the kindness and love of our Savior toward man.

In Johns' Gospel 1:15 NIV "John the Baptist testifies of Jesus. He cries out, saying, this was He of whom I said, He who comes after me has surpassed me because He was before me. From the fullness of His grace we have all received one blessing after another. For the law was given through Moses; grace and truth came through Jesus Christ."

There are, several reason, which make this transition so very important. Under the law God demanded righteousness from man but, under grace, He gives righteousness to man. The law is like a mirror that reveals mans sin, but cannot remove it, for only the blood of Christ, shed on cavalry, can wash the sin away. Another difference is; the law blesses the good, while grace saves the bad. Law demands that blessings be earned; grace is a free gift. This is where there is misunderstanding because human nature seems to want to pay for, or earn everything. The question is, "what must I do to be saved?" The guard of the jail in Philippi, ask Paul and Silas this question: (Acts 16:31) and_they answered, "Believe on the Lord Jesus Christ, and thou shalt be saved, and thy house."

To believe on the Lord Jesus Christ, means to believe that Jesus was born of a virgin, died on the cross for our sins, was buried and rose again the third day, ascended in to heaven and is seated at the right hand of God.

Salvation is a free gift which; cannot be bought, earned, or bargained for in any way. It can only be accepted. This is why joining a church won't save you, or being baptized or confirmed, or being good; but only by believing, are we saved.

"But God, who is rich in mercy, for his great love wherewith he loved us, Even when we were dead in sins, hath quickened us together with Christ, (by grace ye are saved;) And hath raised us up together, and made us sit together in heavenly places in Christ Jesus: That in the ages to come he might shew the exceeding riches of his grace in his kindness toward us through Christ Jesus. For by grace are ye saved through faith; and that not of yourselves: it is the gift of God: Not of works, lest any man should boast."

(Ephesians 2:4-9) This portion of scripture says not of works, but there is a place for works: However the place is not prior to salvation; but it is after. Salvation is by grace through faith. The place for good works; is after salvation: In fact they are very necessary then. "Even so faith, if it hath not works, is dead, being alone. Yea, a man may say thou hast faith, and I have works: Show me thy faith without thy works, and I will show you my faith by my works." In other words, we are justified (declared righteous) before God by faith, but we are justified before men by works. God can see, and know our faith, but men can see only our works. (James 2:17-18) "Let your light so shine before men, that they may see your good works, and glorify your Father which is in heaven. (Matthew 5:16) "That ye might walk worthy of the Lord unto all pleasing, being fruitful in every good work, and increasing in the knowledge of God." (Colossians 1:10)

There is much emphasis on doing good works of all kinds; like being good to others and helping the needy; and bearing fruit, and being of service wherever needs exist.

Grace is not only a method of divine dealing in salvation, but is also the method God uses in the believers life and service. The believer is not under law, but now is under grace. God has, by grace, brought the believer into the highest conceivable position. (Ephesians 1:4-10 NIV) "For He chose us in Him before the creation of the world to be holy and blameless in His sight. In love He predestined us to be adopted as His sons through Jesus Christ, in accordance with His will and pleasure, to the praise of His glorious grace, which He has freely given us in the One He loves. In Him we have redemption through His blood, and the forgiveness of sins, in accordance with the riches of God's grace that He lavished on us with all wisdom and understanding, And He made known to us the mystery of His will according to His good pleasure, which He purposed in Christ to be put into effect when the times will have reached their fulfillment to bring all things in heaven and on earth together under one head, even Christ."

As we have said, Adam sinned, and by doing so brought condemnation upon all men. For as by one man's disobedience many were made sinners, so by the obedience by one man (Jesus), many are made righteous. The introduction of the law caused sin to increase, in that all could see the extent of their failure to obey God's law. But the more we see our sinfulness, the more we see God's abounding grace, forgiving us. Before this, sin ruled over all men and brought them to death, but now God's kindness rules instead, giving us right standing with God, and resulting in eternal life through Jesus Christ our Lord. Well then, shall we keep on sinning so that God can keep on showing us more and more kindness and forgiveness? The answer is, "of course not!" How shall we, who are dead to sin, live any longer therein?

Sin's power over us was broken when we became Christians and became a part of the church of Jesus Christ. Through the death of Christ the power of our sinful nature was shattered, so sin has no place in the life of Christians. Though Christians are free from the Law of Moses, they are not free to break God's moral law.

A large part of being a Christian is a matter of rewards, blessings, and riches; all of which we do not deserve. The Bible speaks much of love, joy, peace, longsuffering, gentleness and goodness. It is interesting that most other religions have little to say about these things; they seem to be more like being under the law. Some one said, "He who falls from faith lands in the law." Of course they may have never been under law, just unbelievers.

In some circles there exists, what is known as legalism, which is defined as, strict, literal, and often excessive adherence to the law. Some Christians become legalistic. They are a stickler for rules, sometimes for others more than for themselves. They are always ready to condemn others for their activities. Let no man therefore judge you in meat, or in drink, or in respect of an holyday, or of the new moon, or of the Sabbath days:" Colossians 2:16 Legalism is the robber here stealing your liberty in Christ and making you live by religious regulations instead of by God's grace. Salvation through belief in Jesus Christ sets us free to live according to His will; not someone else's will, or the will of the world. Jesus said, "If ye love me, keep my commandments." (John 14.15)

But now God has shown us a way to heaven: Not by being good enough and trying to keep His laws, but by a new way (though not new, really, for the Scripture told about it long ago). Now God says He will accept us and acquit us, declare us not guilty, if we trust in Jesus Christ to take away our sins. And we all can be saved in the same way, by coming to Christ, no matter who we are or what we have been. Yes all have sinned; all fall short of God's glorious ideal; yet God declares us not guilty of offending Him if we trust in Jesus Christ, who in His kindness freely takes away our sins. For God sent Christ Jesus to take the punishment for our sins and to end all God's anger against us. He used Christ's blood and our faith as the means of saving us from His wrath. In this way He was being entirely fair, even though He did not punish those who sinned in former times. For He was looking forward to the time when Christ would come and take away those sins. And in these days also He can receive sinners in the same way, because Jesus took away their sins. But isn't this unfair for God to let criminals go free, and say that they are innocent? No, for He does it on the basis of their trust in Jesus who took away their sins, by paying the penalty for their sin.

"Therefore thou art inexcusable, O man, whosoever thou art that judgest: for wherein thou judgest another, thou condemnest thyself; for thou that judgest doest the same things. But we are sure that the judgment of God is according to truth against them which commit such things. And thinkest thou this, O man, that judgest them which do such things, and doest the same, that thou shalt escape the judgment of God? Or despisest thou the riches of his goodness and forbearance and longsuffering; not knowing that the goodness of God leadeth thee to repentance?" (Romans 2:1-4) It is truly strange, and sad, that many people do not understand the grace of God; they have ill feelings, and many times hostility, because they think God is not fair in His dealings, while the truth is He is longsuffering, righteous, and just with man in spite of mans ignorance.

So we see that grace is not only a method of God dealing with man in salvation through a long period of time, but it is also the method of God's dealing in the believer's life and service. As a believer man is not under law, but under grace: God having by grace brought him into the highest conceivable position, which is that He has made us accepted in the Beloved. God ceaselessly works through grace, to impart to, and perfect in him, the many corresponding graces. Grace, therefore, stands connected with service; and with Christian growth. Paul says in, 2Peter 3:17 "Therefore, beloved, seeing you know these things before; beware unless you also, being led away with the error of the wicked, fall from your own steadfastness. But grow in the grace and in the knowledge of our Lord and Savior Jesus Christ. To Him; be glory both now and forever. Amen." (2 Peter 3.18)

Chapter 36

ISRAEL

Some time ago a wise man told me; "if you want to understand the Bible, you have to understand the Jews." Up until that time I, like many people, didn't give much importance to them. I knew the main stories about them, and all that; but I had never studied or tried to put it all together. From that time I started to pay attention and have gradually learned something of their importance. Now my island of knowledge is larger; which makes my shoreline of wonder extensive. In other words I don't know it all, but we will look at what we can find in the Bible, which records the history of Israel.

The word, Jew, is a New Testament word for Israelite. In fact, the words Hebrew, Israel, and Jew are all used to speak of the same people. In order to understand how the Israelites fit in, it will be necessary to go back to the beginning of the early world.

Psalm 93.2: "Thy throne is established of old: thou art from everlasting." Psalm 90.2: "Before the mountains were brought forth, or ever thou hadst formed the earth and the world, even from everlasting to everlasting, thou art God." Colossians 1:17: "And He is before all things, and by Him all things consist." John 1:1: "In the beginning was the word, and the word was with God, and the word was God. And the same was in the beginning with God." Proverbs 8:12-13: "I wisdom dwell with prudence, and find out knowledge of witty inventions. The fear of the LORD is to hate evil: pride, and arrogancy, and the evil way, and the froward mouth, do I hate." V.22-31 "The LORD possessed me in the beginning of his way, before his works of old. I was set up from everlasting, from the beginning, or ever the earth was. When there were no depths, I was brought forth; when there were no fountains abounding with water. Before the mountains were settled, before the hills was I brought forth: While as yet he had not made the earth, nor the fields, nor the highest part of the dust of the world. When he prepared the heavens, I was there: when he set a compass upon the face of the depth: When he established the clouds above: when he strengthened the fountains of the deep: When he gave to the sea his decree, that the waters should not pass his commandment: when he appointed the foundations of the earth: Then I was by him, as one brought up with him: and I was daily his delight, rejoicing always before him; Rejoicing in the habitable part of his earth; and my delights were with the sons of men.

These portions of scripture are speaking of history before the creation of the world; and they refer to the eternity of Jesus and the Holy Spirit. A scripture that bears out the truth concerning the eternity of Jesus is Colossians 1:15-20 "Who is the image of the invisible God, the firstborn of every creature: For by him were all things created, that are in heaven, and that are in earth, visible and invisible, whether they be thrones, or dominions, or principalities, or powers: all things were created by him, and for him: And he is before all things, and by him all things consist. And he is the head of the body, the church: who is the beginning, the firstborn from the dead; that in all things he might have the preeminence. For it pleased the Father that in him should all fulness dwell; And, having made peace through the blood of his cross, by him to reconcile all things unto himself; by him, I say, whether they be things in earth, or things in heaven."

All three: God the Father, Jesus Christ, the Son, and the Holy Spirit existed before the creation; and all three participated in the creation. From the creation to the flood was a period of 1656 years. (These early dated are now, known to not be accurate) During this time divine dealing had been with the whole human race. There had been neither Jew nor Gentile: All had been one race, all descendents from Adam and Eve.

The human race has been compared to a large river, which had been flowing for a little over 2000 years, when God called Abraham: Which was the birth of the nation of Israel which became a small stream branching off from the large river. This large stream flows on, and to distinguish it from Israel is called Gentile.

Israel was called to be a witness to the other nations, so that they could understand that to serve God in the midst of universal idolatry could bring blessing and divine favor. Israel was called to receive and preserve divine revelations. Deuteronomy 4:5-8 "Behold, I have taught you statutes and judgments, even as the LORD my God commanded me, that ye should do so in the land whither ye go to possess it. Keep therefore and do them; for this is your wisdom and your understanding in the sight of the nations, which shall hear all these statutes, and say, Surely this great nation is a wise and understanding people. For what nation is there so great, who hath God so nigh unto them, as the LORD our God is in all things that we call upon him for? And what nation is there so great, that hath statutes and judgments so righteous as all this law, which I set before you this day?"

On the surface what Israel was called upon to do sounds simple. They were to be a witness to the surrounding nations; and they were to take the Divine revelations and the other things they had been taught, to the land they were going to possess, and teach them there. Their witness to the other nations was meant to demonstrate to them the benefits of serving the true God. One other thing this recently formed nation was to accomplish; was to produce the Messiah.

From chapter 12 of Genesis to Matthew 12:45 the Scriptures have Israel, primarily in view, not the large Gentile segment of civilization: Although, this Gentile segment is much larger, with many nations, who have accomplished many things; that are not recorded in the Bible. However many happenings and dates can be harmonized, thus proving the accuracy of the Bible in cases where this is possible.

ABRAHAM

The nation of Israel actually started with one man, Abraham, the Hebrew, whose name at that time was Abram. He was born in Ur of Chaldea, three hundred fifty years after the flood. He was a descendant of Shem: one of Noah's three sons. The study of Abraham is of great importance because he was chosen of God to become the father of a new spiritual race. He was the leader of a great spiritual movement, called God's elect, which means, chosen.

While living with his father in Haran, Abraham received a message from the Lord calling upon him to separate himself from his old associations and go forth into a new country. He was promised the Divine favor, a great posterity, and that he should become a blessing to all the families of the earth. He obeyed the call, and thus became the leader of that innumerable company, of pilgrims: who have sought a city whose builder and maker is God.

Genesis 12:1-4: "Now the LORD had said unto Abram, Get thee out of thy country, and from thy kindred, and from thy father's house, unto a land that I will shew thee: And I will make of thee a great nation, and I will bless thee, and make thy name great; and thou shalt be a blessing: And I will bless them that bless thee, and curse him that curseth thee: and in thee shall all families of the earth be blessed. So Abram departed, as the LORD had spoken unto him; and Lot went with him: and Abram was seventy and five years old when he departed out of Haran." He took his wife Sarah, and Lot, all the possessions they had accumulated and the people they had acquired in Haran, and they set out for the land of Canaan, and they arrived there. Abraham traveled through the land as far as the site of the great tree of Moreh at Shechem, which is near the Mediterranean Sea. The Canaanites lived in the land, "And the LORD appeared unto Abram, and said, unto thy seed will I give this land: and there builded he an altar unto the LORD, who appeared unto him." (Verse 7)

Approximately two thousand years later Paul the Apostle wrote about these same events in Hebrews chapter 11 "By faith Abraham, when called to go to a place he would later receive as his inheritance, obeyed and went, even though he did not know where he was going. By faith he made his home in the Promised Land like a stranger in a foreign country; he lived in tents, as did Isaac and Jacob, his son and grandson, who were heirs with him of the same promise. For he was looking forward to the city with foundations, whose architect and builder is God.

By faith Abraham, even though he was past age; and Sarah herself was barren; was enabled to become a father because he considered Him faithful who had made the promise. And so from this one man, and he as good as dead, came descendants as the stars in the sky, and as countless as the sand of the seashore. All of these people were living by faith when they died.

They did not receive the things promised; they only saw and welcomed them from a distance.

From one man, God's chosen nation became a tribe. But let us back track a little. After the flood there was a new beginning, which started with eight people, Noah and his wife, their three sons, and their wives. Two sons, Ham and Japheth, were the ancestors of the Gentiles, and Shem, the ancestor of the nation of Israel. It was approximately 450 years from the birth of Shem to the birth of Abraham; and it was 1650 years from the creation to the flood. This gives us an idea of how slow things developed. I should mention that these spans, of years, might not be accurate, because the early dates are questionable.

Abraham thought he had a problem; he was childless and his wife was barren. But the word of the Lord came unto him in a vision saying, "After these things the word of the LORD came unto Abram in a vision, saying, Fear not, Abram: I am thy shield, and thy exceeding great reward. And Abram said, Lord GOD, what wilt thou give me, seeing I go childless... And he brought him forth abroad, and said, Look now toward heaven, and tell the stars, if thou be able to number them: and he said unto him, So shall thy seed be. And he believed in the LORD; and he counted it to him for righteousness. And he said unto him, I am the LORD that brought thee out of Ur of the Chaldees, to give thee this land to inherit it.... And he said unto Abram, Know of a surety that thy seed shall be a stranger in a land that is not theirs, and shall serve them; and they shall afflict them four hundred years; And also that nation, whom they shall

serve, will I judge: and afterward shall they come out
with great substance... In the same day the LORD
made a covenant with Abram, saying, unto thy seed
have I given this land, from the river of Egypt unto
the great river, the river Euphrates:" (Genesis 15.1-2,
5-7, 13-14, 18)

Abram, like many of us, was getting impatient,
and the Lord didn't seem to be in a hurry, and Abrams
wife, being impatient also, decided to help the Lord
out. "Now Sarai, Abram's wife, bare him no children:
and she had an handmaid, an Egyptian, whose name
was Hagar. And Sarai said unto Abram, Behold now,
the LORD hath restrained me from bearing: I pray
thee, go in unto my maid; it may be that I may obtain
children by her. And Abram hearkened to the voice
of Sarai. And Sarai, Abram's wife, took Hagar her
maid the Egyptian, after Abram had dwelt ten years
in the land of Canaan, and gave her to her husband
Abram to be his wife. And he went in unto Hagar,
and she conceived: and when she saw that she had
conceived, her mistress was despised in her eyes."
(Genesis 16:1-4) From this union a son was born.
Abram was 86 years old when he was born. He
named him Ishmael. Before Ishmael was born the
angel of the Lord told his mother, "I will multiply
your seed exceedingly, that it shall not be numbered
for multitude." (Genesis 16.10)

"And when Abram was ninety years old and nine,
the LORD appeared to Abram, and said unto him, I
am the Almighty God; walk before me, and be thou
perfect. And I will make my covenant between me
and thee, and will multiply thee exceedingly. And

Abram fell on his face: and God talked with him, saying, As for me, behold, my covenant is with thee, and thou shalt be a father of many nations. Neither shall thy name any more be called Abram, but thy name shall be Abraham; for a father of many nations have I made thee... And I will establish my covenant between me and thee and thy seed after thee in their generations for an everlasting covenant, to be a God unto thee, and to thy seed after thee. And I will give unto thee, and to thy seed after thee, the land wherein thou art a stranger, all the land of Canaan, for an everlasting possession; and I will be their God." (Genesis 17.1-5, 7-8)

"And God said unto Abraham, As for Sarai thy wife, thou shalt not call her name Sarai, but Sarah shall her name be. And I will bless her, and give thee a son also of her: yea, I will bless her, and she shall be a mother of nations; kings of people shall be of her." (Genesis 17.15-16) Abraham couldn't believe, and he laughed, because he was now one hundred years old, and Sarah was ninety. "And God said Sarah thy wife shall bear thee a son indeed; and thou shalt call his name Isaac: and I will establish my covenant with him for an everlasting covenant and with his seed after him. (Genesis 17.19) "And as for Ishmael, I have heard thee: Behold, I have blessed him, and will make him fruitful, and will multiply him exceedingly; twelve princes shall he beget, and I will make him a great nation. But my covenant will I establish with Isaac, which Sarah shall bear unto thee at this set time in the next year." (Genesis 17.20-21)

Isaac was born in 2047 B.C. Ishmael was born 14 years before this.

The key phrase here is, "My covenant will I establish with Isaac." This means that the nation of Israel shall develop from Isaac and his line of descendants, and the covenant is with them, and it is forever.

It is important to remember that from Ishmael also, a great nation is promised. It is interesting to note that Ishmael is half Egyptian; and he married an Egyptian wife, which makes his twelve sons three quarters Egyptian and one quarter Hebrew. They became warlike tribal leaders of their settlements and camps in the area where they settled near the border of Egypt. Sarah died thirty-seven years after Isaac was born, and, Abraham, later married Keturah and she bore six sons.

ISAAC and JACOB

Genesis 25:5-6: "And Abraham gave all that he had unto Isaac. But unto the sons of the concubines, which Abraham had, Abraham gave gifts, and sent them away from Isaac his son, while he yet lived, eastward, unto the east country."

Abraham sent his oldest servant back to Abraham's country, to the city of Nahor, in Mesopotamia, to get a wife for Isaac. Through special guidance he found Rebekah, who was a relative of Abraham's brother. About three years after his mother's death, Isaac and Rebekah were married.

"And these are the generations of Isaac, Abraham's son: Abraham begat Isaac: And Isaac was forty years old when he took Rebekah to wife, the daughter of Bethuel the Syrian of Padanaram, the sister to Laban the Syrian. And Isaac intreated the LORD for his wife, because she was barren: and the LORD was intreated of him, and Rebekah his wife conceived. And the children struggled together within her; and she said, If it be so, why am I thus? And she went to enquire of the LORD. And the LORD said unto her, two nations are in thy womb, and two manner of people shall be separated from thy bowels; and the one people shall be stronger than the other people; and the elder shall serve the younger. And when her days to be delivered were fulfilled, behold, there were twins in her womb. And the first came out red, all over like an hairy garment; and they called his name Esau. And after that came his brother out, and his hand took hold on Esau's heel; and his name was called Jacob: and Isaac was threescore years old when she bare them." (Genesis 25:19-26)

These two boys were as opposite as any you ever saw. And to make things worse Isaac loved the hunter, the man's man and Rebekah loved Jacob, the mama's boy, who, the Bible says, was a plain man dwelling in tents. It doesn't sound like a harmonious home. Through a little trickery Jacob and his mother swindled Esau out of his birthright, which Esau didn't think of it as being very important anyway until later.

There was another famine in the land, and when Isaac was considering going down to Egypt the Lord stopped him. "And the LORD appeared unto him, and said, Go not down into Egypt; dwell in the land which I shall tell thee of: Sojourn in this land, and I will be with thee, and will bless thee; for unto thee, and unto thy seed, I will give all these countries, and I will perform the oath which I sware unto Abraham thy father; And I will make thy seed to multiply as the stars of heaven, and will give unto thy seed all these countries; and in thy seed shall all the nations of the earth be blessed; Because that Abraham obeyed my voice, and kept my charge, my commandments, my statutes, and my laws." (Genesis 26:2-5)

Jacob with the help of his mother cheated his brother, Esau, two times, and when Rebekah heard that Esau was planning to kill Jacob; she began to plan for Jacob to escape. Rebekah told Jacob to flee to her brother Laban who lived in Haran. She said, "tarry with him a few days, until your brother's fury turn away from you, and he forgets that which you have done unto him: then I will send, for you, for why should I be deprived of you both the same day?

Jacob left Beersheba and went toward Haran, the first night as he slept he saw a vision. "And, behold, the LORD stood above it, and said, I am the LORD God of Abraham thy father, and the God of Isaac: the land whereon thou liest, to thee will I give it, and to thy seed; And thy seed shall be as the dust of the earth, and thou shalt spread abroad to the west, and to the east, and to the north, and to the south: and in thee and in thy seed shall all the families of the earth be blessed. And, behold, I am with thee, and will keep thee in all places whither thou goest, and will bring thee again into this land; for I will not leave thee, until I have done that which I have spoken to thee of. (Genesis 28.13-15)

Arriving in Haran, Jacob found Laban, Rebekah's brother, and went to work for him. Laban had two daughters so Jacob agreed to work seven years for Rachel, the younger daughter. When the seven years were passed, Laban, on the wedding night, substituted the older daughter; consequently Jacob ended up working another seven years for Rachel. He now had two wives and he loved Rachel more than Leah, which created problems in the family life. "And when the Lord saw that Leah was hated, he opened her womb: but Rachel was barren." (Gen. 29:31) After four sons were born, Leah stopped bearing. Rachel was distressed, and like Sarah before her, she suggested that her husband, Jacob, take her maid, Bilhah, for a wife, which he did. And later he took the handmaid of his other wife, as his wife. From the four wives he had twelve sons who became the heads of the twelve tribes of Israel.

To Leah were born, Ruben, Simeon, Levi, Judah, Issachar, and Zebulun: To Rachel, Joseph, and Benjamin: To Bilah, Dan, and Naphtali: And to Zilpah, Gad, and Asher.

Even though, Laban, Jacob's father in law, cheated him and changed his wages ten times, Jacob out smarted him, and with God's help, left him a wealthy man. Now, after many years, Jacob was on his way back to, Canaan, his home country, with all his family and workers, and an abundance of livestock. But he had a big problem: What about brother Esau? He still would have to face him, so Jacob sent messengers to Esau unto the land of Seir, the country of Edom, and when the messengers returned, they said, "We came to thy brother Esau, and also he cometh to meet thee, and four hundred men with him. Then Jacob was greatly afraid and distressed: and he divided the people that was with him, and the flocks, and herds, and the camels, into two bands; And said, If Esau come to the one company, and smite it, then the other company which is left shall escape. And Jacob said, O God of my father Abraham, and God of my father Isaac, the LORD which saidst unto me, Return unto thy country, and to thy kindred, and I will deal well with thee: I am not worthy of the least of all the mercies, and of all the truth, which thou hast shewed unto thy servant; for with my staff I passed over this Jordan; and now I am become two bands. Deliver me, I pray thee, from the hand of my brother, from the hand of Esau: for I fear him, lest he will come and smite me, and the mother with the children. And thou saidst, I will surely do thee good, and make thy seed as the sand of the sea, which cannot be numbered for multitude" (Genesis 32.6-12)

He stayed there that night: Then he took what ever was handy for a present for Esau: Two hundred she goats, and twenty he goats, two hundred ewes, and twenty rams, thirty milk camels with their colts, forty cows, and ten bulls, twenty she asses, and ten foals. And he gave them to his servants to drive ahead, and to tell Esau they are a present. They stayed another night, and during the night while Jacob was alone he wrestled with a man. "And Jacob was left alone; and there wrestled a man with him until the breaking of the day. And when he saw that he prevailed not against him, he touched the hollow of his thigh; and the hollow of Jacob's thigh was out of joint, as he wrestled with him. And he said, Let me go, for the day breaketh. And he said, I will not let thee go, except thou bless me. And he said unto him, what is thy name? And he said, Jacob. And he said, Thy name shall be called no more Jacob, but Israel: for as a prince hast thou power with God and with men, and hast prevailed. And Jacob asked him, and said; tell me, I pray thee, thy name. And he said, wherefore is it that thou dost ask after my name? And he blessed him there. And Jacob called the name of the place Peniel: for I have seen God face to face and my life is preserved. And as he passed over Penuel the sun rose upon him, and he halted upon his thigh. Therefore the children of Israel eat not of the sinew which shrank, which is upon the hollow of the thigh, unto this day: because he touched the hollow of Jacob's thigh in the sinew that shrank." (Genesis 32:24-32)

Jacob looked up and there was Esau, coming with his four hundred men; Jacob went ahead and bowed to the ground seven times as he approached his brother. But Esau ran to meet Jacob and embraced him; he threw his arms around his neck and kissed him. And they wept. Then Esau looked up and saw the women and children. "Who are these with you?" And he said, "They are the children God has graciously given your servant." The women came with their children and bowed. Esau asked, "What do you mean by all these droves of livestock I met?" "To find favor in your eyes, my lord." He said. Jacob finally persuaded

Esau to take them even though he said he already had plenty. But because Jacob insisted Esau accepted. "And God appeared unto Jacob again, when he came out of Padanaram, and blessed him. And God said unto him, Thy name is Jacob: thy name shall not be called any more Jacob, but Israel shall be thy name: and he called his name Israel. And God said unto him, I am God Almighty: be fruitful and multiply; a nation and a company of nations shall be of thee, and kings shall come out of thy loins; And the land which I gave Abraham and Isaac, to thee I will give it, and to thy seed after thee will I give the land. And God went up from him in the place where he talked with him. And Jacob set up a pillar in the place where he talked with him, even a pillar of stone: and he poured a drink offering thereon, and he poured oil thereon. And Jacob called the name of the place where God spake with him, Bethel." (Gen. 35:9-15)

Notice that the promises, also called covenant, made to Jacob are the same as God had promised to Abraham and Isaac before him. The promise was in two parts; God would make of them a nation and a community of nations, and kings: The other part concerned the land, which is the big problem in the world today, but God promised it, starting with Abraham, and God says over and over again, the promise is forever. Israel has yet to posses all of the Promised Land.

As Jacob traveled from Bethel, his wife, Rachel, died in giving birth to Benjamin, Jacob's twelfth son. Jacob continued living in the Promised Land with his twelve sons.

JOSEPH

Of Jacob's twelve sons Joseph was his favorite; He was the first born of his favorite wife Rachel, and he was the son of his old age, and he made him a coat of many colors, and when his brothers saw that their father loved him more than all the rest, they hated him. Joseph had a dream. "And he said unto them, Hear, I pray you, this dream which I have dreamed: For, behold, we were binding sheaves in the field, and, lo, my sheaf arose, and also stood upright; and, behold, your sheaves stood round about, and made obeisance to my sheaf. And his brethren said to him, Shalt thou indeed reign over us? or shalt thou indeed have dominion over us? And they hated him yet the more for his dreams, and for his words. And he dreamed yet another dream, and told it his brethren, and said, Behold, I have dreamed a dream more; and, behold, the sun and the moon and the eleven stars made obeisance to me. And he told it to his father, and to his brethren: and his father rebuked him, and said unto him, What is this dream that thou hast dreamed? Shall I and thy mother and thy brethren indeed come to bow down ourselves to thee to the earth? And his brethren envied him; but his father observed the saying." (Genesis 37.6-11)

His brothers wanted to kill Joseph, but Reuben, said "don't kill him. Throw him into this pit." So that is what they did, they took off his coat of many colors, and cast him in the pit. As they sat down to eat lunch, a company of When some Ishmaelite traders passed by on their way to Egypt Judah suggested that they sell Joseph to them and they all agreed, so they sold him for twenty pieces of silver: and they brought Joseph into Egypt; where he was bought by Potiphar, an officer of Pharaoh, captain of the guard, an Egyptian.

The story of Joseph's life is very eventful: and it is interesting, and it is worth any one's time to read it: But it is too long to cover here, so we will just hit the high points. He started by being a slave in Potiphar's house; from there he ended up in prison as the result of false accusation by Potiphar's wife. While in prison Joseph, with God's help, gave the interpretation of the dreams of Pharaoh's chief butler and chief baker. Two years later Pharaoh had a dream, himself, which none of his wise men and magicians could interpret. The chief butler told about Joseph interpreting his dream: Joseph interpreted Pharaoh's dream, so Pharaoh rewarded him. "And Pharaoh said unto his servants, Can we find such a one as this is, a man in whom the Spirit of God is? And Pharaoh said unto Joseph, Forasmuch as God hath shewed thee all this, there is none so discreet and wise as thou art: Thou shalt be over my house, and according unto thy word shall all my people be ruled: only in the throne will I be greater than thou. And Pharaoh said unto Joseph, See, I have set thee over all the land of Egypt." (Genesis 41:38-41) The interpretation of Pharaoh's dream was that there would be seven good years followed by seven years of famine. "And Pharaoh called Joseph's name Zaphnathpaaneah; and he gave him to wife Asenath the daughter of Potipherah priest of On. And Joseph went out over all the land of Egypt. And Joseph was thirty years old when he stood before Pharaoh King of Egypt." (Genesis 41:45-46) Thirteen years had passed since he dreamed his dreams. It is interesting that Joseph, an Israelite, now has a Gentile wife, and before the seven years of famine came, two sons were born to them, Manasseh and Epharaim.

During the seven years of plenty Joseph gathered all of the food around each city and stored it in the cities. The famine, when it came, was world wide, and all the countries came to Joseph, in Egypt to buy corn.

When Jacob heard there was corn in Egypt he sent all of Joseph's brothers except Benjamin, down to buy some. At first they didn't recognize Joseph, but later he revealed his identity to them. "And Joseph said unto his brethren, Come near to me, I pray you. And they came near. And he said, I am Joseph your brother, whom ye sold into Egypt. Now therefore be not grieved, nor angry with yourselves, that ye sold me hither: for God did send me before you to preserve life. For these two years hath the famine been in the land: and yet there are five years, in the which there shall neither be earing nor harvest. And God sent me before you to preserve you a posterity in the earth, and to save your lives by a great deliverance. So now it was not you that sent me hither, but God: and he hath made me a father to Pharaoh, and lord of all his house, and a ruler throughout all the land of Egypt." (Genesis 45:4-8)

When Pharaoh and his servants heard about Joseph's brothers and father, they were pleased, and

Pharaoh sent wagons to move them down to Egypt. On the way down they stopped at Beersheba and offered sacrifices to the God of his father Isaac. So Israel and his descendants, numbering seventy people in all, loaded every thing they owned in to the wagons and moved to Egypt. Thirteen years later Israel died, and Joseph took him to Canaan for burial.

Joseph lived forty-four years after his father's death, and he died in the year 1772 B.C. "And Joseph died, and all his brethren, and all that generation. And the children of Israel were fruitful, and increased abundantly, and multiplied, and waxed exceeding mighty; and the land was filled with them." (Exodus 1.6-7)

We have been considering the development of Israel as a tribe. This covered the period of time between 2133 and 1570 B.C. a period of 563YRS. Now we will look at the development of Israel as a Nation from 1570 to 1043 B.C. a period of 527YRS.

MOSES

"Now there arose up a new king over Egypt, which knew not Joseph. And he said unto his people, Behold, the people of the children of Israel are more and mightier than we: Come on, let us deal wisely with them; lest they multiply, and it come to pass, that, when there falleth out any war, they join also unto our enemies, and fight against us, and so get them up out of the land." (Exodus 1:8-10)

One solution the Egyptians came up with was to put taskmasters over the Israelites, and force them to work harder, but the more they afflicted them, the more they multiplied, and grew. Next, the king spoke to the Hebrew midwives, and told them to kill the male babies. "But the midwives feared God, and did not as the king of Egypt commanded them, but saved the men children alive. And the king of Egypt called for the midwives, and said unto them, Why have ye done this thing, and have saved the men children alive? And the midwives said unto Pharaoh, because the Hebrew women are not as the Egyptian women; for they are lively, and are delivered ere the midwives come in unto them. Therefore God dealt well with the midwives: and the people multiplied, and waxed very mighty." (Exodus 1.17-20)

Two plans failed, first the taskmasters with severe affliction, followed by his plan with the midwives: Now in the last verse of Exodus chapter one the king has another solution: "And Pharaoh charged all his people, saying, every son that is born ye shall cast into the river, and every daughter ye shall save alive." (Exodus 1.22)

At this time a young couple of the tribe of Levi, had a baby son born to them, his mother hid him at home for three months: Then when she could no longer hide him, she took a basket and water-proofed it with pitch; put the baby in it and placed it in the reeds at the edge of the river. The baby's sister (Miriam) watched from a distance to see what would happen to him. This is what happened: A princess, one of the kings daughters, came down to the river to bathe, and as she and her maid were walking along the river bank, she saw the basket in the reeds and sent one of her maids to bring it to her. When she opened it, the baby was crying; this touched her heart. "He must be one of the Hebrew children!" she said. Then the baby's, sister, approached the princess and ask her: "Shall I go find one of the Hebrew women to nurse the baby for you? "Yes," she replied. So the sister rushed home and told her mother. "Take this child and nurse him for me, and I will pay you," said the Princess. So she took him and nursed him. Later when he was older, she brought him back to the princess and he became her son. She named him Moses, which means, "to draw out" because she had drawn him out of the water.

When Moses was grown, he went out to check on the conditions of the Hebrew slaves, and when he saw an Egyptian beating up on a Hebrew, he killed the Egyptian and buried him in the sand. When Moses found that what he had done was discovered, he was frightened. And when Pharaoh heard about it he wanted to kill Moses, so Moses fled to the land of Midian. While sitting by a well, seven daughters of the priest of Midian came and filled the troughs to water their father's flock. And the shepherds came and drove them away: but Moses stood up and helped them, and watered their flock. As a result Moses, in process of time, married Zipporah, one of the daughters, (who was a Gentile) and they had a son and Moses named him Gershom, which means foreigner, because Moses was in a foreign land.

Exodus 2:23-25: "And it came to pass in process of time that the king of Egypt died: and the children of Israel sighed by reason of the bondage, and they cried, and their cry came up unto God by reason of the bondage. And God heard their groaning, and God remembered his covenant with Abraham, with Isaac, and with Jacob. And God looked upon the children of Israel, and God had respect unto them."

At this time Moses kept the flock of Jethro, his father in law, the priest of Midian: one day as he lead the flock to the backside of the desert, he saw a bush burning, but it was not burned up, so Moses turned aside to take a look. Exodus 3:4-15: "Now Moses kept the flock of Jethro his father in law, the priest of Midian: and he led the flock to the backside of the desert, and came to the mountain of God, even to Horeb. And the angel of the LORD appeared unto him in a flame of fire out of the midst of a bush: and he looked, and, behold, the bush burned with fire, and the bush was not consumed. And Moses said, I will now turn aside, and see this great sight, why the bush is not burnt. And when the LORD saw that he turned aside to see, God called unto him out of the midst of the bush, and said, Moses, Moses. And he said, here am I. And he said, Draw not nigh hither: put off thy shoes from off thy feet, for the place whereon thou standest is holy ground. Moreover he said, I am the God of thy father, the God of Abraham, the God of Isaac, and the God of Jacob. And Moses hid his face; for he was afraid to look upon God. And the LORD said, I have surely seen the affliction of my people which are in Egypt, and have heard their cry by reason of their taskmasters; for I know their sorrows; And I am come down to deliver them out of the hand of the Egyptians, and to bring them up out of that land unto a good land and a large, unto a land flowing with milk and honey; unto the place of the Canaanites, and the Hittites, and the Amorites, and the Perizzites, and the Hivites, and the Jebusites. Now therefore, behold, the cry of the children of Israel is come unto me: and I have also seen the oppression wherewith the Egyptians oppress them. Come now therefore, and I will send thee unto Pharaoh, that thou mayest bring forth my people the children of Israel out of Egypt. And Moses said unto God, Who am I, that I should go unto Pharaoh, and that I should bring forth the children of Israel out of Egypt? And he said, Certainly I will be with thee; and this shall be a token unto thee, that I have sent thee: When thou hast brought forth the people out of Egypt, ye shall serve God upon this mountain. And Moses said unto God, Behold, when I come unto the children of Israel, and shall say unto them, The God of your fathers hath sent me unto you; and they shall say to me, what is his name? What shall I say unto them? And God said unto Moses, I AM THAT I AM: and he said, Thus shalt thou say unto the children of Israel, I AM hath sent me unto you. And God said moreover unto Moses, Thus shalt thou say unto the children of Israel, The LORD God of your fathers, the God of Abraham, the God of Isaac, and the God of Jacob, hath sent me unto you: this is my name for ever, and this is my memorial unto all generations."

After much persuasion, and God allowing him to have Aaron, his brother, as his spokesman, Moses agreed to do God's bidding. So Moses went to his father in law, Jethro, who encouraged him to go ahead back to Egypt, because all of those who had wanted to kill him were dead. Moses took his wife and sons and returned to Egypt. There he found the Israelites continuing to labor under severe conditions. And each time he and Aaron urged the King to let the people go, their work conditions grew worse: And each time the King refused; God sent another plague upon Egypt. In the end Pharaoh let them go; and the Israelites, as instructed by God, borrowed from the Egyptians, jewels of silver, and jewels of gold, and raiment; which the Egyptians were glad to do in order to be rid of them. In addition Pharaoh told them to take all their belongings, including their flocks and their herds.

Exodus 12:37, 41: "And the children of Israel journeyed from Rameses to Succoth, about six hundred thousand on foot that were men, beside children....And it came to pass at the end of the four hundred and thirty years, even the selfsame day it came to pass, that all the hosts of the LORD went out from the land of Egypt." They crossed the Red Sea and went into the desert and wandered for forty years. However in their wandering, they did many things, both good and bad: But more bad than good. Right off they began to murmur, they didn't have enough water or food and they wished they were back in Egypt. They said Moses brought them out in the desert to die.

Exodus 16:2-4: "And the whole congregation of the children of Israel murmured against Moses and Aaron in the wilderness: And the children of Israel said unto them, Would to God we had died by the hand of the LORD in the land of Egypt, when we sat by the flesh pots, and when we did eat bread to the full; for ye have brought us forth into this wilderness, to kill this whole assembly with hunger. Then said the LORD unto Moses, Behold, I will rain bread from heaven for you; and the people shall go out and gather a certain rate every day, that I may prove them, whether they will walk in my law, or no."

The people were given specific instructions; they were to gather only a specific amount each day, and not keep any over until the next day: Except on Friday, when they were to gather enough for two days so they wouldn't have to gather on the Sabbath. God gave them these instructions like he did in order to test them; and they didn't do very well on the test: Because they kept some over until the next day and it did stink, and had worms in it. However what they kept over for the Sabbath didn't spoil. Some went out on the Sabbath to gather and found nothing: And that which others kept over for the Sabbath did not spoil. "And the LORD said unto Moses, How long refuse ye to keep my commandments and my laws? (Exodus 16.28)

So far God had made several covenants which primarily told what He would do for Israel: But there was one thing he required of them: That was obedience. That was the one thing that was hard for them to learn because they wanted their own way.

Three months after leaving Egypt they have come to Mount Sinai, and are camped near the mountain. And Moses went up on the mountain and God told him what to tell the people. Exodus 19:3-8: "And Moses went up unto God, and the LORD called unto him out of the mountain, saying, Thus shalt thou say to the house of Jacob, and tell the children of Israel; Ye have seen what I did unto the Egyptians, and how I bare you on eagles' wings, and brought you unto myself. Now therefore, if ye will obey my voice indeed, and keep my covenant, then ye shall be a peculiar treasure unto me above all people: for all the earth is mine: And ye shall be unto me a kingdom of priests, and an holy nation. These are the words which thou shalt speak unto the children of Israel. And Moses came and called for the elders of the people, and laid before their faces all these words which the LORD commanded him. And all the people answered together, and said, All that the LORD hath spoken we will do. And Moses returned the words of the people unto the LORD."

Three days later Moses went up to the mountain, and God gave him the Ten Commandments." 1. You shall have no other gods before me. 2. You shall not make any graven images, or any likeness of anything that is in heaven above, or that is in the earth beneath, or that is in the water of the earth. You shall not bow down before them, nor serve them: 3. You shall not take the name of the Lord your God in vain. 4. Remember the Sabbath day, to keep it wholly. 5. Honor your father and mother: that your days shall be long upon the land which the Lord your

God gives you. 6. You shall not kill. 7. You shall not commit adultery. 8. You shall not steal. 9. You shall not bear false witness. 10. You shall not covet. These are the ten- commandments: And, as someone has pointed out, they are not the ten suggestions. God is serious.

It is of interest that the first four commandments deal with our relationship with God while the other six deal with our relationship with other people. If we Love God and obey him, we will love others and serve them.

The initiation of the Mosaic Law is a big and a long lasting transition for the nation of Israel. It lasted until the crucifixion of Jesus, over fourteen hundred years later. The law does not save sinners: It reveals God's holiness and mans need for salvation. Israel was not saved from Egypt by the law; but now obedience of the law enabled them to receive and enjoy the blessings God has promised them. To be sanctified means to be set apart for God's use and pleasure. At the Red Sea, God separated his people from their old life: At Sinai, he brought them into a new life; a covenant relationship with himself. It was like a wedding ceremony, with God as the husband and Israel as the wife. Whenever the nation turned from God to Idols, God accused them of committing adultery.

When Moses went up on the mountain and God talked to him and gave him the Ten Commandments, God impressed the people with quite a display of signs and wonders. Exodus 20:18-21: "And all the people saw the thunderings, and the lightnings, and the noise of the trumpet, and the mountain smoking: and when the people saw it, they removed, and stood afar off. And they said unto Moses, Speak thou with us, and we will hear: but let not God speak with us, lest we die. And Moses said unto the people, Fear not: for God is come to prove you, and that his fear may be before your faces, that ye sin not. And the people stood afar off, and Moses drew near unto the thick darkness where God was."

After everything was explained to the people, and they had agreed to it, Moses wrote it all down in what came to be called the Book of the Covenant: The ratification of the covenant was complete: But it wasn't long until the children of Israel failed. Moses went up the mountain to meet God, and when he came down they were worshiping a calf, made of gold jewelry, which they had brought from Egypt.

Exodus 32:1: "And when the people saw that Moses delayed to come down out of the mount, the people gathered themselves together unto Aaron, and said unto him, Up, make us gods, which shall go before us; for as for this Moses, the man that brought us up out of the land of Egypt, we wot not what is become of him." As a result of the long absence of Moses, and the lack of faith on their part the new nation failed miserably. God in his grace forgives the sinner, but in his government, he must punish the sin. The punishment may seem cruel to us, but the people had been warned against idolatry and had willfully disobeyed God. God had to teach them early not to act like the nations around them. Israel had to remain a separated people, or God could not work out his great purposes through them.

Because God is gracious and longsuffering, He was willing to give them another chance, so He renewed the covenant with them. Exodus 34:10-16: "And he said, Behold, I make a covenant: before all thy people I will do marvels, such as have not been done in all the earth, nor in any nation: and all the people among which thou art shall see the work of the LORD: for it is a terrible thing that I will do with thee. Observe thou that which I command thee this day: behold, I drive out before thee the Amorite, and the Canaanite, and the Hittite, and the Perizzite, and the Hivite, and the Jebusite. Take heed to thyself, lest thou make a covenant with the inhabitants of the land whither thou goest, lest it be for a snare in the midst of thee: But ye shall destroy their altars, break their images, and cut down their groves: For thou shalt worship no other god: for the LORD, whose name is Jealous, is a jealous God: Lest thou make a covenant with the inhabitants of the land, and they go a whoring after their gods, and do sacrifice unto their gods, and one call thee, and thou eat of his sacrifice; And thou take of their daughters unto thy sons, and their daughters go a whoring after their gods, and make thy sons go a whoring after their gods." The Israelites were given many do's and don't, under the law; but idolatry and the worship of other gods, were the ones that they had the most trouble keeping, even though the penalty for some other offenses, such as breaking the Sabbath, was death.

During their stay at Mt. Sinai they built the tabernacle; and the Lord told Moses to bring the tribe of Levi and present them to Aaron the priest to assist him. They are to perform duties for him and for the whole community by doing the work of the tabernacle. Give the Levites to Aaron and his sons; they are the Israelites who are given wholly to him. Appoint Aaron and his sons to serve as priests; any one else who approaches the sanctuary must be put to death.

The whole tribe of Levi was dedicated for this purpose; consequently they were no longer listed with the other tribes, so at this time to take their place, Joseph's two sons replaced the tribe of Levi.

The time had come to leave Mt. Sinai and start their journey to the Plains of Moab. Deuteronomy 1:6-8: "The LORD our God spake unto us in Horeb, saying, Ye have dwelt long enough in this mount: Turn you, and take your journey, and go to the mount of the Amorites, and unto all the places nigh thereunto, in the plain, in the hills, and in the vale, and in the south, and by the sea side, to the land of the Canaanites, and unto Lebanon, unto the great river, the river Euphrates. Behold, I have set the land before you: go in and possess the land which the LORD sware unto your fathers, Abraham, Isaac, and Jacob, to give unto them and to their seed after them."

On their journey they began to complain, they had been living on the manna that God sent from heaven; and they began to say, "Who shall give us flesh to eat? We remember the fish, which we did eat in Egypt freely; the cucumbers, and the melons, and the leeks, and the onions, and the garlick: But now our soul is dried away: there is nothing at all, beside this manna, before our eyes."(Numbers 11.4-6) When Moses heard them crying and complaining, he went to God with his problems. He said, "I am not able to bear all this people alone, because it is too heavy for me. And if thou deal thus with me, kill me, I pray thee, out of hand, if I have found favour in thy sight; and let me not see my wretchedness. And the LORD said unto Moses, Gather unto me seventy men of the elders of Israel, whom thou knowest to be the elders of the people, and officers over them; and bring them unto the tabernacle of the congregation, that they may stand there with thee. And I will come down and talk with thee there: and I will take of the spirit which is upon thee, and will put it upon them; and they shall bear the burden of the people with thee, that thou bear it not thyself alone." (Numbers 11.14-17)

God did not increase the power: He only distributed the Spirit that Moses had onto seventy other men. God originally gave Moses power in proportion to the burden; but Moses thought he was over burdened, and complained about it. At any rate that is how God handled the complaint, and a different method of judging the people's disagreements and problems was initiated.

The Israelites left the area around Mt. Sinai where they had been for awhile; and Moses said, "And when we departed from Horeb, we went through all that great and terrible wilderness, which ye saw by the way of the mountain of the Amorites, as the LORD our God commanded us; and we came to Kadeshbarnea. And I said unto you, Ye are come unto the mountain of the Amorites, which the LORD our God doth give unto us. Behold, the LORD thy God hath set the land before thee: go up and possess it, as the LORD God of thy fathers hath said unto thee; fear not, neither be discouraged. (Deuteronomy 1:19-21)

They came to Moses and said, we will send men to search the land; and the idea pleased Moses, so he selected twelve men, one man from each tribe, and they went up the mountain, and came to the valley Eschol, and searched it out. They came back after forty days and showed them the fruit of the land and told them that surely the land flowed with milk and honey.

Then they begin to change from the positive to the negative. "Nevertheless the people be strong that dwell in the land, and the cities are walled, and very great: and moreover we saw the children of Anak there. The Amalekites dwell in the land of the south: and the Hittites, and the Jebusites, and the Amorites, dwell in the mountains: and the Canaanites dwell by the sea, and by the coast of Jordan. And Caleb stilled the people before Moses, and said, Let us go up at once, and possess it; for we are well able to overcome it. But the men that went up with him said, We be not able to go up against the people; for they are stronger than we. And they brought up an evil report of the land which they had searched unto the children of Israel, saying, The land, through which we have gone to search it, is a land that eateth up the inhabitants thereof; and all the people that we saw in it are men of a great stature. And there we saw the giants, the sons of Anak, which come of the giants: and we were in our own sight as grasshoppers, and so we were in their sight." (Numbers 13:28-33)

They told them that the land was a land that eats up its inhabitance, and all the men they saw were giants, and that they were like grasshoppers compared to them. As a result of this report the people were distressed and wept that night. "And all the children of Israel murmured against Moses and against Aaron: and the whole congregation said unto them, Would God that we had died in the land of Egypt! Or would God we had died in this wilderness! And wherefore hath the LORD brought us unto this land, to fall by the sword, that our wives and our children should be a prey? Were it not better for us to return into Egypt? And they said one to another, Let us make a captain, and let us return into Egypt." (Numbers 14.2-4) But Caleb and Joshua, two of the twelve who searched out the land tore their clothes and told the people that the land they passed through was a good land.

Numbers 14:11-12: "And the LORD said unto Moses, How long will this people provoke me? and how long will it be ere they believe me, for all the signs which I have shewed among them? I will smite them with the pestilence, and disinherit them, and will make of thee a greater nation and mightier than they.

Moses interceded for the people: his reasoning was that God had chosen Israel as a nation to show to the other nations that Israel's God truly was with them and talked face to face with them, and that he lead them with a cloud over them: and now if God carried out His threat, then the Egyptians, where they had just been delivered from, would hear of it, and spread it to all the surrounding nations. "Now if thou shalt kill all this people as one man, then the nations which have heard the fame of thee will speak, saying, Because the LORD was not able to bring this people into the land which he sware unto them, therefore he hath slain them in the wilderness." (Numbers 14.15-16) The outcome was that the Lord did not destroy them. However, He told them they would not enter the land, He had promised them. Numbers 14:27-31: "How long shall I bear with this evil congregation, which murmur against me? I have heard the murmurings of the children of Israel, which they murmur against me. Say unto them, As truly as I live, saith the LORD, as ye have spoken in mine ears, so will I do to you: Your carcases shall fall in this wilderness; and all that were numbered of you, according to your whole number, from twenty years old and upward, which have murmured against me, Doubtless ye shall not come into the land, concerning which I sware to make you dwell therein, save Caleb the son of Jephunneh, and Joshua the son of Nun. But your little ones, which ye said should be a prey, them will I bring in, and they shall know the land which ye have despised."

Of the six hundred thousand who were over twenty years of age when they came out of Egypt, all except the two men who told the truth were to die in the wilderness, after wandering for forty years in the wild desert. That was one year for each of the forty days the spies spent searching out the land. This refusal to enter Canaan happened in the year 1445 B.C. Many things transpired in the next forty years as they wandered around and back and forth in the desert. Many ordinances were given: Ordinances concerning the Levites, ordinances of purification, and inheritance and the inheritance rights for women. They fought many wars, and won most of the time, for God was with them. From time to time they didn't win, usually because they got involved in idolatry and immorality. In Numbers 26:1-2 the Lord spoke to Moses and Eleazar the son of the priest, saying, "Take the sum of all the congregation of the children of Israel, from twenty years old and upward, through their fathers' house, all that are able to go to war in Israel." The number was 601,730 this was the second census: The number of the first census, when they came out of Egypt, was, 603,550.

Israel, with its forty years of wandering almost ended, has moved up the Jordan River to a position just across the river from the city of Jericho. "And the LORD spake unto Moses in the plains of Moab by Jordan near Jericho, saying, Speak unto the children of Israel, and say unto them, When ye are passed over Jordan into the land of Canaan; Then ye shall drive out all the inhabitants of the land from before you, and destroy all their pictures, and destroy all their molten images, and quite pluck down all their high places: And ye shall dispossess the inhabitants of the land, and dwell therein: for I have given you the land to possess it. And ye shall divide the land by lot for an inheritance among your families: and to the more ye shall give the more inheritance, and to the fewer ye shall give the less inheritance: every man's inheritance shall be in the place where his lot falleth; according to the tribes of your fathers ye shall inherit." (Numbers 33:50-54)

Moses climbed up Mount Nebo from the plains of Moab to the top of Pisgah, across from Jericho. And the Lord showed him all of the Promised Land. "And the LORD said unto him, This is the land which I sware unto Abraham, unto Isaac, and unto Jacob, saying, I will give it unto thy seed: I have caused thee to see it with thine eyes, but thou shalt not go over thither. So Moses the servant of the LORD died there in the land of Moab, according to the word of the LORD. And the children of Israel wept for Moses in the plains of Moab thirty days: so the days of weeping and mourning for Moses were ended. And Joshua the son of Nun was full of the spirit of wisdom; for Moses had laid his hands upon him: and the children of Israel hearkened unto him, and did as the LORD commanded Moses. And there arose not a prophet since in Israel like unto Moses, whom the LORD knew face to face, In all the signs and the wonders, which the LORD sent him to do in the land of Egypt to Pharaoh, and to all his servants, and to all his land," (Deuteronomy 34.4, 5, 8-11)

Moses had been a great leader: When Israel was in trouble with the Lord: Moses would plead with the Lord in their behalf, and soften the wrath of God. Joshua is Israel's leader now: He is a man of faith, and true consecration as well as a man, known for his obedience and decision.

JOSHUA

"Now after the death of Moses the servant of the LORD it came to pass, that the LORD spake unto Joshua the son of Nun, Moses' minister, saying, Moses my servant is dead; now therefore arise, go over this Jordan, thou, and all this people, unto the land which I do give to them, even to the children of Israel. Every place that the sole of your foot shall tread upon, that have I given unto you, as I said unto Moses. From the wilderness and this Lebanon even unto the great river, the river Euphrates, all the land of the Hittites, and unto the great sea toward the going down of the sun, shall be your coast. There shall not any man be able to stand before thee all the days of thy life: as I was with Moses, so I will be with thee: I will not fail thee, nor forsake thee. Be strong and of a good courage: for unto this people shalt thou divide for an inheritance the land, which I sware unto their fathers to give them. Only be thou strong and very courageous, that thou mayest observe to do according to all the law, which Moses my servant commanded thee: turn not from it to the right hand or to the left, that thou mayest prosper whithersoever thou goest. This book of the law shall not depart out of thy mouth; but thou shalt meditate therein day and night, that thou mayest observe to do according to all that is written therein: for then thou shalt make thy way prosperous, and then thou shalt have good success." (Joshua 1.1-8)

Joshua told the people to prepare food, for they would pass over the Jordan River in three days. Then he told the Reubenites, the Gadites, and half tribe of Manasseh, the Lord has given you land on this side of the river, your wives and children shall remain here with your herds. But you shall crossover the river, armed, before your brothers, all the mighty men of valor, and help them. Then you can return to your own land.

After the three days they arrived at the river and received further instructions for crossing the river, which was overflowing its banks at this time of year. Joshua told them to sanctify themselves: "for tomorrow the Lord will do wonders among you." (Joshua 3.5) Then Joshua gave the priests, the Levites, instructions because they were to lead out, carrying the ark, and go before the multitude. The Lord told Joshua, "This day I will begin to magnify you in the sight of all Israel, that they may know that, as I was with Moses, so I will be with you." (Joshua 3.7) The priests were instructed to go to the brink of the Jordan and stand still in the Jordan. "And Joshua said unto the children of Israel, Come hither, and hear the words of the LORD your God. And Joshua said, Hereby ye shall know that the living God is among you, and that he will without fail drive out from before you the Canaanites, and the Hittites, and the Hivites, and the Perizzites, and the Girgashites, and the Amorites, and the Jebusites. Behold, the ark of the covenant of the Lord of all the earth passeth over before you into Jordan. (Joshua 3.9-11)

Twelve men, one from each tribe, was instructed to pick up a stone from the river bed, as they went across, and take it with them, to make a memorial.

It would be for a sign among them; that when their children ask their fathers in time to come. Saying, what do these stones mean?" "Then ye shall answer them, That the waters of Jordan were cut off before the ark of the covenant of the LORD; when it passed over Jordan, the waters of Jordan were cut off: and these stones shall be for a memorial unto the children of Israel for ever." (Joshua 4.7)

When the nations west of the Jordan river: the Amorites and Canaanites who lived along the Mediterranean coast, heard that the Lord had dried up the Jordan river so the people of Israel could cross, their courage melted away completely and they were paralyzed with fear.

Joshua led Israel in their occupation of the land, which God had promised them. It was a time of wars, but it was a time, in which God was with them: Except for a few times, when they disobeyed, at which times God punished them severely, and sometimes allowed them to be defeated temporarily.

Moses had led Israel for forty-one years, and at his death, his assistant, Joshua was put in charge, and now after sixteen years his time is coming to an end and in Joshua 23:14-16 he says, "And, behold, this day I am going the way of all the earth: and ye know in all your hearts and in all your souls, that not one thing hath failed of all the good things which the LORD your God spake concerning you; all are come to pass unto you, and not one thing hath failed thereof. Therefore it shall come to pass, that as all good things are come upon you, which the LORD your God promised you; so shall the LORD bring upon you all evil things, until he have destroyed you from off this good land which the LORD your God hath given you. When ye have transgressed the covenant of The LORD your God, which he commanded you, and have gone and served other gods, and bowed yourselves to them; then shall the anger of the LORD be kindled against you, and ye shall perish quickly from off the good land which he hath given unto you."

Moses and Joshua both had a part in the redemption of Israel out of Egypt: This redemption, like New Testament redemption through Christ, was in two parts; "out" and "into" Moses brought Israel out of Egypt; and Joshua took them into the Promised Land, where they had victory, and blessing. Redemption through belief in Christ is similar, in that sinful man is delivered out of a life of bondage to sin and Satan into a life of victory and blessing.

Almost sixty years, after their deliverance out of Egypt, Israel is in a good situation: The Lord has given them all the land He had sworn to give to their fathers; and they possessed it and were dwelling in it. And the Lord has given them rest and peace all around, like He had promised to their fathers. They had no enemies, and they had every thing that the Lord had promised. Now we will see how they fare from here.

THE JUDGES

After the death of Joshua, Israel moves into the period of the Judges; Which covers a period of three hundred and five years and thirteen judges, who are raised up to guide Israel, in what turns out to be a time of declension and confusion; where every man did what was right in his own eyes. Two things stand out: the utter failure of Israel, and the persistent grace of God.

Along with Joshua all of the older generation died. Judges 2:10-19: "And also all that generation were gathered unto their fathers: and there arose another generation after them, which knew not the LORD, nor yet the works which he had done for Israel. And the children of Israel did evil in the sight of the LORD, and served Baalim: And they forsook the LORD God of their fathers, which brought them out of the land of Egypt, and followed other gods, of the gods of the people that were round about them, and bowed themselves unto them, and provoked the LORD to anger. And they forsook the LORD, and served Baal and Ashtaroth. And the anger of the LORD was hot against Israel, and he delivered them into the hands of spoilers that spoiled them, and he sold them into the hands of their enemies round about, so that they could not any longer stand before their enemies. Whithersoever they went out, the hand of the LORD was against them for evil, as the LORD had said, and as the LORD had sworn unto them: and they were greatly distressed. Nevertheless the LORD raised up judges, which delivered them out of the hand of those that spoiled them. And yet they would not hearken unto their judges, but they went a whoring after other gods, and bowed themselves unto them: they turned quickly out of the way which their fathers walked in, obeying the commandments of the LORD; but they did not so. And when the LORD raised them up judges, then the LORD was with the judge, and delivered them out of the hand of their enemies all the days of the judge: for it repented the LORD because of their groanings by reason of them that oppressed them and vexed them. And it came to pass, when the judge was dead, that they returned, and corrupted themselves more than their fathers, in following other gods to serve them, and to bow down unto them; they ceased not from their own doings, nor from their stubborn way."

As Israel entered the Promised Land they were doing fine for awhile: But shortly after the death of Joshua they began to compromise, by allowing some of the enemy to remain among them which was strictly forbidden. This soon led to intermarriage, which in turn led to the worship of other gods, which was the thing that a jealous God hated most. The first of the Ten Commandments says you shall have no other gods before me.

In the time of Joshua God was with the nation as a whole, as they conquered the land: Now God turned to a system whereby He gave victory to individuals He called and empowered by His Spirit. These individuals were Judges, who were tribesmen in Israel, upon whom the Lord laid the burden of Israel's apostate and oppressed state. The Judges were the spiritual ancestors of the Prophets, who were to play a very important part in the life of Israel. The Judges were both patriotic and spiritual leaders because national security and prosperity were inseparably connected with loyalty and obedience to Jehovah God, the theocratic King of Israel. These people who God chose to serve as Judges, were ordinary people who God equipped by His Spirit to accomplish God's will.

Samuel was the last of the Judges and in him begins the line of the writing Prophets: In his prophetic office, Samuel was faithful, but there was moral failure in his attempt to make the office of Judge hereditary. 1 Samuel 8:1-7: "And it came to pass, when Samuel was old, that he made his sons judges over Israel. Now the name of his firstborn was Joel; and the name of his second, Abiah: they were judges in Beersheba. And his sons walked not in his ways, but turned aside after lucre, and took bribes, and perverted judgment. Then all the elders of Israel gathered themselves together, and came to Samuel unto Ramah, And said unto him, Behold, thou art old, and thy sons walk not in thy ways: now make us a king to judge us like all the nations. But the thing displeased Samuel, when they said, Give us a king to judge us. And Samuel prayed unto the LORD. And the LORD said unto Samuel, Hearken unto the voice of the people in all that they say unto thee: for they have not rejected thee, but they have rejected me, that I should not reign over them."

Here is a very important statement: God says, "that I should not reign over them." (verse 7) This is the thing that causes many problems throughout the world. There is no doubt in my mind, that this is what causes the atheist to become an atheist, whether they realize it or not: the same applies to many others who are anti God, or as the Bible mentions; there are many antichrists. It has been a trait of mankind, going back to Adam and Eve.

For approximately five hundred years God worked with Israel as a tribe: Then for about that long as a nation. Now Israel wants to be like other nations; and have a king. From now on God will be working with them as a kingdom.

Samuel, the last of the judges, was displeased when Israel said, give us a king, and he went to the Lord in prayer. God told him to listen to them, howbeit at the same time protest and tell them the kind of king they will have over them. So he painted them a dismal picture: their sons and daughters would be taken from them, and be made to serve the king, they would be taxed, and the king would take the best of their vineyards, olive-yards, and fields. But the people refused to listen to Samuel; and they said, "We will have a king over us." (Verse 19) And the Lord told Samuel to make them a king.

Samuel set a king over them. Then Samuel recounted to them how their fathers had failed God many times by forgetting Him and serving idols: and he reminded them of how God punished them by turning them over to their enemies. Samuel also reminded them how the Lord had delivered them from their enemies on every side, so that they lived securely.

Samuel gave them a good explanation concerning punishment. God administers, what seems to be, severe punishment. But when God is dealing with His people He is endeavoring to correct their actions and teach them obedience. But they truly, are a rebellious and stiff-necked people.

SAUL

Israel got their way and now they have their king; His name is Saul; he is a man of fine personal appearance, humility, and self-control; and he is thirty years of age. From his shoulders and up he was taller than any of the people. When he became King he didn't have confidence that a person like himself was capable of ruling over a nation like Israel. However soon after he was anointed by Samuel to be King, Samuel gave him a number of instructions to build his confidence: A leader must trust God to solve problems, to provide needs, and to provide power needed to serve the nation. A leader must be able to listen to God and wait patiently for His instructions and carefully obey them. Saul began his reign in the strength of these assurances, but as time went on he trusted more and more in himself and eventually ended in rebelling against God's word.

Toward the end of Saul's reign God gave him instructions to destroy Amalek who laid in ambush and attacked Israel as they came up out of Egypt. Saul disobeyed: Then he lied and gave excuses for what he had done. "Then came the word of the LORD unto Samuel, saying, It repenteth me that I have set up Saul to be king: for he is turned back from following me, and hath not performed my commandments...And Samuel said, When thou wast little in thine own sight, wast thou not made the head of the tribes of Israel, and the LORD anointed thee king over Israel? ...For rebellion is as the sin of witchcraft, and stubbornness is as iniquity and idolatry. Because thou hast rejected the word of the LORD, he hath also rejected thee from being king...And Samuel said unto him; The LORD hath rent the kingdom of Israel from thee this day, and hath given it to a neighbour of thine, that is better than thou." (1 Samuel 15:10, 11, 17, 23, 28)

DAVID

That neighbor was a young shepherd boy named David, the youngest son of Jesse from Bethlehem. And the LORD said, Arise, anoint him: for this is he. Then Samuel took the horn of oil, and anointed him in the midst of his brethren: and the Spirit of the LORD came upon David from that day forward." (1 Samuel 16:12-13)

God had Samuel anoint David king long before he took the throne and ruled. He was already king, as far as God was concerned, when he fought and killed Goliath, the nine foot six inch giant. Saul was still acting king; even though he was declining rapidly in power and authority. He was in command of Israel's army when David went down and accepted the giant's challenge: Saul was the one that offered David his armor: But David refused the offer because he thought it wise to do it God's way. It worked: And David grew up to be a very courageous warrior.

For about ten years David lived in exile, while Saul tried to kill him. During this time, Saul and his followers lied about David, causing many people in

Israel to believe David was a rebel against the king, and that David was trying to destroy Saul. David left his reputation in God's hands; and trusted Him to take care of his accusers.

Back to King David: He was faced with a formidable enemy. The Bible said there was an evil spirit upon Saul; and he tried to kill David several times. David wrote several of the Psalms during this time.

Psalms 59.1-4: "Deliver me from mine enemies, O my God: defend me from them that rise up against me. Deliver me from the workers of iniquity, and save me from bloody men. For, lo, they lie in wait for my soul: the mighty are gathered against me; not for my transgression, nor for my sin, O LORD. They run and prepare themselves without my fault: awake to help me."

Psalm 57.1-5: "Be merciful unto me, O God, be merciful unto me: for my soul trusteth in thee: yea, in the shadow of thy wings will I make my refuge, until these calamities be overpast. I will cry unto God most high; unto God that performeth all things for me. He shall send from heaven, and save me from the reproach of him that would swallow me up. Selah. God shall send forth his mercy and his truth. My soul is among lions: and I lie even among them that are set on fire, even the sons of men, whose teeth are spears and arrows, and their tongue a sharp sword. Be thou exalted, O God, above the heavens; let thy glory be above all the earth."

For several years David with a rag tag army was in hiding because Saul, who was still acting as king, was trying to kill him, and David the anointed king was abiding by the rules; which didn't allow him to fight back. We have a good description of David's army in 1 Samuel 22.1-2: "David therefore departed thence, and escaped to the cave Adullam: and when his brethren and all his father's house heard it, they went down thither to him. And every one that was in distress, and every one that was in debt, and every one that was discontented, gathered themselves unto him; and he became a captain over them: and there were with him about four hundred men."

"And it came to pass, when Saul was returned from following the Philistines, that it was told him, saying, Behold, David is in the wilderness of Engedi. Then Saul took three thousand chosen men out of all Israel, and went to seek David and his men upon the rocks of the wild goats." (1 Samuel 24.1-2)

Two times David had opportunity to kill Saul; and even though he was encouraged to do so by some of his men, David refused because he didn't consider Saul his enemy; he still consider him to be king, and respected him for that reason. David even felt bad about cutting off part of Saul's robe. David was living by the scripture, "for it is written, Vengeance is mine; I will repay, saith the Lord." (Romans 12.19)

Saul remained king, until he and his three sons, were killed in battle. "So Saul died for his transgression which he committed against the LORD, even against the word of the LORD, which he kept not, and also for asking counsel of one that had a familiar spirit, to enquire of it; And enquired not of the LORD: therefore he slew him, and turned the kingdom unto David the son of Jesse." (1 Chronicles 10.13-14)

Most people make mistakes: And both David and Saul made their share: But there is a difference: Some times when David was in danger and fleeing for his life, he stopped depending on the Lord, who had promised to protect him, and started thinking about survival. He made some foolish mistakes; when he could have inquired of the Lord. With Saul it was different, in that when he was in trouble, he went to the witch of Endor: instead of going to God, he went to demonic forces. Saul had been fighting the wrong enemy, David and the Lord, for so long, that when the real enemy appeared he was not prepared.

David, the second king in Israel's development as a kingdom, is probably Israel's greatest king. He obeyed God and God was with him in all that he did. Now we want to look at the covenant the Lord made with him, called the Davidic Covenant. 2 Samuel 7:8-17 "Now therefore so shalt thou say unto my servant David, Thus saith the LORD of hosts, I took thee from the sheepcote, from following the sheep, to be ruler over my people, over Israel: And I was with thee whithersoever thou wentest, and have cut off all thine enemies out of thy sight, and have made thee a great name, like unto the name of the great men that are in the earth. Moreover I will appoint a place for my people Israel, and will plant them, that they may dwell in a place of their own, and move no more; neither shall the children of wickedness afflict them any more, as beforetime, And as since the time that I commanded judges to be over my people Israel, and have caused thee to rest from all thine enemies. Also the LORD telleth thee that he will make thee an house. And when thy days be fulfilled, and thou shalt sleep with thy fathers, I will set up thy seed after thee, which shall proceed out of thy bowels, and I will establish his kingdom. He shall build an house for my name, and I will stablish the throne of his kingdom for ever. I will be his father, and he shall be my son. If he commit iniquity, I will chasten him with the rod of men, and with the stripes of the children of men: But my mercy shall not depart away from him, as I took it from Saul, whom I put away before thee. And thine house and thy kingdom shall be established for ever before thee: thy throne shall be established for ever. According to all these words, and according to all this vision, so did Nathan speak unto David."

SOLOMON

David died, in 970 B.C. after reigning over Israel forty years: And his son Solomon became the third king over Israel, and like David he was a good king, but not without faults. At that time the children of Israel sacrificed their offerings on altars in the hills; because the Temple of the Lord hadn't yet been built. They had no temple since they first came out of Egypt years ago. While Solomon was up in the hills worshiping, the Lord appeared unto him in a dream that night and told him to ask for anything he wanted, and it would be given to him. 1 Kings 3:9, 11-14: "Give therefore thy servant an understanding heart to judge thy people, that I may discern between good and bad: for who is able to judge this thy so great a people?" "And God said unto him, Because thou hast asked this thing, and hast not asked for thyself long life; neither hast asked riches for thyself, nor hast asked the life of thine enemies; but hast asked for thyself understanding to discern judgment; Behold, I have done according to thy words: lo, I have given thee a wise and an understanding heart; so that there was none like thee before thee, neither after thee shall any arise like unto thee. And I have also given thee that which thou hast not asked, both riches, and honour: so that there shall not be any among the kings like unto thee all thy days. And if thou wilt walk in my ways, to keep my statutes and my commandments, as thy father David did walk, then I will lengthen thy days."

The trouble was, Solomon came up short in keeping God's laws like his father did. Solomon, largely, because of his father, was highly favored by the Lord, and he was a great king, who built a great kingdom: And he built the temple, which David was forbidden to do because he was a warrior; and had shed so much blood: But he did two things that were specifically forbidden for the king: Do not multiply to yourself horses; And do not multiply to yourself wives. But if you read the story you will hardly believe the number he had. The reason for not having a large number of horses was that in time of war, horses and chariots were a great advantage: But the Lord wanted the king to depend on Him to fight his battles. And God was using Israel to show the heathen nations what it was like to serve the living God. To multiply to yourself wives was never God's plan: and in addition to that Solomon had wives from several different nations; and they served other gods, and soon they had Solomon building a place to worship their gods. 1 Kings 11:4-6: "For it came to pass, when Solomon was old, that his wives turned away his heart after other gods: and his heart was not perfect with the LORD his God, as was the heart of David his father. For Solomon went after Ashtoreth the goddess of the Zidonians, and after Milcom the abomination of the Ammonites. And Solomon did evil in the sight of the LORD, and went not fully after the LORD, as did David his father."

So we can see that Solomon with all his wisdom; didn't use commonsense where it really counted. There is an interesting phrase in verse six: "and went not fully after the Lord," Solomon, had the same shortcoming that many church going people have: He didn't sell out for God; especially, where it was the most important thing. Idolatry was Israel's greatest failure: just like conforming to the world is the biggest problem of Christianity today. Both stem from wanting to be like the nations: or the people, by which we are surrounded.

Because of his failure Solomon lost most of his control over the kingdom. 1 Kings 11:11-13: "Wherefore the LORD said unto Solomon, Forasmuch as this is done of thee, and thou hast not kept my covenant and my statutes, which I have commanded thee, I will surely rend the kingdom from thee, and will give it to thy servant. Notwithstanding in thy days I will not do it for David thy father's sake: but I will rend it out of the hand of thy son. Howbeit I will not rend away all the kingdom; but will give one tribe to thy son for David my servant's sake, and for Jerusalem's sake which I have chosen."

TWO KINGDOMS

At this time the twelve tribes of Israel were divided in to a dual kingdom: The northern kingdom of Israel and the southern kingdom of Judah. The north kingdom of Israel consisted of ten tribes, and the southern kingdom, the remaining two. They each lasted some three hundred years: and both ended by being taken in to captivity by other nations: Israel by Assyria; and Judah by Babylon. The captivities were God's punishment upon Israel. 2 Kings 17:7-12: "For so it was, that the children of Israel had sinned against the LORD their God, which had brought them up out of the land of Egypt, from under the hand of Pharaoh king of Egypt, and had feared other gods, And walked in the statutes of the heathen, whom the LORD cast out from before the children of Israel, and of the kings of Israel, which they had made. And the children of Israel did secretly those things that were not right against the LORD their God, and they built them high places in all their cities, from the tower of the watchmen to the fenced city. And they set them up images and groves in every high hill, and under every green tree: And there they burnt incense in all the high places, as did the heathen whom the LORD carried away before them; and wrought wicked things to provoke the LORD to anger: For they served idols, whereof the LORD had said unto them, Ye shall not do this thing."

They disobeyed other commands and statutes; but here again the worse infraction was worshiping other gods. God hated all sin and disobedience: But, because He is a jealous God, He hates spiritual adultery worse.

They were without excuse: God had warned their fathers, and He warned them through the Prophets and Seers, for years and years they pleaded with them, and warned them of the consequence of disobedience. 2 Kings 17:13-15: "Yet the LORD testified against Israel, and against Judah, by all the prophets, and by all the seers, saying, Turn ye from your evil ways, and keep my commandments and my statutes, according to all the law which I commanded your fathers, and which I sent to you by my servants the prophets. Notwithstanding they would not hear, but hardened their necks, like to the neck of their fathers, that did not believe in the LORD their God. And they rejected his statutes, and his covenant that he made with their fathers, and his testimonies which he testified against them; and they followed vanity, and became vain, and went after the heathen that were round about them, concerning whom the LORD had charged them, that they should not do like them.

From the time that the kingdom was taken from Solomon, the kingdom became a divided kingdom. It was divided into Israel, the northern kingdom, and Judah the southern kingdom. As a united nation Israel had three kings; Saul, David and Solomon: Between the divided kingdoms, they had approximately forty kings: Of the three kings of the united, kingdom two were good, and the other started out good but ended up bad. In the divided kingdom Israel had all evil kings, while Judah had six good and the rest were evil kings.

Each division of the kingdom survived for about two hundred years before the Lord punished them by sending them in to captivity. Both had disobeyed God continually, and they were in war much of the time, even among themselves. Judah was in captivity in Babylonia for forty- eight years. Babylon was the world's dominant power at that time. Israel, the northern kingdom, spent approximately the same amount of time as captives in Assyria.

People have many questions about God and punishment, like, why me Lord, why did this happen to me? Or how can a loving God send anyone to hell? Well, we know God is a just God, and He is fair, for the Bible tells us He is: So let us look at how He dealt with Israel, leading up to the point that He caused His chosen nation to go into captivity; it progressed by degrees. First, when Israel gave herself up to ungodliness, the Lord would appoint over them 'terror,' this consisted of disease, famine and defeat. "And if ye will not yet for all this hearken unto me, then I will punish you seven times more for your sins. And I will break the pride of your power; and I will make your heaven as iron, and your earth as brass: And your strength shall be spent in vain: for your land shall not yield her increase, neither shall the trees of the land yield their fruits. And if ye walk contrary unto me, and will not hearken unto me; I will bring seven times more plagues upon you according to your sins. I will also send wild beasts among you, which shall rob you of your children, and destroy your cattle, and make you few in number; and your high ways shall be desolate." (Leviticus 26.18-22) This was much the picture of the Holy Land until recent years, which has long been a desolate desert, brought about by the sins of the ancient Jews.

Israel remained in captivity from 586 B.C. to 538 B.C. While there, they had their Prophets who gave them God's messages; but they still didn't listen very well, so they had some troubled experiences, as well as some in which the Lord worked miracles for them. However over all they seem to have deteriorated as a nation. But the Prophets were able to keep their hope alive to the point that they were able to maintain their national spirit and their spiritual identity.

When Israel was taken captive, Nebucadnezzar was king of Babylon: Toward the end of their captivity Cyrus king of Persia had taken over the Babylonian empire. "Now in the first year of Cyrus king of Persia, that the word of the LORD spoken by the mouth of Jeremiah might be accomplished, the LORD stirred up the spirit of Cyrus king of Persia, that he made a proclamation throughout all his kingdom, and put it also in writing, saying, Thus saith Cyrus king of Persia, All the kingdoms of the earth hath the LORD God of heaven given me; and he hath charged me to build him an house in Jerusalem, which is in Judah. Who is there among you of all his people? The LORD his God be with him, and let him go up." (2 Chronicles 36:22-23) "And whosoever remaineth in any place where he sojourneth, let the men of his place help him with silver, and with gold, and with goods, and with beasts, beside the freewill offering for the house of God that is in Jerusalem. Then rose up the chief of the fathers of Judah and Benjamin, and the priests, and the Levites, with all them whose spirit God had raised, to go up to build the house of the LORD which is in Jerusalem." (Ezra 1.4-5)

All the people around them helped just as the King had asked. Also King Cyrus brought the vessels of the house of the Lord, which Nebuchadnezzar had brought forth out of Jerusalem, and had put them in the house of his gods. All the vessels of gold and silver were five thousand and four hundred: all of these they took from Babylon back to Jerusalem. All of this happened like clockwork because the Lord moved upon the hearts of people and they responded.

After being gone seventy years they were going back to a desolate land and a destroyed temple: And there were enemies in the land who didn't want them to build it back. Consequently it was a struggle: They would work and make progress for a while; and then they would have to stop for a while. This happened several times, but they were determined and kept working at it.

They had built an altar, the first thing before they started building, so they were worshipping the Lord, and the Lord was helping them. Ezra 6:14-15: "And the elders of the Jews builded, and they prospered through the prophesying of Haggai the prophet and Zechariah the son of Iddo. And they builded, and finished it, according to the commandment of the

God of Israel, and according to the commandment of Cyrus, and Darius, and Artaxerxes king of Persia. And this house was finished on the third day of the month Adar, which was in the sixth year of the reign of Darius the king." It took twenty- three years, and they finished it in 515 B.C.

However they had much work ahead: they still had the destruction of the city to repair, and the wall of the city, which was their next step in the restoration of Israel as a nation. Nehemiah, who was the cupbearer of the king, was God's pick for the man to be in charge of the task of building the wall.

Nehemiah 2:1-6: "And it came to pass in the month Nisan, in the twentieth year of Artaxerxes the king, that wine was before him: and I took up the wine, and gave it unto the king. Now I had not been beforetime sad in his presence. Wherefore the king said unto me, Why is thy countenance sad, seeing thou art not sick? this is nothing else but sorrow of heart. Then I was very sore afraid, And said unto the king, Let the king live for ever: why should not my countenance be sad, when the city, the place of my fathers' sepulchres, lieth waste, and the gates thereof are consumed with fire? Then the king said unto me, For what dost thou make request? So I prayed to the God of heaven. And I said unto the king, If it please the king, and if thy servant have found favour in thy sight, that thou wouldest send me unto Judah, unto the city of my fathers' sepulchres, that I may build it. And the king said unto me, (the queen also sitting by him,) For how long shall thy journey be? and when wilt thou return? So it pleased the king to send me; and I set him a time."

The king gave Nehemiah letters to the Governors beyond the river so he could pass through to Judah. And to the keeper of the king's forest so he could get timbers for beams for the gates of the palace by the temple, and for the walls of the city. Nehemiah took a few men with him and surveyed the damage, in order to understand the situation. He did this for three nights, unbeknown to the rulers and the people. "Then said I unto them, Ye see the distress that we are in, how Jerusalem lieth waste, and the gates thereof are burned with fire: come, and let us build up the wall of Jerusalem, that we be no more a reproach. Then I told them of the hand of my God which was good upon me; as also the king's words that he had spoken unto me. And they said, Let us rise up and build. So they strengthened their hands for this good work." (Nehemiah 2.17-18)

The Nation of Israel at this time was at a very low point. They are the chosen people of the Lord: chosen to be an example to the nations everywhere. But here they are, this is a day of reproach, they are the, remnant that have escaped the captivity, Jerusalem is no longer the beautiful and important city, and the Jews were no longer powerful, and they were now few in number. Israel was fortunate to have a man of God like Nehemiah who not only prayed, and believed God for the answer to prayer, he wanted to be the answer to prayer. The people were willing, and Nehemiah was a good organizer so they soon had crews working at different places around the wall of the city. The wall was completed 444 B.C. and they gave thanks to God, and had a dedication with much celebration.

At the time that the wall was completed the number of exiles who had returned to the province was forty two thousand three hundred sixty. The rulers of the people dwelt at Jerusalem and the rest of the people cast lots, to bring one of ten people to dwell in the holy city, and nine parts to live in the other cities.

We need to keep in mind the fact that many Jews remained scattered in many countries throughout the world. Only a comparative small number have returned at this time. This is important as we look to the future, and consider how the Jews fit in. Now that they are back in their land, they have repented for their failures, and have agreed to keep their side of the covenant that God had made with their fathers. Their leaders felt the need to review what the Lord had done for the nation of Israel, because this was a younger generation.

"Thou, even thou, art LORD alone; thou hast made heaven, the heaven of heavens, with all their host, the earth, and all things that are therein, the seas, and all that is therein, and thou preservest them all; and the host of heaven worshippeth thee. Thou art the LORD the God, who didst choose Abram, and broughtest him forth out of Ur of the Chaldees, and gavest him the name of Abraham; And foundest his heart faithful before thee, and madest a covenant with him to give the land of the Canaanites, the Hittites, the Amorites, and the Perizzites, and the Jebusites, and the Girgashites, to give it, I say, to his seed, and hast performed thy words; for thou art righteous: And didst see the affliction of our fathers in Egypt, and heardest their cry by the Red sea; And shewedst signs and wonders upon Pharaoh, and on all his servants, and on all the people of his land: for thou knewest that they dealt proudly against them. So didst thou get thee a name, as it is this day. And thou didst divide the sea before them, so that they went through the midst of the sea on the dry land; and their persecutors thou threwest into the deeps, as a stone into the mighty waters. Moreover thou leddest them in the day by a cloudy pillar; and in the night by a pillar of fire, to give them light in the way wherein they should go. Thou camest down also upon mount Sinai, and spakest with them from heaven, and gavest them right judgments, and true laws, good statutes and commandments: And madest known unto them thy holy sabbath, and commandedst them precepts, statutes, and laws, by the hand of Moses thy servant: And gavest them bread from heaven for their hunger, and broughtest forth water for them out of the rock for their thirst, and promisedst them that they should go in to possess the land which thou hadst sworn to give them. But they and our fathers dealt proudly, and hardened their necks, and hearkened not to thy commandments, And refused to obey, neither were mindful of thy wonders that thou didst among them; but hardened their necks, and in their rebellion appointed a captain to return to their bondage: but thou art a God ready to pardon, gracious and merciful, slow to anger, and of great kindness, and forsookest them not. Yea, when they had made them a molten calf, and said, This is thy God that brought thee up out of Egypt, and had wrought great provocations; Yet thou in thy manifold mercies forsookest them not in the wilderness: the pillar of the cloud departed not from them by day, to lead them in the way; neither the pillar of fire by night, to shew them light, and the way wherein they should go. Thou gavest also thy good spirit to instruct them, and withheldest not thy manna from their mouth, and gavest them water for their thirst. Yea, forty years didst thou sustain them in the wilderness, so that they lacked nothing; their clothes waxed not old, and their feet swelled not. Moreover thou gavest them kingdoms and nations, and didst divide them into corners: so they possessed the land of Sihon, and the land of the king of Heshbon, and the land of Og king of Bashan. Their children also multipliedst thou as the stars of heaven, and broughtest them into the land, concerning which thou hadst promised to their fathers, that they should go in to possess it. So the children went in and possessed the land, and thou subduedst before them the inhabitants of the land, the Canaanites, and gavest them into their hands, with their kings, and the people of the land, that they might do with them as they would. And they took strong cities, and a fat land, and possessed houses full of all goods, wells digged, vineyards, and oliveyards, and fruit trees in abundance: so they did eat, and were filled, and became fat, and delighted themselves in thy great goodness. Nevertheless they were disobedient, and rebelled against thee, and cast thy law behind their backs, and slew thy prophets which testified against them to turn them to thee, and they wrought great provocations. Therefore thou deliveredst them into the hand of their enemies, who vexed them: and in the time of their trouble, when they cried unto thee, thou heardest them from heaven; and according to thy manifold mercies thou gavest them saviours, who saved them out of the hand of their enemies. But after they had rest, they did evil again before thee: therefore leftest thou them in the hand of their enemies, so that they had the dominion over them: yet when they returned, and cried unto thee, thou heardest them from heaven; and many times didst thou deliver them according to thy mercies; And testifiedst against them, that thou mightest bring them again unto thy law: yet they dealt proudly, and hearkened not unto thy commandments, but sinned against thy judgments, (which if a man do, he shall live in them;) and withdrew the shoulder, and hardened their neck, and would not hear. Yet many years didst thou forbear them, and testifiedst against them by thy spirit in thy prophets: yet would they not give ear: therefore gavest thou them into the hand of the people of the lands. Nevertheless for thy great mercies' sake thou didst not utterly consume them, nor forsake them; for thou art a gracious and merciful God. Now therefore, our God, the great, the mighty, and the terrible God, who keepest covenant and mercy, let not all the trouble seem little before thee, that hath come upon us, on our kings, on our princes, and on our priests, and on our prophets, and on our fathers, and on all thy people, since the time of the kings of Assyria unto this day. Howbeit thou art just in all that is brought upon us; for thou hast done right, but we have done wickedly: Neither have our kings, our princes, our priests, nor our fathers, kept thy law, nor hearkened unto thy commandments and thy testimonies, wherewith thou didst testify against them. For they have not served thee in their kingdom, and in thy great goodness that thou gavest them, and in the large and fat land which thou gavest before them, neither turned they from their wicked works. Behold, we are servants this day, and for the land that thou gavest unto our fathers to eat the fruit thereof and the good thereof, behold, we are servants in it: And it yieldeth much increase unto the kings whom thou hast set over us because of our sins: also they have dominion over our bodies, and over our cattle, at their pleasure, and we are in great distress. And because of all this we make a sure covenant, and write it; and our princes, Levites, and priests, seal unto it. (Nehemiah 9:6-38)

We have just considered what is called the Restoration of Israel as a Nation: But in reality, Israel is now a nation in a nation, because Persia is the world power in 400 B.C. And will continue to be for the next sixty-eight years. We have been following the development of Israel and have ignored the Gentile world except where it affected our account of Israel. However now at this time the Old Testament has ended, and it will be four hundred years to the beginning of the New Testament, therefore we have to depend on the Gentile kingdoms' history for what information is recorded about Israel. During this, sixty-eight years of Persian rule, little is known with regard to the Jewish community of Judah. There were no significant events and exact dates. However there were two important developments of this period of Jewish history: the prominence of the High Priest increased to the point that he became the head of the Jewish state. This development was natural since the civil government of Judah was in the hands of a non-Jewish representative of the Persian king. The other development of this period was for the Jews to emphasize the outward rituals of their religion rather than the internal holiness of the heart. This came about as a result of them making a special effort to keep free of the foreign religious practices of those around them. It was easier to observe the outward rituals than to know what was taking place with the peoples' inward spiritual condition.

In 331 B.C. Alexander the Great conquered Persia, making Greece the dominant world power. He annexed Judah to the newly established empire, which meant that the Jews would pay their annual tax to Greece instead of Persia. Alexander the Great died of a fever, in 323 B.C. At which time the kingdom was divided into four parts, under four of his military chiefs. At first, Judah was under the control of a family of Greek rulers known as the Ptolemies who ruled from Egypt. The Jews were treated well under these Greek rulers and many of them started using the Greek language. Judah soon became known by the Greek pronunciation of Judea. Later the Old Testament was translated into Greek for the benefit of the Jews who no longer spoke or read Hebrew.

In 198 B.C. Trouble developed between the Greek kingdoms: And Antiochus III of the Seleucid family added Palestine to his kingdom, and became the next Greek ruler of Judea. For a few years the Jews were treated well, and then things changed, as the result of a financial crisis, which Antiochus III found himself in: caused by heavy financial losses suffered in expanding his kingdom. When Antiochus III died, his youngest son, AntiochusIV followed him on the throne. It became his obligation to pay his fathers' debts. He raised money any way he could, including robbing the temples, excessive taxation, and selling royal appointments to the highest bidder. These policies brought him into open conflict with the Jews of Judea: Especially, over the appointment of Jason, as the High Priest, in exchange for a bribe.

Their new ruler tried to fix things by eliminating their religion: He desecrated their temple and outlawed all religious observance: Any Jew that remained faithful to the religion of their forefathers' was risking his life. In order to survive, some Jews abandoned the practice of their religion, while others kept the law secretly; but not all Jews accepted this brutality. Thousands of them took up the sword in order to defend their faith: they rallied around the priestly family of Mattathias and became known as the Maccabees. Their military success brought a halt to the religious persecution in 164 B.C. The temple was repaired and rededicated to God. Judaism had survived a great assault but thousands of Jews had laid down their lives for their faith.

By 142 B.C. the Maccabees had established political independence for Judea as well as religious freedom, which lasted until 65 B.C. When the Romans conquered the Seleucids and annexed Palestine to the Roman Empire. General Pompey annexed all of Syria and Palestine: therefore Rome became the new overlord of Judea, after almost a century of independence. Roman dominion was primarily political and the Jews were allowed to practice their religion without interference. The internal affairs of Judea continued to be governed by the High Priest with the aid of the Sanhedrin: Therefore most of the Jews adapted to the new overlord.

Herod the Great established himself as the Roman-appointed "king of the Jews" in 37 B.C. And he continued in that position until his death in 4 B.C. It was in this Roman context that the Lord Jesus Christ was born, the true "King of the Jews", and all mankind. That fairly well covers what is known about the Jews during the three hundred ninety four years between the Old and the New Testament: referred to as the Inter-testament Period.

We have sort of skimmed through the Old Testament hitting the high points, with the thought of showing how God dealt with Israel. God chose Israel, primarily to do four things. First, to be His witnesses to the other nations, that He is the one and only true God. Isaiah 43:10-12 "Ye are my witnesses, saith the LORD, and my servant whom I have chosen: that ye may know and believe me, and understand that I am he: before me there was no God formed, neither shall there be after me. I, even I, am the LORD; and beside me there is no saviour. I have declared, and have saved, and I have shewed, when there was no strange god among you: therefore ye are my witnesses, saith the LORD, that I am God."

The second, connected to the first, was to illustrate to the nations; the blessedness of serving the true God. Third, this chosen nation was to, receive, preserve, and transmit the scriptures. The fourth, is to produce, as to His humanity, the Messiah.

In the Old Testament, Israel is called God's elect: likewise in the four Gospels of the New Testament, it's the Jews that are called elect: in the Epistles, letters to the churches and some to people, elect is applied to the church. I mention this because there has been some confusion concerning the elect, and election. But in both Testaments the Hebrew and Greek words are rendered elect, election, choose, chosen: in all cases they mean, simply chosen or to choose; and are used of both human and divine choices.

One thing needs to be stressed; that it is a very serious matter of how people and nations treat the Jews. "I will bless them that bless you, and curse him that curses you." (Genesis 12:3) This is stated many times throughout the Bible: And it has proven to be true, time and time again, to the nations that have taken Israel captive, or those that have fought against them. Today many nations and many individuals as well, are headed for trouble, because of their hatred toward Israel.

Up to this point we have covered the preparation of the Kingdom of God, in God's activities with the nation of Israel. Now we will consider the coming of the Kingdom of God to earth with the person of Jesus Christ. This is recorded in the New Testament, and covers a span of approximately thirty-six years from 6 B.C. to 30A.D.

THE NEW TESTAMENT

The first book of the New Testament begins with this statement, "The book of the generation of Jesus Christ, the son of David, the son of Abraham."(Matthew 1:1) This connects Jesus at once to two of the most important of the Old Testament covenants: the Davidic covenant of kingship, and the Abrahamic covenant of promise. These two covenants boil down to two things; a promised land for the Jews; and a promised kingdom for all of the redeemed. And both are promised forever.

As a reminder; remember that the great stream of civilization, years ago divided into two streams when Israel branched off. Now imagine that we draw on a chalkboard these two streams going down with a space between, now draw a line from each stream to the center of the space between them, and where these two lines meet draw a line straight down, thus creating three streams flowing down, this is what we will now have, as we introduce the Kingdom of God on earth: the middle line will be the Church of Jesus Christ; with Christ as it's head. This new stream will consist of those individuals from the other two streams, who believe on the Lord Jesus Christ.

In preparation for the Kingdom of God there were two miraculous births; that of John the Baptist, and that of Jesus, in the days of Herod king of Judea. John the Baptist's parents were Zacharias and his wife Elizabeth, who had been barren for years, as they were both well along in years. As Zacharias was praying an angel appeared to him, "the angel said unto him, Fear not, Zacharias: for thy prayer is heard; and thy wife Elisabeth shall bear thee a son, and thou shalt call his name John...And many of the children of Israel shall he turn to the Lord their God."(Luke 1:13, 16)

A virgin named Mary was engaged to a man named Joseph, of the house of David. An angel came to Mary, and said, "Hail, thou that art highly favoured, the Lord is with thee: blessed art thou among women...And, behold, thou shalt conceive in thy womb, and bring forth a son, and shalt call his name JESUS. He shall be great, and shall be called the Son of the Highest: and the Lord God shall give unto him the throne of his father David: And he shall reign over the house of Jacob for ever; and of his kingdom there shall be no end." (Luke 1:28, 31-33)

John the Baptist was born about six months before Jesus and his father Zacharias prophesied. "Blessed be the Lord God of Israel; for he hath visited and redeemed his people, And hath raised up an horn of salvation for us in the house of his servant David; As he spake by the mouth of his holy prophets, which have been since the world began: That we should be saved from our enemies, and from the hand of all that hate us; To perform the mercy promised to our fathers, and to remember his holy covenant; The oath which he sware to our father Abraham," (Luke 1:68-73)

Not much is told of the boyhood of Jesus, except that He grew, and waxed strong in the Spirit, filled with wisdom: and the grace of God was upon Him. When He was twelve, He went with His parents to the Passover at Jerusalem. When it was over and they were returning home they found that Jesus was not in the company. They returned to Jerusalem and found Him in the temple, sitting among the doctors, listening to them, and asking them questions. "And all that heard him were astonished at his under-standing and answers. And when they saw him, they were amazed: and his mother said unto him, Son, why hast thou thus dealt with us? behold, thy father and I have sought thee sorrowing. And he said unto them, How is it that ye sought me? wist ye not that I must be about my Father's business? And they under-stood not the saying which he spake unto them. And he went down with them, and came to Nazareth, and was subject unto them: but his mother kept all these sayings in her heart." (Luke 2:47-51)

Jesus was born about 5 B.C. And after the inci-dent at the temple nothing is recorded concerning Jesus until 26 A.D. This is referred to as the silent years of Jesus. Then came the Introduction of the Kingdom of God: And the presentation of Jesus the King. Matthew 3:1-6: "In those days came John the Baptist, preaching in the wilderness of Judaea, And saying, Repent ye: for the kingdom of heaven is at hand. For this is he that was spoken of by the prophet Esaias, saying, The voice of one crying in the wilderness, Prepare ye the way of the Lord, make his paths straight. And the same John had his raiment of camel's hair, and a leathern girdle about his loins; and his meat was locusts and wild honey. Then went out to him Jerusalem, and all Judaea, and all the region round about Jordan, And were baptized of him in Jordan, confessing their sins."

The ministry of John was to prepare the nation of Israel for their Messiah and then present Him to the people of the nation. To accomplish this John had to get right down to the fundamentals of the truth: he preached against sin, and told them they needed to repent, and warned if they didn't they faced the wrath which was to come. He said for them to bring forth fruits worthy of repentance, and not to use being Abraham's descendants as an excuse. Like some today who are counting on getting to heaven on their parents or grandparents righteousness, instead of getting down to the root of sin. John was attracting attention and many were repenting and being baptized: And many were curious and confused as to who John was: was he the Messiah, or Elias, or some other prophet? But John told them he was not the Christ, or a prophet, or Elias: He said, "He said, I am the voice of one crying in the wilderness, Make straight the way of the Lord.... I baptize with water: but there standeth one among you, whom ye know not; He it is, who coming after me is preferred before me, whose shoe's latchet I am not worthy to unloose... The next day John seeth Jesus coming unto him, and saith, Behold the Lamb of God, which taketh away the sin of the world. This is he of whom

I said, After me cometh a man which is preferred before me: for he was before me. And I knew him not: but that he should be made manifest to Israel, therefore am I come baptizing with water. And John bare record, saying, I saw the Spirit descending from heaven like a dove, and it abode upon him. And I knew him not: but he that sent me to baptize with water, the same said unto me, Upon whom thou shalt see the Spirit descending, and remaining on him, the same is he which baptizeth with the Holy Ghost. And I saw, and bare record that this is the Son of God." (John 1:23, 26-27, 29-34)

Just previous to this Jesus had come to John while he was baptizing and ask John to baptize Him. John told Jesus he was the one that needed to be baptized by Jesus, but Jesus convinced John it was necessary, and while John was baptizing Him, is when John saw the Holy Spirit descend upon Jesus.

Jesus has been introduced, and is now ready to begin His ministry, that is to the Jews primarily, who are living in their promised land: But as mentioned before, Rome is ruling over that part of the country. The Jews, however, are free to worship in the restored temple in Jerusalem; as well as the synagogues in other cities. Jesus did much of His teaching in the synagogues.

Matthew, one of the original twelve Apostles, in his gospel, proves that Jesus Christ is the son of David, the Messiah, and the rightful heir to David's throne. Matthew's gospel acts as a bridge between the Old Testament and the New Testament: between the old covenant and the new.

Jesus, the King of the Jews, presented Himself to His people: He said, "I am not sent but unto the lost sheep of the house of Israel." (Matthew 15:24) But the Jewish religious leaders rejected Him. The scripture says, "He came unto his own, and his own received him not." (John 1:11) The religious leaders were called "lost sheep" because they were exalting their traditions above divine law. Jesus, asked them, "Why do ye also transgress the commandment of God by your tradition?...This people draweth nigh unto me with their mouth, and honoureth me with their lips; but their heart is far from me.But in vain they do worship me, teaching for doctrines the commandments of men." (Matthew 15:3, 8-9)

Teaching for doctrines the commandments of men: this is an interesting statement. Jesus said that to the religious leaders long ago: But it is common knowledge today that some men in Christian churches are guilty of doing the same thing. Some times it may not be too serious, but if those commandments of men are contrary to God's word it is extremely serious, and we need to be very careful.

Luke 6:12-13: "And it came to pass in those days, that he went out into a mountain to pray, and continued all night in prayer to God. And when it was day, he called unto him his disciples: and of them he chose twelve, whom also he named apostles;" These were men from several different walks of life, who later became the foundation of the New Testament Church. They followed Jesus the rest of His time on earth, and He was their teacher, so they received excellent on the job training. Later Jesus sent them out, and they preached the word with signs following, and many became believers. These Apostles played a big part in building the Kingdom of God on earth.

At the heart of building the Kingdom of God is a proper understanding of the importance of Jesus Christ, the Son of God. This is the one thing above all else that the Jews were not willing to believe. This is also true of many throughout the world today. The Gospels repeatedly tell how violent the struggle was, and how intense was the hatred of the Jews toward Jesus.

One Sabbath day, Jesus healed a man who had been paralyzed for thirty-eight years: Jesus simply said to him, "Take up thy bed and walk," (John 5:8) and the man was made well, and took up his bed, and walked. "And therefore did the Jews persecute Jesus, and sought to slay him, because he had done these things on the sabbath day. But Jesus answered them, My Father worketh hitherto, and I work. Therefore the Jews sought the more to kill him, because he not only had broken the sabbath, but said also that God was his Father, making himself equal with God.(John 5:16-18) Then Jesus answered them by instructing them about eternal life.

John 5:19-29: "Then answered Jesus and said unto them, Verily, verily, I say unto you, The Son can do nothing of himself, but what he seeth the Father do: for what things soever he doeth, these also doeth the Son likewise. For the Father loveth the Son, and sheweth him all things that himself doeth: and he will shew him greater works than these, that ye may marvel. For as the Father raiseth up the dead, and quickeneth them; even so the Son quickeneth whom he will. For the Father judgeth no man, but hath committed all judgment unto the Son: That all men should honour the Son, even as they honour the Father. He that honoureth not the Son honoureth not the Father which hath sent him. Verily, verily, I say unto you, He that heareth my word, and believeth on him that sent me, hath everlasting life, and shall not come into condemnation; but is passed from death unto life. Verily, verily, I say unto you, The hour is coming, and now is, when the dead shall hear the voice of the Son of God: and they that hear shall live. For as the Father hath life in himself; so hath he given to the Son to have life in himself; And hath given him authority to execute judgment also, because he is the Son of man. Marvel not at this: for the hour is coming, in the which all that are in the graves shall hear his voice, And shall come forth; they that have done good, unto the resurrection of life; and they that have done evil, unto the resurrection of damnation."

What the Jews didn't understand was that you can not just worship God and ignore the Son of God: Not after God gave His Son to die on the cross to pay the penalty for their sins, and ours. John 3:16-18, the key verses of the Bible says it best: "For God so loved the world, that he gave his only begotten Son, that whosoever believeth in him should not perish, but have everlasting life. For God sent not his Son into the world to condemn the world; but that the world through him might be saved. He that believeth on him is not condemned: but he that believeth not is

263

condemned already, because he hath not believed in the name of the only begotten Son of God."

Many people, and many religions, leave Jesus out, or consider Him as being a prophet, or just a good man. Have you noticed that many people will talk about God, but draw back at the mention of Jesus? It is amazing that so many can deny that Jesus is the Son of God when there are so many witnesses that say He is. John the Baptist said He was: the many miracles, the Father, the Scriptures, and Moses, all said He was, and when people believed on Him, they have the witness within themselves.

1 John 5:10-12: "He that believeth on the Son of God hath the witness in himself: he that believeth not God hath made him a liar; because he believeth not the record that God gave of his Son. And this is the record, that God hath given to us eternal life, and this life is in his Son. He that hath the Son hath life; and he that hath not the Son of God hath not life."

These scriptures make it very plain that Jesus Christ is extremely important. The scribes and the chief priests had nothing to say, when ask if they had read the scripture: "The stone which the builders refused is become the head stone of the corner." (Ps 118:22) Jesus is the chief corner stone, the most important stone of the building.

Matthew 16:13-17: "When Jesus came into the coasts of Caesarea Philippi, he asked his disciples, saying, Whom do men say that I the Son of man am? And they said, Some say that thou art John the Baptist: some, Elias; and others, Jeremias, or one of the prophets. He saith unto them, But whom say ye that I am? And Simon Peter answered and said, Thou art the Christ, the Son of the living God. And Jesus answered and said unto him, Blessed art thou, Simon Barjona: for flesh and blood hath not revealed it unto thee, but my Father which is in heaven."

This was the revelation of Jesus as Messiah. The Jews had studied and had been taught about the Messiah: The Prophets foretold of the coming Messiah, so this was not something new: It was just very different from what they thought it would be. They were expecting the Messiah to come as a conquering King and set up a kingdom on earth immediately.

When the prophets were telling what was to come to pass in the future they were covering a long space of time: They covered from the birth of Christ, all the way to the last days, as recorded in Revelation. The Jews didn't see the two thousand year plus span of time between the birth of their Messiah and the setting up of His kingdom.

In John 8:43-47 Jesus said to the Jews, "Why do ye not understand my speech? even because ye cannot hear my word. Ye are of your father the devil, and the lusts of your father ye will do. He was a murderer from the beginning, and abode not in the truth, because there is no truth in him. When he speaketh a lie, he speaketh of his own: for he is a liar, and the father of it. And because I tell you the truth, ye believe me not. Which of you convinceth me of sin? And if I say the truth, why do ye not believe me? He that is of God heareth God's words: ye therefore hear them not, because ye are not of God."

Ignorance is rampant in the world today, because many people everywhere are rejecting the truth: They reject the book that contains the truth, and they reject the author of the book, and they reject His Son that He sent to die in their place. They believe, instead the lies, which come from the father of lies, the devil. However the truth is going forth at a rapid pace, and modern technology makes it both easier and faster.

Jesus continued teaching many things concerning the Kingdom of God, and many people were receiving and believing what He taught: But many of "the lost sheep of the house of Israel" were opposing all that Jesus taught: And these were the ones to whom He was sent. "These twelve Jesus sent forth, and commanded them, saying, Go not into the way of the Gentiles, and into any city of the Samaritans enter ye not: But go rather to the lost sheep of the house of Israel." (Matthew 10:5-6) The ones, who needed it most, were the very ones who were the most resistant to His message.

"Jesus continued from city to city and village to village, teaching as He went, always pressing toward Jerusalem. Someone asked Him, Will only a few be saved? And He answered, The door to heaven is narrow. Work hard to get in, for the truth is that many will try to enter but when the head of the house has locked the door, it will be too late. Then if you stand outside knocking, and pleading, Lord open the door for us, He will reply, I do not know you. But we ate with you, and you taught in our streets, And He will reply, I tell you I do not know you. You can't come in here as guilty as you are. Go away. And there will be weeping and gnashing of teeth as you stand outside and see Abraham, and Isaac, and Jacob, and all of the Prophets within the Kingdom of God: for people shall come from all over the world to take their places there. And note this: some who are despised now will be greatly honored; and some who are greatly thought of now will be least important then. A few minutes later some Pharisees said to Him. Get out of here if you want to live, for King Herod is after you! Jesus replied, "Go tell that fox that I will keep on casting out demons and doing miracles of healing today and tomorrow; and the third day I will reach My destination. Yes, today, tomorrow, and the next day! For it wouldn't do for a prophet of God to be killed except in Jerusalem." (Luke 13:22-33 The Living Bible)

John 12:12, 13, 17-19 "On the next day much people that were come to the feast, when they heard that Jesus was coming to Jerusalem, Took branches of palm trees, and went forth to meet him, and cried, Hosanna: Blessed is the King of Israel that cometh in the name of the Lord... The people therefore that was with him when he called Lazarus out of his grave, and raised him from the dead, bare record. For this cause the people also met him, for that they heard that he had done this miracle. The Pharisees therefore said among themselves, Perceive ye how ye prevail nothing? behold, the world is gone after him." As Jesus was coming close to the end of His ministry here on earth He used parables describing the religious leaders. "Hear another parable: There was a certain householder, which planted a vineyard, and hedged it round about, and digged a winepress in it, and built a tower, and let it out to husbandmen, and went into a far country: And when the time of the fruit drew near, he sent his servants to the husbandmen, that they might receive the fruits of it. And the husbandmen took his servants, and beat one, and killed another, and stoned another. Again, he sent other servants more than the first: and they did unto them likewise. But last of all he sent unto them his son, saying, They will reverence my son. But when the husbandmen saw the son, they said among themselves, This is the heir; come, let us kill him, and let us seize on his inheritance. And they caught him, and cast him out of the vineyard, and slew him. When the lord therefore of the vineyard cometh, what will he do unto those husbandmen? They say unto him, He will miserably destroy those wicked men, and will let out his vineyard unto other husbandmen, which shall render him the fruits in their seasons. Jesus saith unto them, Did ye never read in the scriptures, The stone which the builders rejected, the same is become the head of the corner: this is the Lord's doing, and it is marvellous in our eyes? (Matthew 21:33-42) This parable sets forth exactly what the Jews had done, when God sent them Prophets, they mistreated some and killed others: and now they will soon kill the Son of God. They knew Jesus had spoken this parable against them. "Therefore say I unto you, The kingdom of God shall be taken from you, and given to a nation bringing forth the fruits thereof." (Matthew 21:43)

In saying this, Jesus is foretelling what will happen, later when the Kingdom is transferred from the nation of Israel to the Gentiles. We will discuss this in detail when we come to it.

Another story is found in Matthew 22:15-22, "Then went the Pharisees, and took counsel how they might entangle him in his talk. And they sent out unto him their disciples with the Herodians, saying, Master, we know that thou art true, and teachest the way of God in truth, neither carest thou for any man: for thou regardest not the person of men. Tell us therefore, What thinkest thou? Is it lawful to give tribute unto Caesar, or not? But Jesus perceived their wickedness, and said, Why tempt ye me, ye hypocrites? Shew me the tribute money. And they brought unto him a penny. And he saith unto them, Whose is this image and superscription? They say unto him, Caesar's. Then saith he unto them, Render therefore unto Caesar the things which are Caesar's; and unto God the things that are God's. When they had heard these words, they marvelled, and left him, and went their way." Jesus told them the truth: He told them they were hypocrites, and He told them to give the government of the land, due respect: But He also told them to give God and His laws, due respect, which they were not doing.

There are a few other very important things that Jesus was getting cleared up before He went back to heaven, which He knew would be soon. One of those was concerning the resurrection, which was a matter of division among the Jews. "The same day came to him the Sadducees, which say that there is no resurrection, and asked him, Saying, Master, Moses said, If a man die, having no children, his brother shall marry his wife, and raise up seed unto his brother. Now there were with us seven brethren: and the first, when he had married a wife, deceased, and, having no issue, left his wife unto his brother: Likewise the second also, and the third, unto the seventh. And last of all the woman died also. Therefore in the resurrection whose wife shall she be of the seven? for they all had her. Jesus answered and said unto them, Ye do err, not knowing the scriptures, nor the power of God. For in the resurrection they neither marry, nor are given in marriage, but are as the angels of God in heaven. But as touching the resurrection of the dead, have ye not read that which was spoken unto you by God, saying, I am the God of Abraham, and the God of Isaac, and the God of Jacob? God is not the God of the dead, but of the living. And when the multitude heard this, they were astonished at his doctrine." (Matthew 22:23-33) It is good to ponder the great questions of life, it is also good to worship Christ; in whom are hidden all the treasures of wisdom and knowledge.

Matthew 22:34-40: "But when the Pharisees had heard that he had put the Sadducees to silence, they were gathered together. Then one of them, which was a lawyer, asked him a question, tempting him, and saying, Master, which is the great commandment in the law? Jesus said unto him, Thou shalt love the Lord thy God with all thy heart, and with all thy soul, and with all thy mind. This is the first and great commandment. And the second is like unto it, Thou shalt love thy neighbour as thyself. On these two commandments hang all the law and the prophets."

This means that every thing is covered by these two commandments: The whole Law of Moses is covered, and all the ministry of the Prophets is covered. To love God takes care of our vertical relationship, and to love our neighbor takes care of the horizontal relationships, which includes those we come in contact with in every day life.

Then Jesus explained to the multitude, and to His Disciples, that the Scribes and the Pharisees sit in the seat of Moses: Which meant that they were in authority. Therefore they should obey and do what they tell them. But he told them not to do as they do, because they do all their works to be seen of men.

Jesus continued teaching as He moved toward the cross that awaited Him. He instructed His followers concerning the end-time, so they would know what to expect. He told them about the persecution ahead, and the destruction of the temple, which happened in 70 A.D. And He also told them about the great tribulation, and His second coming at the end of the age.

The Jewish authorities consult to put Jesus to death, and they plotted with Judas, when he came asking what they would give him to deliver Jesus to them. And they bargained with him for thirty pieces of silver. Jesus instituted the Lord's Supper, and as they were eating, Jesus took bread and blessed it, and He took the cup of wine, and gave thanks, and after they had partaken Jesus said, "But I say unto you, I will not drink henceforth of this fruit of the vine, until that day when I drink it new with you in my Father's kingdom." (Matthew 26:29)

Afterward they went to The Garden of Gethsemane, where Jesus was betrayed, arrested, and taken away, to be tried: and then condemned, and crucified.

Let's take a look at the trial of Jesus: Probably the most devious and sinful trial on record. They led Jesus away to Annas first for he was father- in-law to Caiaphas who was the high priest at that time. The scribes and the elders who were assembled there, sought false witnesses against Jesus, to put Him to death; but they weren't finding any; until at last two false witnesses came forward, and said, "This fellow said, I am able to destroy the temple of God, and build it in three days." The high priest questioned Jesus, but He remained silent. Then the high priest said, "I adjure thee by the living God, that thou tell us whether thou be the Christ, the Son of God. Jesus saith unto him, Thou hast said: nevertheless I say unto you, Hereafter shall ye see the Son of man sitting on the right hand of power, and coming in the clouds of heaven. Then the high priest rent his clothes, saying, He hath spoken blasphemy; what further need have we of witnesses? behold, now ye have heard his blasphemy. What think ye? They answered and said, He is guilty of death. Then did they spit in his face, and buffeted him; and others smote him with the palms of their hands, Saying, Prophesy unto us, thou Christ, Who is he that smote thee? (Matthew 26:61-68)

They bound Jesus and took Him from Caiaphas to Pilate, the Governor, who was at the judgment hall: But the Jews couldn't go in because they would be defiled and would be unable to eat the Passover.

Therefore Pilate went out to them, and asked them what accusations they brought against Jesus. They replied, "if He wasn't a criminal we would not have brought Him to you." Pilate told them to take Jesus and judge Him themselves, according to their law. The Jews told him, it was not lawful for them to put any man to death.

"Then Pilate entered into the judgment hall again, and called Jesus, and said unto him, Art thou the King of the Jews? Jesus answered him, Sayest thou this thing of thyself, or did others tell it thee of me? Pilate answered, Am I a Jew? Thine own nation and the chief priests have delivered thee unto me: what hast thou done? Jesus answered, My kingdom is not of this world: if my kingdom were of this world, then would my servants fight, that I should not be delivered to the Jews: but now is my kingdom not from hence. Pilate therefore said unto him, Art thou a king then? Jesus answered, Thou sayest that I am a king. To this end was I born, and for this cause came I into the world, that I should bear witness unto the truth. Every one that is of the truth heareth my voice. Pilate saith unto him, What is truth? And when he had said this, he went out again unto the Jews, and saith unto them, I find in him no fault at all." (John 18:33-38) "When Pilate saw that he could prevail nothing, but that rather a tumult was made, he took water, and washed his hands before the multitude, saying, I am innocent of the blood of this just person: see ye to it. Then answered all the people, and said, His blood be on us, and on our children. (Matthew 27: 24-25)

The crucifixion of Jesus Christ was the high point in the building of the Kingdom of God. From Moses up to this point in time God's chosen nation, Israel, lived under the Law: Which was given in three parts, the commandments, which expressed the righteous will of God, the ordinances, which governed the religious life of Israel, and the judgments governing the social life of Israel. When Israel sinned they were held blameless if they brought the required offerings.

The death of Christ was the beginning of what has been called the dispensation of grace, which was a contrast to the law. Under law God demanded righteousness, while under grace, God bestows righteousness: The righteousness, which comes through belief in Jesus Christ. Law is connected with Moses and works: Grace with Christ and faith. Grace is the kindness and love of our Savior toward man.

At the same time that grace began, law ended. The law had been God's way of bringing Israel to the place that they could accept the blessings of God through faith. "But before faith came, we were kept under the law, shut up unto the faith which should afterwards be revealed. Wherefore the law was our schoolmaster to bring us unto Christ, that we might be justified by faith. But after that faith is come, we are no longer under a schoolmaster." (Galatians 3:23-25) In other words the law was their teacher, preparing them to move out into new territory. Jesus explained it when He said, "Think not that I am come to destroy the law, or the prophets: I am not come to destroy, but to fulfil. For verily I say unto you, Till heaven and earth pass, one jot or one tittle shall in no wise pass from the law, till all be fulfilled." (Matthew 5:17-18)

Wuest, in his expanded translation, gives further explanation in Galatians, in chapter four and verse four, "As long as the heir is in his minority, he does not differ one bit from a slave, even though he is owner of all, but is under guardians and stewards until the time fixed by his father. In like manner, the Jews also, when they were in their minority, were in a permanent state of servitude under the rudimentary first principles of mankind. But when there came the fullness of time, God sent His Son, woman-born, made subject to the law, in order that He might deliver those under law to the end that they might be placed as adult sons. And because they are sons, God sent forth the Spirit of His Son into your hearts crying, my Father. So that no longer are they a slave but a son, and since they are sons, they are also heirs through God." This means they are joint-heirs with Christ.

The Resurrection of Christ must be included with His Crucifixion, or we miss an important part of the picture, because His resurrection is a central truth of the gospel. Jesus died on the cross for the sins of the world, and God, with His infinite power raised Him from the dead, for the believer's justification: Which means the slate is wiped clean, and the believer comes out just like he had never sinned.

In Acts, Luke, the writer of the Gospel of Luke, says, "Dear friend who loves God: In my first letter I told you about Jesus' life and teachings and how He returned to heaven after giving His chosen Apostles further instructions through the Holy Spirit. During the forty days after His crucifixion and resurrection He appeared to the Apostles from time to time, actually alive (which they didn't believe at first) and proved to them in many ways that it was really Himself they were seeing. And on these occasions He talked to them about the Kingdom of God. In one of these meetings He told them not to leave Jerusalem until the Holy Spirit came upon them in fulfillment of the Father's promise, a matter He had previously discussed with them. John baptized you with water He reminded them, but you shall be baptized with the Holy Spirit in just a few days. Another time when He appeared to them, they ask Him, Lord, are you going to free Israel from Rome now and restore us as an independent nation? The Father sets those dates, He replied, and they are not for you to know. But when the Holy Spirit comes upon you, you will receive power to testify about Me with great effect, to the people in Jerusalem, throughout Judea, in Samaria, and to the ends of the earth, about My death and resurrection. It was not long afterward that He rose into the sky and disappeared into a cloud, leaving then staring after Him. As they were straining their eyes for another glimpse of Him, suddenly two white robed men were standing there among them, and said, Men of Galilee, why are you standing here looking into the sky? (Acts 1:1-11 The Living Bible)Jesus has gone away in to heaven, and some day, just as He went, He will return!"

These Jewish followers of Jesus didn't understand: They had been looking for the Messiah to come and set them free and set up His Kingdom. Jesus had come and they believed Him to be the Messiah but things were not coming about as they had expected. Jesus was going back to heaven, and wouldn't set up His Kingdom on earth until He came back again. They were confused, but they were obedient because they went to Jerusalem, to wait for the next important event, as Jesus had instructed them.

Acts chapter two: Seven weeks had gone by since Jesus' death and resurrection: and the Day of Pentecost had now arrived. As the believers (one hundred and twenty of them) met together that day, suddenly there was the sound like the roaring of a mighty wind in the skies above them and it filled the house where they were meeting. Then what looked like flames or tongues of fire appeared and settled upon their heads. And every one present was filled with the Holy Spirit and began speaking in languages they didn't know, for the Holy Spirit gave them this ability. Many godly Jews were in Jerusalem that day for the religious celebrations, having arrived from many nations. And when they heard the noise and the wind the crowds came running to see what it was all about, and were stunned to hear their own languages being spoken by the disciples. How can this be? They exclaimed: For these people are all from Galilee, and yet we hear them speaking the languages of the lands where we were born! Here we are—Parthians, Medes, Elamites, men from Mesopotamia, Judea, Cppadocia, Pontus, Asia, Phrygia, Pamphilia, Egypt, the Cyrene language area of Lybia, visitors from Rome; both Jews and Jewish converts; Cretans, and Arabians. And we all hear them telling in our own languages about the mighty miracles of God! They stood there amazed and perplexed. What can this mean? They asked each other. But others in the crowd were mocking. They are drunk, that's all, they said.

Then Peter stepped forward with the eleven Apostles, and shouted to the crowd, listen all of you, visitors and residents of Jerusalem alike! Some of you are saying these people are drunk! It isn't true! It's much too early for that! People don't get drunk by 9 A.M.! No! What you see this morning was predicted centuries ago, by the Prophet Joel. In the last days, God said I will pour out My Holy Spirit upon all mankind, and your sons and daughters shall prophesy, and your young men shall see visions, and your old men shall dream dreams. Yes the Holy Spirit shall come upon all My servants, men and women alike, and they shall prophesy. And I will cause strange demonstrations in the heavens, and on earth: Blood and fire and clouds of smoke: the sun shall turn black and the moon blood red before that terrible day of the Lord arrives. But anyone who asks for mercy from the Lord shall have it and shall be saved. Oh men of Israel, listen! God publicly endorsed Jesus of Nazareth by doing tremendous miracles through Him, as you well know. But God, following His prearranged plan, let you use the Roman government to nail Him to the cross and murder Him. Then God released Him from the horrors of death and brought Him back to life again, for death could not keep this man, Jesus, within its grip. We all are witnesses that

Jesus rose from the dead, and now He sits on the throne, of highest honor, in heaven, next to God; And just as promised, the Father gave Him authority to send the Holy Spirit with the results you are seeing and hearing today. I clearly state to everyone in Israel that God has made this Jesus you crucified to be the Lord, and the Messiah!

These words of Peter's moved them deeply, and they said to him and to the other Apostles, Brothers what shall we do? And Peter replied, each one of you must turn from sin, return to God, and be baptized in the name of Jesus Christ for the forgiveness of your sins; then you shall receive the gift of the Holy Spirit. For Christ promised Him to each one of you who has been called by the Lord our God, and to your children and even those in distant lands! Then Peter preached a long sermon, telling them about Jesus and urging them to save themselves from the evils of their nation. And those who believed Peter were baptized: About 3,000 in all! They joined with the other believers in regular attendance at the Apostles teaching sessions and at the communion services and prayer meetings. A deep sense of awe was on them all, and the Apostles did many miracles." (Acts 2:14-42)

After this all the believers met together constantly, and worshiped together in the temple, and met in their homes in small groups, fellowshipping and eating together, with great joy and thankfulness: praising God with great enthusiasm. The whole city was filled with good will toward them, and each day God added to them many that were being saved.

Jesus had instructed His followers concerning the Holy Spirit, just before He ascended back into heaven. Since He would no longer be here on earth with them, to teach, and help, and comfort them, Jesus was asking His Father to send them the Holy Spirit to do all these things for them. John 14:16-17: "And I will pray the Father, and he shall give you another Comforter, that he may abide with you for ever; Even the Spirit of truth; whom the world cannot receive, because it seeth him not, neither knoweth him: but ye know him; for he dwelleth with you, and shall be in you."(Notice, the Holy Spirit was already with them, because they were saved; but after they were all filled and spoke in other languages, the Holy Spirit was in them: There to abide, forever).

Jesus had been hated and treated very badly, and then killed by those He came to save: So now He was warning His followers that they could expect the same. John 15:18-21: "If the world hate you, ye know that it hated me before it hated you. If ye were of the world, the world would love his own: but because ye are not of the world, but I have chosen you out of the world, therefore the world hateth you. Remember the word that I said unto you, The servant is not greater than his lord. If they have persecuted me, they will also persecute you; if they have kept my saying, they will keep yours also. But all these things will they do unto you for my name's sake, because they know not him that sent me."

Jesus didn't paint them a very pretty picture, but He was telling them the truth, and by giving them the Holy Spirit He was equipping them properly for the job. With the help of the Holy Spirit they would be able to reveal to the world, Jesus, as Savior and Lord in a supernatural manner. The primary purpose for Spirit filled Disciples is to preach the Gospel: all else is supportive.

After Pentecost the Lord of the church made it clear that He was the head of the church, and He would build it when, how, and with whom ever He wanted. The church must contend for the faith, and respond to the leadership of the Holy Spirit. This continues to be of the utmost importance today.

A sinner is dead to the Kingdom of God: his mind is dead to truth, and it is by the Holy Spirit that the sinner is brought face to face with the spiritual and eternal consequence of the sinful life. It is necessary, through the working of the Holy Spirit, for the sinner to be convinced of spiritual death and judgment to come, and of the saving grace of Christ. When this is accomplished the Spirit completes the process by putting the new believer into the Church of Jesus Christ.

1 Corinthians 12:12-13: "For as the body is one and has many members, but all the members of that one body, being many, are one body, so also is Christ. For by one Spirit we were all baptized into one body, whether Jews or Greeks, whether slaves or free, and have all been made to drink into one Spirit." The things the scriptures tell us are extremely important because they explain how the Church is built: And to build the Church is to build the Kingdom of God. Jesus, while He was here on earth ministered to the Jews primarily, but while He was doing that He was

laying the substructure of the Church, by training the twelve Apostles, and by teaching them, and the multitudes of other Jews, who had believed, and followed Him. These make up the substructure, while Jesus is the foundation upon which the Church is built.

Let us keep in mind that this Early Church is strictly Jewish and it is surrounded by unfriendly rulers and by hostile religious leaders, and it is attacked from without and from within. The fourth chapter of The Acts of the Apostles gives an interesting account of how they proceeded.

After Peter and John had healed a man who had been lame for forty years, they went into the temple, and were speaking to the crowd that had gathered. Acts 4:1-10: "And as they spake unto the people, the priests, and the captain of the temple, and the Sadducees, came upon them, Being grieved that they taught the people, and preached through Jesus the resurrection from the dead. And they laid hands on them, and put them in hold unto the next day: for it was now eventide. Howbeit many of them which heard the word believed; and the number of the men was about five thousand. And it came to pass on the morrow, that their rulers, and elders, and scribes, and Annas the high priest, and Caiaphas, and John, and Alexander, and as many as were of the kindred of the high priest, were gathered together at Jerusalem. And when they had set them in the midst, they asked, By what power, or by what name, have ye done this? Then Peter, filled with the Holy Ghost, said unto them, Ye rulers of the people, and elders of Israel, If we this day be examined of the good deed done to the impotent man, by what means he is made whole; Be it known unto you all, and to all the people of Israel, that by the name of Jesus Christ of Nazareth, whom ye crucified, whom God raised from the dead, even by him doth this man stand here before you whole."

"Now when they saw the boldness of Peter and John, and perceived that they were unlearned and ignorant men, they marvelled; and they took knowledge of them, that they had been with Jesus. And beholding the man which was healed standing with them, they could say nothing against it. But when they had commanded them to go aside out of the council, they conferred among themselves, Saying, What shall we do to these men? for that indeed a notable miracle hath been done by them is manifest to all them that dwell in Jerusalem; and we cannot deny it. But that it spread no further among the people, let us straitly threaten them, that they speak henceforth to no man in this name. And they called them, and commanded them not to speak at all nor teach in the name of Jesus. But Peter and John answered and said unto them, Whether it be right in the sight of God to hearken unto you more than unto God, judge ye. For we cannot but speak the things which we have seen and heard." (Acts 4:13-20)

Peter and John returned to their own people when they were released, and reported what had happened to them, and how they had threatened them. These two Apostles may have been ignorant and unlearned, but they certainly were not lacking in courage. Starting with verse twenty four we are given the reason for their attitude, and their courage: "And when they heard that, they lifted up their voice to God with one accord, and said, Lord, thou art God, which hast made heaven, and earth, and the sea, and all that in them is: Who by the mouth of thy servant David hast said, Why did the heathen rage, and the people imagine vain things? The kings of the earth stood up, and the rulers were gathered together against the Lord, and against his Christ. For of a truth against thy holy child Jesus, whom thou hast anointed, both Herod, and Pontius Pilate, with the Gentiles, and the people of Israel, were gathered together, For to do whatsoever thy hand and thy counsel determined before to be done. And now, Lord, behold their threatenings: and grant unto thy servants, that with all boldness they may speak thy word, By stretching forth thine hand to heal; and that signs and wonders may be done by the name of thy holy child Jesus. And when they had prayed, the place was shaken where they were assembled together; and they were all filled with the Holy Ghost, and they spake the word of God with boldness. (Acts 4:24-31)

This was their first miracle, as well as their first persecution: But they had many more ahead of them. And the disciples multiplied greatly in Jerusalem; and many of the priests were obedient to the faith: and when this happened, the opposition became very riled, just like they say, "When the Lord begins to move, the devil rises up against Him." In this case the devil worked through the synagogue of the Libertines, and the Cyrenians, and Alexanderians, and them of Cilicia and of Aisia. They were disputing with Stephen, and they were not able to resist the wisdom and the Spirit by which he spoke, so they stirred up the people, and the elders, and the scribes, and they arrested him and brought him to the council, where they falsely accused him and set up false witnesses. Stephen gave them a run-down on the history of Israel, with all their failures and wickedness; ending with their crucifying of Jesus. Acts 7:54-8:3 "When they heard these things, they were cut to the heart, and they gnashed on him with their teeth. But he, being full of the Holy Ghost, looked up stedfastly into heaven, and saw the glory of God, and Jesus standing on the right hand of God, And said, Behold, I see the heavens opened, and the Son of man standing on the right hand of God. Then they cried out with a loud voice, and stopped their ears, and ran upon him with one accord, And cast him out of the city, and stoned him: and the witnesses laid down their clothes at a young man's feet, whose name was Saul. And they stoned Stephen, calling upon God, and saying, Lord Jesus, receive my spirit. And he kneeled down, and cried with a loud voice, Lord, lay not this sin to their charge. And when he had said this, he fell asleep. And Saul was consenting unto his death. And at that time there was a great persecution against the church which was at Jerusalem; and they were all scattered abroad throughout the regions of Judaea and Samaria, except the apostles. And devout men carried Stephen to his burial, and made great lamentation over him. As for Saul, he made havock of the church, entering into every house, and haling men and women committed them to prison." Keep this man Saul in mind: we will soon be looking at the important part he played in the building of the Kingdom of God.

After the martyrdom of Stephen the Kingdom of God was expanded in Samaria, and Judea, and along the Mediterranean. As this was happening, Saul continued doing what he could to tear down what the Christians were doing. Acts 9:1-20 "And Saul, yet breathing out threatenings and slaughter against the disciples of the Lord, went unto the high priest, And desired of him letters to Damascus to the synagogues, that if he found any of this way, whether they were men or women, he might bring them bound unto Jerusalem. And as he journeyed, he came near Damascus: and suddenly there shined round about him a light from heaven: And he fell to the earth, and heard a voice saying unto him, Saul, Saul, why persecutest thou me? And he said, Who art thou, Lord? And the Lord said, I am Jesus whom thou persecutest: it is hard for thee to kick against the pricks. And he trembling and astonished said, Lord, what wilt thou have me to do? And the Lord said unto him, Arise, and go into the city, and it shall be told thee what thou must do. And the men which journeyed with him stood speechless, hearing a voice, but seeing no man. And Saul arose from the earth; and when his eyes were opened, he saw no man: but they led him by the hand, and brought him into Damascus. And he was three days without sight, and neither did eat nor drink. And there was a certain disciple at Damascus, named Ananias; and to him said the Lord in a vision, Ananias. And he said, Behold, I am here, Lord. And the Lord said unto him, Arise, and go into the street which is called Straight, and enquire in the house of Judas for one called Saul, of Tarsus: for, behold, he prayeth, And hath seen in a vision a man named Ananias coming in, and putting his hand on him, that he might receive his sight. Then Ananias answered, Lord, I have heard by many of this man, how much evil he hath done to thy saints at Jerusalem: And here he hath authority from the chief priests to bind all that call on thy name. But the Lord said unto him, Go thy way: for he is a chosen vessel unto me, to bear my name before the Gentiles, and kings, and the children of Israel: For I will shew him how great things he must suffer for my name's sake. And Ananias went his way, and entered into the house; and putting his hands on him said, Brother Saul, the Lord, even Jesus, that appeared unto thee in the way as thou camest, hath sent me, that thou mightest receive thy sight, and be filled with the Holy Ghost. And immediately there fell from his eyes as it had been scales: and he received sight forthwith, and arose, and was baptized. And when he had received meat, he was strengthened. Then was Saul certain days with the disciples which were at Damascus. And straightway he preached Christ in the synagogues, that he is the Son of God."

The central thought concerning the growth of the Kingdom of God is found in verse fifteen which says Saul is a chosen instrument, or a chosen means to take the Lord's name and His message to the Gentile nations, and before kings, and to the children of Israel. This means that God's plan for His Kingdom will no longer be only a Jewish institution: But, also will now include Gentiles.

After three years Saul went to Jerusalem to see Peter, and lived with him for fifteen days. He didn't see any other Apostle except James, the Lord's brother. Later when Saul came to Jerusalem he tried to join the Disciples, they were afraid of him, and didn't believe he was a Disciple. But Barnabas took him and brought him to the Apostles, and declared to them how he had seen the Lord, and how the Lord had spoken to him, and how he had preached boldly at Damascus in the name of Jesus. Saul remained with them for a while, and he spoke boldly in the name of the Lord Jesus, and disputed against the Grecians: but they planed to slay him. When the others knew about it they brought him down to Caesarea, and sent him to Tarsus.

Then, at the end of five years of severe persecution the churches had rest throughout Judea, and Galilee, and Samaria, and were edified; and walking in the fear of the Lord, and in the comfort of the Holy Spirit, they were multiplied. It had been about eleven years since Jesus was baptized by John, and started His public ministry: And all through this period of time many had believed, and had become followers of Jesus. This had been happening throughout the country, but the headquarters remains in Jerusalem, where the Apostles remained when the others were scattered by the great persecution.

We want to look at another story which shows again how God worked through dreams and visions in difficult situations: The big problem that was coming forth was; the Jewish believers who were clinging to things they were taught under the law; were about to be faced with Gentile believers, who knew nothing about the law and the Jews customs.

The Living Bible: Acts 10:1 "In Caesarea there lived a Roman army officer, Cornelius, a captain of an Italian regiment. He was a godly man, deeply reverent, as was his entire household. He gave generously to charity and was a man of prayer. While wide-awake one afternoon, he had a vision; it was about three o'clock: and in this vision he saw an angel of the Lord coming toward him. Cornelius, the angel said. Cornelius stared at him in terror. What do you want, sir? He asked the angel. And the angel replied. Your prayers and charities have not gone unnoticed by God! Now send some men to Joppa to find a man named Simon Peter, who is staying with Simon the tanner, down by the shore, and ask him to come and visit you. As soon as the angel was gone, Cornelius called two of his household servants and a goodly soldier, one of his personal bodyguards, and told them what had happened and sent them off to Joppa. The next day as they were nearing the city, Peter went up on the flat roof of his house to pray. It was noon and he was hungry, but while lunch was being prepared he fell into a trance. He saw the sky open, and a great canvas sheet, suspended by its four corners; settle to the ground. In the sheet were all sorts of animals, snakes and birds (forbidden to the Jews for food). Then a voice said to him, Go kill and eat any of them you wish. Never, Lord, Peter declared, I have never in all my life eaten such creatures: For they are forbidden by our Jewish, laws. The voice spoke again, don't contradict God! If He says something is kosher, then it is. The same vision was repeated three times. Then the sheet was pulled up again to heaven. Peter was very perplexed. What could the vision mean? What was he supposed to do?

Just then the men sent by Cornelius had found the house and were standing outside the gate, and inquiring whether this was the place where Simon Peter lived! Meanwhile, as Peter was puzzling over the vision, the Holy Spirit said to him, three men have come to see you, Go down and meet them and go with them. All is well I have sent them. So Peter went down, I am the man you are looking for, he said. Now what is it you want? Then they told him about Cornelius the Roman officer, a good and godly man, well thought of by the Jews, and how an angel instructed him to send for Peter to come and tell him what God wanted him to do. So Peter invited them in and lodged them over night. And the next day he went with them, accompanied by some other believers from Joppa. They arrived in Caesarea the following day, and Cornelius was waiting for him, and had called together his relatives and close friends to meet Peter. As Peter entered his home, Cornelius fell to the floor before him to worship. But Peter said, stand up! I am not a god! So he got up and they talked together for a while and then went in where the others were assembled. Peter told them, you know it is against the Jewish laws for me to come into a Gentile home like this. But God has shown me in a vision that I should never think of anyone as inferior. So I came as soon as I was sent for. Now tell me what you want.

Cornelius replied, four days ago I was praying as usual at this time of the afternoon, when suddenly a man was standing before me clothed in a radiant robe! He told me, Cornelius, your prayers, have been heard, and your acts of charity have been noticed, by God. Now send some men to Joppa and summon Simon Peter, who is staying in the house of Simon the tanner down by the shore. So I sent for you at once, and you have done well to come so soon. Now here we are waiting before the Lord, anxious to hear what He has told you to tell us! Then Peter replied, I see very clearly that the Jews are not God's only favorites. In every nation He has those who worship Him and do good deeds and are acceptable to Him. I am sure you have heard about the Good News for the people of Israel: That there is peace with God through Jesus, the Messiah who is Lord of all creation.

This message has spread all through Judea, beginning with John the Baptist in Galilee. And you no doubt know that Jesus of Nazareth was anointed by God with the Holy Spirit and with power and went around doing good and healing all who were possessed with demons, for God was with Him. And we Apostles are witnesses of all that He did throughout Israel and in Jerusalem, where He was murdered on a cross. But God brought Him back to life again three days later and showed Him to certain witnesses God had selected beforehand: Not to the general public, but us who ate and drank with Him after He rose from the dead. And He sent us to preach the Good News everywhere and to testify that Jesus is ordained of God to be judge of all: living and dead. And all of the Prophets have written about Him, saying that everyone who believes in Him shall have their sins forgiven through His name.

Even as Peter was saying these things, the Holy Spirit fell upon all those listening! The Jews who came with Peter were amazed that the Holy Spirit would be given to Gentiles too! But there could be no doubt about it, because they heard them speaking in tongues and praising God. Peter asked: Can anyone object to my baptizing them, now that they have received the Holy Spirit just as we did? So he did, baptizing them in the name of Jesus the Messiah. Afterwards Cornelius begged him to stay with them for several days.

Soon the news reached the Apostles and other believers in Judea that Gentiles also were being converted. But when Peter arrived back in Jerusalem, the Jewish believers argued with him. You fellow-shipped with Gentiles and even ate with them, they accused. Then Peter told them the whole story. One day in Joppa, he said. While I was praying, I saw a vision: a huge sheet was let down, by its four corners, from the sky. Inside the sheet were all sorts of animals, reptiles and birds; which we are not to eat. And I heard a voice say: Kill and eat whatever you wish. Never, Lord, I replied. For I have never eaten anything forbidden by our Jewish laws. But the voice came again: Don't say it isn't right when God declares it is! This happened three times before the sheet disappeared into heaven. Just then three men who had come to take me with them to Caesarea arrived at the house where I was staying. The Holy Spirit told me to go with them and not to worry about them being Gentiles. These six brothers here accompanied me, and we soon arrived at the home of the man who had sent the messengers. He told us how an angel had appeared to him and had told him to send messengers to Joppa to find Simon Peter. He will tell you how you and all your, household can be saved, the angel told him.

Well, I began telling them the Good News, but just as I was getting started with my sermon, the Holy Spirit fell on them, just as He fell on us at the beginning. Then I thought of the Lord's words when He said, Yes, John baptized with water, but you will be baptized with the Holy Spirit. And since it was God who gave these Gentiles the same gift He gave to us when we believed on the Lord Jesus Christ, who was I to argue. When the others heard this, all their objections were answered and they began praising God. Yes, they said, God has given to the Gentiles, too, the privilege of turning to Him and receiving eternal life."

This was a new revelation to the Jewish believers: Up until this time Gentiles were considered low class citizens, or worse. So it was hard for them to make adjustments and they had to be convinced. However, Peter had taken other believing Jews with him, as witnesses, and God had worked through angels, and dreams and visions, in a supernatural way; to the point that they were convinced.

I have read recently, that God is using dreams and visions, similar to this, in the salvation of Muslims, in different parts of the world: Jesus appears to them in a dream or vision and tells then to contact a certain Christian or a missionary, who will give them more instructions. This is believed to be successful because Muslims believe that Jesus is a Prophet: therefore they obey Him. This shows us that God is continuing to use signs and wonders to convince mankind, and to save some.

Just after Saul's conversion the Lord said, "He is a chosen vessel unto Me, to bear My name before the Gentiles, and kings, and the children of Israel." (Acts 9:15) Now, Saul has an important part in the expansion of the Kingdom of God in, all, the world. Acts 13:1-4: "Now there were in the church that was at Antioch certain prophets and teachers; as Barnabas, and Simeon that was called Niger, and Lucius of Cyrene, and Manaen, which had been brought up with Herod the tetrarch, and Saul. As they ministered to the Lord, and fasted, the Holy Ghost said, Separate me Barnabas and Saul for the work whereunto I have called them. And when they had fasted and prayed, and laid their hands on them, they sent them away. So they, being sent forth by the Holy Ghost, departed unto Seleucia; and from thence they sailed to Cyprus."

They traveled around from place to place, preaching primarily in the synagogues, to the Jews. Acts13:14-15: "But when they departed from Perga, they came to Antioch in Pisidia, and went into the synagogue on the Sabbath day, and sat down. And after the reading of the law and the prophets the rulers of the synagogue sent unto them, saying, Ye men and brethren, if ye have any word of exhortation for the people, say on." Saul, whose name had now been changed to Paul, stood up and preached them a sermon about how God had delivered them from Egypt and brought them into the promised land. And he continued in verse 21 "And afterward they desired a king: and God gave unto them Saul the son of Cis, a man of the tribe of Benjamin, by the space of forty years. And when he had removed him, he raised up unto them David to be their king; to whom also he gave testimony, and said, I have found David the son of Jesse, a man after mine own heart, which shall fulfil all my will. Of this man's seed hath God according to his promise raised unto Israel a Saviour, Jesus:" (Acts 13:21-23) David holds a very important place in History: He is said to be a mountain peak among Bible characters, as he is one of the most prominent figures in the History of the world. He is the most famous ancestor of Christ. Jesus is not called the son of Abraham, or the son of Jacob, but the Son of David.

Paul continued to tell them the story of the Gospel; how Jesus was crucified, and buried, and how He was raised from the dead. Then he said, "Be it known unto you therefore, men and brethren, that through this man is preached unto you the forgiveness of sins: And by him all that believe are justified from all things, from which ye could not be justified by the law of Moses. Beware therefore, lest that come upon you, which is spoken of in the prophets;

Behold, ye despisers, and wonder, and perish: for I work a work in your days, a work which ye shall in no wise believe, though a man declare it unto you. And when the Jews were gone out of the synagogue, the Gentiles besought that these words might be preached to them the next sabbath." (Acts 13:38-41)

"And the next sabbath day came almost the whole city together to hear the word of God. But when the Jews saw the multitudes, they were filled with envy, and spake against those things which were spoken by Paul, contradicting and blaspheming. Then Paul and Barnabas waxed bold, and said, It was necessary that the word of God should first have been spoken to you: but seeing ye put it from you, and judge your-selves unworthy of everlasting life, lo, we turn to the Gentiles. For so hath the Lord commanded us, saying, I have set thee to be a light of the Gentiles, that thou shouldest be for salvation unto the ends of the earth. And when the Gentiles heard this, they were glad, and glorified the word of the Lord: and as many as were ordained to eternal life believed. And the word of the Lord was published throughout all the region. But the Jews stirred up the devout and honourable women, and the chief men of the city, and raised persecution against Paul and Barnabas, and expelled them out of their coasts. But they shook off the dust of their feet against them, and came unto Iconium." (Acts 13:44-51)

They traveled to several other cities, preaching the word where they went. Then on their return to Antioch they stopped at the churches, and confirmed the souls of the Disciples, and exhorting them to continue in the faith, and that we must through much tribulation enter into the Kingdom of God. And when they had ordained Elders in every church, and had prayed with fasting they commended them to the Lord, on whom they believed. When they arrived at Antioch the church gathered together, and they reported all that God had done, and how He had opened the door of faith to the Gentiles. They stayed a long time with the Disciples.

The next problem was with some men who came down from Judaea, teaching that unless new believers were circumcised according to the Law they couldn't be saved. The scripture says, "Paul and Barnabas had no small dissension and disputation with them." (Acts 15:2) They decided to take the dispute to the Apostles and Elders at Jerusalem. On their way there, as they came to the churches they spread the news of the conversion of the Gentiles, which caused great joy among the believers. Upon arriving, they were welcomed by the church. And they reported what the Lord had done with them. Then they told them about certain of the sect of Pharisees who were saying it was needful that believers be circumcised and keep the law.

The Apostles and Elders came together to consider the matter. "And when there had been much disputing, Peter rose up, and said unto them, Men and brethren, ye know how that a good while ago God made choice among us, that the Gentiles by my mouth should hear the word of the gospel, and believe. And God, which knoweth the hearts, bare them witness, giving them the Holy Ghost, even as he did unto us; And put no difference between us and them, purifying their hearts by faith. Now therefore why tempt ye God, to put a yoke upon the neck of the disciples, which neither our fathers nor we were able to bear? But we believe that through the grace of the Lord Jesus Christ we shall be saved, even as they. Then all the multitude kept silence, and gave audience to Barnabas and Paul, declaring what miracles and wonders God had wrought among the Gentiles by them. And after they had held their peace, James answered, saying, Men and brethren, hearken unto me: Simeon hath declared how God at the first did visit the Gentiles, to take out of them a people for his name. And to this agree the words of the prophets; as it is written, After this I will return, and will build again the tabernacle of David, which is fallen down; and I will build again the ruins thereof, and I will set it up: That the residue of men might seek after the Lord, and all the Gentiles, upon whom my name is called, saith the Lord, who doeth all these things. Known unto God are all his works from the beginning of the world. Wherefore my sentence is, that we trouble not them, which from among the Gentiles are turned to God: But that we write unto them, that they abstain from pollutions of idols, and from fornication, and from things strangled, and from blood. For Moses of old time hath in every city them that preach him, being read in the synagogues every sabbath day. (Acts 15:7-21

This decision involves the whole question of the relation of the law to Gentile believers: And their exemption meant that they were not under the law, but under grace. However the Gentile believers were to show consideration to the Jews by abstaining from the practices that were offensive to godly Jews. The forbidden things were, abstain from meats offered to idols, from blood and things strangled, and from fornication: These are things strictly forbidden by God, and stressed every Sabbath, year after year.

The Jews, during this time of transition, had the idea that the way it should work, was for the Gentiles to become Jews: Then they could become Christians. But that wasn't God's way. It was very difficult for the Jews to understand that their glorious religious system, which had been given to them by God, had been fulfilled by Christ, and was now out dated. The solution seemed to be, just blend the old religion with the new: And that caused many problems, for a long time, because false teachers continued to stir up trouble and confusion.

The Kingdom of God continued to expand in all the world, as Paul and many other believers preached the Gospel message throughout the nations: But there were other struggles to be faced: They had to cope with persecution, while training pastors and other workers: They had to work at avoiding apostasy, and heresy: But God was with them and the Kingdom grew, and continues to grow throughout the world today: And will continue until Jesus returns, like he said He would.

We have followed through the Bible considering the building of the Kingdom of God and the activities of God with the nation of Israel. This has been immense; but at the same time straightforward and uncomplicated, for the most part: But with the coming of Jesus and His death, burial, resurrection and ascension into heaven: And the coming of the Holy Spirit and the birth of the Church, things become more complex, and sometimes hard to be understood.

Before we come to the place where the Kingdom of God comes to the earth in its fullest manifestation at the end of time, there are several things we want to consider: Because now we have the Church, and Israel, and the Gentile nations to consider as we approach the end times. The big question is where and how do they all fit? We won't be able to fit all the pieces together, to the satisfaction of everyone: But there are some key points that may help.

In studying the Bible we should free our minds, as far as possible, from mere theological concepts and presuppositions: One of those is that the Church is true Israel, another is that the Old Testament foreview of the Kingdom of God is fulfilled in the Church. Do not assume interpretations to be true because they are familiar.

Realize that the Old Testament is an introduction to the four Gospels, divinely provided by God. It gives a fore-view of Christ: His work and Kingdom, this makes the Gospels more easily understood: But remember to expect, in the Gospels, a strong legal and Jewish coloring up to the death of Jesus on the cross, which was the point of transition from law to grace: This means that the Sermon on the Mount is law not grace. Many have thought it was grace, and this can make a difference: Take forgiveness as an example, under the law of the Kingdom no one can hope for forgiveness who has not forgiven: Under grace the Christian is exhorted to forgive because he, himself, is already forgiven. "And be ye kind one to another, tenderhearted, forgiving one another, even as God for Christ's sake hath forgiven you." (Ephesians 4:32) Law demands perfect character, while grace, through divine power, creates it. Galatians 5:22-23 "But the fruit of the Spirit is love, joy, peace, longsuffering, gentleness, goodness, faith, meekness, temperance: against such there is no law. Christian character is not mere moral or legal correctness, but the possession and manifestation of these nine graces. Taken together they present a moral portrait of Christ: And the Christian is to be like Christ.

The doctrines of grace are found in the Epistles, not in the Gospels; but the doctrines of grace rest back upon the death and resurrection of Christ, and upon the great truths of His teaching and preaching, upon which the Epistles expand. Furthermore, the only perfect example of grace is the Christ of the Gospels. Another truth is that the Gospels do not unfold the doctrine of the Church. The word Church is, mentioned in Matthew, only after His rejection as King and Savior, by the Jews. That was in the sixteenth chapter, verse eighteen where Jesus told His Apostles, "and upon this rock I will build my church; and the gates of hell shall not prevail against it." He does not promise to build His Church upon Peter, but upon Himself, as Peter himself is careful to tell us in his Epistle.

The Gospels present a group of Jewish Disciples, associated with a Messiah who is being rejected by His nation. The Epistles present a Church, which is the body of Christ, while The Acts of the Apostles tells us how the Church was brought into being on the Day of Pentecost. The Holy Spirit fill the scene: As the presence of the Son, exalting and revealing the Father, is the great fact of the Gospels, so the presence of the Holy Spirit, exalting and revealing Jesus, the Son, is the great fact of the Acts.

The Jews, since the call of Abraham, have had a covenant relationship with God. Even in the Acts, which covers thirty-two years, the first nine chapters are devoted to ministry to the Jews. Peter is the prominent character, Jerusalem is the center, and the message is to the Jews, who had sinned in rejecting Jesus as the Messiah. The preaching was therefore directed to that point, and repentance (that is a change of mind) was demanded. The Jews didn't understand that the Davidic Kingdom would be set up at Christ's second coming. The Apostles indicated this by the question, Lord, wilt thou at this time restore again the kingdom to Israel? (Acts 1:6) For forty days the risen Lord had been instructing the Apostles of the things pertaining to the Kingdom of God. This point had been left untouched, because, "And he said unto them, It is not for you to know the times or the seasons, which the Father hath put in his own power." (Acts 1:7) The time was God's secret.

The problem the Jews had was the same that we sometimes have in understanding the prophesy of future events. They saw the first coming of Christ, and they saw the second coming of Christ, but they could not see the large valley between the two mountains. The valley is this period of time we are now in, called, "the time of the Gentiles."

In the remaining part of Acts Paul is prominent, a new center is established at Antioch, and the ministry is chiefly to the Gentiles, who are strangers to the covenants, which God made with Abraham, Noah and David, as well as others. The Gentiles, however, had only to believe on the Lord Jesus to be saved. Ephesians 2:11 NIV: "Remember that formerly you who are Gentiles by birth and called "uncircumcised" by those who call themselves "the circumcision" remember that at that time you were separated from Christ, excluded from citizenship in Israel and foreigners to the covenants of promise, without hope and without God in the world. But now in Christ Jesus you who were far away have been brought near through the blood of Christ... (Verse 19) Consequently, you are no longer foreigners and aliens, but fellow citizens with God's people and members of God's household, built on the foundation of the Apostles, and Prophets, with Jesus Himself as the chief cornerstone. In Him the whole building is joined together and rises to become the holy temple in the Lord. And in Him you to are being built together to become a dwelling in which God lives by His Spirit." (Ephesians 2:19-22)

God's plan, which is in operation during this present age, is that individuals are to be saved out from among the Gentiles and added to the Church that Jesus is building. From Pentecost to now these believers from among the Gentiles have been put together with the believing Jews: Thus the Kingdom of God continues to grow.

Another important thing to consider concerning the chosen nation of Israel is that it is divided: There are two parts, as explained by the Apostle Paul in the epistle of Romans 9:1-16: "I say the truth in Christ, I lie not, my conscience also bearing me witness in the Holy Ghost, That I have great heaviness and continual sorrow in my heart. For I could wish that myself were accursed from Christ for my brethren, my kinsmen according to the flesh: Who are Israelites; to whom pertaineth the adoption, and the glory, and the covenants, and the giving of the law, and the service of God, and the promises; Whose are the fathers, and of whom as concerning the flesh Christ came, who is over all, God blessed for ever. Amen. Not as though the word of God hath taken none effect. For they are not all Israel, which are of Israel: Neither, because they are the seed of Abraham, are they all children: but, In Isaac shall thy seed be called. That is, They which are the children of the flesh, these are not the children of God: but the children of the promise are counted for the seed. For this is the word of promise, At this time will I come, and Sara shall have a son. And not only this; but when Rebecca also had conceived by one, even by our father Isaac; (For the children being not yet born, neither having done any good or evil, that the purpose of God according to election might stand, not of works, but of him that calleth;) It was said unto her, The elder shall serve the younger. As it is written, Jacob have I loved, but

Esau have I hated. What shall we say then? Is there unrighteousness with God? God forbid. For he saith to Moses, I will have mercy on whom I will have mercy, and I will have compassion on whom I will have compassion.So then it is not of him that willeth, nor of him that runneth, but of God that sheweth mercy"

This portion of scripture makes it plain that there is a godly line starting with Abraham who believed and obeyed God. This was the beginning of Christian faith. It was with Abraham that two lines of descendants got their start.

This lineage of Abraham, and Isaac, and Jacob is the one that extends down to our Lord and Savior, Jesus Christ. This is the spiritual line to which the promises pertain. Ishmael and Esau were in the natural, as contrasted to the spiritual, line: And each of them had many descendants, which contributed to Abraham realizing the promise, "And I will make thy seed as the dust of the earth:" (Genesis 13:16) This was saying that the Hebrew people would be so numerous that they could not be counted.

Jacob became the father of twelve sons who in time became the twelve tribes of Israel, which were God's chosen instruments to accomplish God's will on earth. The twelve tribes began developing while they were spending four hundred years in captivity: After that they spent forty years wandering in the wilderness. This was a difficult way to get an education however they survived and were able to accomplish what God had for them, and became a great nation numbering well over six hundred thousand, not counting the women and children: And it has continued growing for approximately three thousand years.

It is easy for Christians to forget the Jew, for many Christians actually know very little about the Jews and God's dealings with them. A very important question today is: "What is the relation of Judaism to the Church?" This was a vital question to Paul, and it is to us. The interpretation of the Old Testament was very much affected by it, and the Messiahship of the Lord Jesus hung upon it. Faith seemed to blot out all distinction among men, religious and national, because of faulty understanding of scripture like Galatians 3:28-29: "There is neither Jew nor Greek, there is neither bond nor free, there is neither male nor female: for ye are all one in Christ Jesus. And if ye be Christ's, then are ye Abraham's seed, and heirs according to the promise." This scripture is describing the Church: And it is simply saying there is no distinction between those who are members of the Church; through faith in Jesus Christ. They are not Jews or Gentiles: They are Christians who are one in Christ. The point is that there are many Jews, and many Gentiles, who are in the world, but outside of the Church.

When we were considering Paul and his ministry we saw how he turned from the Jews and began preaching the Gospel, primarily, to the Gentiles: Many believed on Christ and the Church, which had been Jewish, began to be both Jewish and Gentile. But there is a future for Israel: Paul is proof of that and so is Israel's past history. Romans 11:1-24 NIV:

Paul says, "I ask then? Did God reject His people? By no means! I am an Israelite myself, a descendant of Abraham, from the tribe of Benjamin. God did not reject His people, whom He foreknew. Don't you know what the scripture says in the passage about Elijah: how he appealed to God against Israel: Lord they have killed your prophets and torn down your altars; I am the only one left, and they are trying to kill me. And what was God's answer to him? I have reserved for Myself seven thousand who have not bowed the knee to Baal. So to at the present time there is a remnant chosen by grace. And if by grace, then it is no more by works; if it were, grace would no longer be grace. What then? What Israel sought so earnestly it did not obtain, but the elect, did. The others were hardened, as it is written. God gave them a spirit of stupor, eyes so that they could not see and ears that they could not hear, to this very day. And David says: May their table become a snare and a trap, a stumbling block, and, a retribution, to them. May their eyes be darkened so that they cannot see, and their backs be bent forever.

Again I ask, did they stumble to fall beyond recovery? Not at all! Rather, because of their transgression, salvation has come to the Gentiles to make Israel envious. But if their transgression means riches for the world, and their loss means riches for the Gentiles, how much greater riches will their fullness bring! I am talking to you Gentiles. Inasmuch as I am the Apostle to the Gentiles, I make much of my ministry in the hope that I may somehow arouse my own people to envy and save some of them. For if their rejection is the reconciliation of the world, what will their acceptance be but life from the dead? If the part of the dough offered as first fruits is holy, then the whole batch is holy; if the root is holy, so are the branches. If some of the branches have been broken off, and you though a wild olive shoot, have been grafted in among the others and now share in the nourishing sap from the olive root, do not boast over those branches. If you do consider this: You do not support the root, but the root supports you. You will say then, branches were broken off that I could be grafted in. Granted, but they were broken off because of unbelief, and you stand by faith. Do not be arrogant but be afraid. For, if God, did not spare the natural branches, He will not spare you either. Consider therefore the kindness and sternness of God: sternness to those who fell, but kindness to you, provided that you continue in His kindness. Otherwise, you also will be cut off. And if they do not persist in unbelief, they will be grafted in, for God is able to graft them in again. After all, if you were cut out of an olive tree that is wild by nature, and contrary to nature were grafted into a cultivated olive tree, how much more readily will these, the natural branches, be grafted into their own olive tree."

That Israel has not been forever set aside is the theme of this portion of scripture. Through Israel's lapse, God's grace has abounded, and will continue to abound throughout this present age, for the whole world. That means that anyone in the whole world has the opportunity to become a true Christian by simply believing the truth about Jesus Christ and following

Him. This however, does not set-aside the distinctive covenant obligations and promises of God to Israel.

Paul said, "For I am not ashamed of the gospel of Christ: for it is the power of God unto salvation to every one that believeth; to the Jew first, and also to the Greek." (Romans 1:16) And Jesus told the Samaritan woman at the well, "Ye worship ye know not what: we know what we worship: for salvation is of the Jews." (John 4:22) We know that salvation is through Jesus, however Jesus came through the Jews, so salvation is of the Jews, and salvation for the nations of the earth will find its completion in the restoration of Israel, to divine favor and the righteous rule of Jesus of Nazareth, the King of the Jews.

The Jews had a problem, because in their study of the Scripture, almost everywhere they found promises to the seed of Abraham of a universal Kingdom of righteousness: But the Church was not a Kingdom, and at that time it was not universal. And we must remember that the Gospel does not set aside, except the Mosaic, any of the covenants that God made with Israel: Also we must not forget that those covenants were with them and their seed forever.

The Church had its beginning at Pentecost and it is primarily a calling out from among the Gentiles, by God, a people for His name. "And to this agree the words of the prophets; as it is written, After this I will return, and will build again the tabernacle of David, which is fallen down; and I will build again the ruins thereof, and I will set it up: That the residue of men might seek after the Lord, and all the Gentiles, upon whom my name is called, saith the Lord, who doeth all these things."(Acts 15:15-17)

Never has the Gospel, anywhere, converted all, but everywhere has called out some: After the out-calling Jesus says, "I will return." And then will be the fulfilling of the covenant God made with David. The eighty-ninth Psalm is both a confirmation, and an exposition of the Davidic covenant. Verse twenty-seven tells us that the covenant looks far beyond David and his son Solomon.

Psalm 89:20-37: "I have found David my servant; with my holy oil have I anointed him: With whom my hand shall be established: mine arm also shall strengthen him. The enemy shall not exact upon him; (subject him to tribute) nor the son of wickedness afflict him. And I will beat down his foes before his face, and plague them that hate him. But my faithfulness and my mercy shall be with him: and in my name shall his horn be exalted. I will set his hand also in the sea, and his right hand in the rivers. He shall cry unto me, Thou art my father, my God, and the rock of my salvation. Also I will make him my firstborn, higher than the kings of the earth. My mercy will I keep for him for evermore, and my covenant shall stand fast with him. His seed also will I make to endure for ever, and his throne as the days of heaven. If his children forsake my law, and walk not in my judgments; If they break my statutes, and keep not my commandments; Then will I visit their transgression with the rod, and their iniquity with stripes. Nevertheless my lovingkindness will I not utterly take from him, nor suffer my faithfulness to fail. My covenant will I not break, nor alter the thing that is gone out of my lips. Once have I sworn by my holiness that I will not lie unto David. His seed shall endure for ever, and his throne as the sun before me. It shall be established for ever as the moon, and as a faithful witness in heaven. Selah"

One important thing, among others, is the way God will deal with disobedience and failure, in the descendants of David. God will punish them but not forsake them. "2 Samuel 7:14-17: (Speaking of Solomon, David's son) "I will be his father, and he shall be my son. If he commit iniquity, I will chasten him with the rod of men, and with the stripes of the children of men: But my mercy shall not depart away from him, as I took it from Saul, whom I put away before thee. And thine house and thy kingdom shall be established for ever before thee: thy throne shall be established for ever.According to all these words, and according to all this vision, so did Nathan speak unto David."

In reading the covenants, which God has made with His people, one thing that cannot be ignored is, they are forever. Therefore we know that the building of the Church, by the Lord Jesus Christ, doesn't divert or eradicate Judaism, which is made up of God's chosen people.

Paul, in the book of Romans, gives us a view of the big picture: He calls it the "Gospel of God" the very widest possible designation of the whole body of redemption truth: it is with God, that there is no respect (partiality) of persons; and He is not, the God of the Jews only: But of the Gentiles also: Therefore, before God, all are found guilty, but there is redemption, by faith, as great as the need: Not only that, in the fullest way, the doctrines of grace in relation to salvation, and the great promises to Israel are reconciled with the promises concerning the Gentiles, and the fulfillment of the former must wait for the completion of the Church and the coming of Jesus the Deliverer, out of Zion. Which is the second coming of Christ,

We need to consider the Davidic covenant: we mentioned it before: now we need to find how it fits in. The Angel Gabriel, when he came to Mary to announce the birth of Jesus, confirmed the Davidic covenant. Luke 1:30 "And the angel said unto her, Fear not, Mary: for thou hast found favour with God. And, behold, thou shalt conceive in thy womb, and bring forth a son, and shalt call his name JESUS. He shall be great, and shall be called the Son of the Highest: and the Lord God shall give unto him the throne of his father David: And he shall reign over the house of Jacob for ever; and of his kingdom there shall be no end."

The covenants are promises: God's salvation promises were made to Abraham: His kingdom promises were made to David, and no promises, as such, were made to the Gentile nations. The Gospel, proclaimed to them is not a promise, but rather is the announcement of a fact to be believed, while many promises were made to Israel as a nation: And the great honor of being the nation from whom the Messiah came outranks all other honors. But several things brought up questions in the Jewish minds. The distinction between the natural and spiritual seed of Abraham, the proclamation of salvation by grace through faith in Christ naturally provoked a question in the Jewish minds as to whether or not God's word had failed. The Gospel was not bringing national salvation to Israel; the fulfilling of the covenants and the promises of the Prophets were not being realized: Romans 9:6-15 gives the answer: Rejection by Israel was not complete; in fact the Israel that rejected Christ was not the true Israel. The spiritual seed of Israel are not lost, and through them God's purpose is being fulfilled.

Here is what the scripture says, "Not as though the word of God hath taken none effect. For they are not all Israel, which are of Israel: Neither, because they are the seed of Abraham, are they all children: but, In Isaac shall thy seed be called. That is, They which are the children of the flesh, these are not the children of God: but the children of the promise are counted for the seed. For this is the word of promise, At this time will I come, and Sara shall have a son. And not only this; but when Rebecca also had conceived by one, even by our father Isaac; (For the children being not yet born, neither having done any good or evil, that the purpose of God according to election might stand, not of works, but of him that calleth;) It was said unto her, The elder shall serve the younger. As it is written, Jacob have I loved, but Esau have I hated. What shall we say then? Is there unrighteousness with God? God forbid. For he saith to Moses, I will have mercy on whom I will have mercy, and I will have compassion on whom I will have compassion."

This is the scripture which, to the utter confusion of all interpretation of the Old Testament: Has been perverted to teach that Gentiles became true Israel by believing on Christ. However scripture distinctly teaches that believers, without distinction of race, are sons of Abraham. Galatians 3:7, 8 "Know ye therefore that they which are of faith, the same are the children of Abraham. And the scripture, foreseeing that God would justify the heathen through faith, preached before the gospel unto Abraham, saying, In thee shall all nations be blessed."

Other things to be considered are that Christians are never said to be sons of Jacob, or sons of Israel. The Church is not a kingdom: it is a body with many members with Christ as the head: But He is never the king of the church. However the Church will rule and reign with Him. The Holy Spirit is calling out from the Gentiles, not subjects for the kingdom, but co-heirs and co-rulers of the kingdom. Jesus was crowned with thorns at His first coming to earth: But the Davidic covenant, confirmed to David by an oath of Jehovah, and renewed to Mary by the angel Gabriel is unchangeable and the Lord God will yet give to that thorn-crowned one, the throne of his father David. David's throne is not to be confused with the throne of God. Revelation 3:21 "To him that overcometh will I grant to sit with me in my throne, even as I also overcame, and am set down with my Father in his throne. This, verse, along with a number of others, tells us that Christ is not now seated upon

His throne. The Davidic covenant, and the promises of God through the Prophets and the Angel Gabriel, concerning the Messianic Kingdom of Christ, is yet to be fulfilled in the future.

Scripture indicates that Israel is the wife of Jehovah: And that the Church is the Bride of Christ. The New Testament speaks of the Church as a virgin espoused to Christ, which could never be said of an adulterous wife restored in grace. Israel is then to be the restored and forgiven wife of Jehovah: The Church the virgin bride of the Lamb.

At this present time, Israel, the unfaithful wife, has not been restored, and will not be until "The Fullness of the Gentiles" which is a term used in Scripture to indicate the completion of the out-calling, in this age, from among the Gentiles, of a people for Christ's name, "the Church which is His body." This is the distinctive work of the present church age. This has been in progress since Pentecost: After this out-calling Jesus says, "I will return." The Apostle Paul explains this in his Epistle to the Romans 11:25-32 NIV "I do not want you to be ignorant of this mystery, brothers, so that you may not be conceited: Israel has experienced a hardening in part until the full number of the Gentiles has come in. And so all Israel shall be saved, as it is written: The deliverer will come from Zion; He shall turn ungodliness away from Jacob. And this is My covenant with them when I take away their sin. As far as the gospel is concerned, they are enemies on your account; but as far as election is concerned, they are loved on account of the Patriarchs, for God's gifts and His call are irrevocable. Just as you who were at one time disobedient to God have now received mercy as a result of their disobedience, so they too have now become disobedient in order that they too may now receive mercy as a result of God's mercy to you. For God has bound all men over to disobedience so that He may have mercy on them all."

Paul was talking to Gentiles in the Church when he said I don't want you to be Ignorant. The problem was that the Gentiles were in danger of becoming conceited in thinking they were better, in God's sight, than the Jews, because they thought God had forsaken the Jews. Things haven't changed much because I understand that some today believe the Church is everything and the Jews are out of the picture. I have never met any myself; But I can understand, since this is the Church Age, and this is where the action is, that there is confusion among the uninformed.

A study of Romans, chapters 9,10, and 11 reveals that Paul's discussion of Israel is not an interruption but an illustration of his theme. In chapter nine he explains Israel's election: God had chosen Israel in the past, to be His chosen people. Chapter ten explains Israel's present rejection: Chapter eleven tells of God's future reception of Israel, and he proves that God has been righteous in all His dealings with Israel. God has not failed to work out His divine purpose for the Jews, nor will He fail to work out His purpose for the Church.

A proper understanding of God's dealings with Israel is necessary for two important reasons: For the understanding of the Old Testament, and for help in understanding the future, and end-time events:

This includes a proper understanding of covenants, both old and new, and blessings, and promises: And the inter-relationships, and effects they have on each-other.

An interesting study is the relation of Christ to each of the covenants: To the Edenic Covenant, Christ as the second man, the last Adam, takes the place over all things, which the first Adam lost: In the Adamic Covenant Christ is the seed of the woman, and fulfilled its conditions of toil and obedience: As the greatest son of Shem, in Christ was fulfilled supremely the promise to Shem in the Noahic Covenant: Christ is the seed to whom the promises were made in the Abrahamic Covenant, the son of Abraham obedient unto death: Christ lived sinless under the Mosaic Covenant and bore for us its curse: Christ lived obediently as a Jew in the promised land under the Palestinian Covenant, and will yet perform its gracious promises: Christ is the seed, the heir, and the King under the Davidic Covenant: Christ's sacrifice of Himself on the cross is the foundation of the New Covenant.

Someone else pointed out that four Covenants are fundamental, they are: Edenic, Adamic, Noahic, and Abrahamic: The other four Covenants are related chiefly as adding detail and development. In a profound sense, therefore, the roots, of all subsequent revelation are, planted in the book of Genesis. However, two Covenants standout as different in some respects: they are the Mosaic and the New Covenant: The Mosaic Covenant (also called the Law) was different in that it was a whole system of rules and regulations on how Israel was to live: And the New Covenant was different in many ways: first it fulfilled the Mosaic Covenant, or in a sense it brought the Mosaic Covenant to an end and completes its desired results. It is the eighth covenant, thus speaking of resurrection and eternal completeness.

The New Covenant is superior in many ways: It had a better mediator, Jesus, of a better covenant which was much superior to the old covenant. It was established upon better promises: It depends on forgiveness on the part of God: and does not depend on man, which is where the old covenant failed: not the covenant its self, but that it depended on man keeping his part, which is where the failure came about. The New Covenant rests upon the sacrifice of Christ, of Himself on the cross, and secures the blessings of the Abrahamic Covenant for all who believe. It is absolutely unconditional: and since no responsibility is committed to man, it is final and irreversible. The following scripture elaborates on the subjects of being final and irreversible.

Galatians 3:11 The Living Bible: "It is clear that no one can ever win God's favor by trying to keep the Jewish laws, because God has said that the only way we can be right in His sight is by faith. As the Prophet Habakkuk says it, the man who finds life will find it through trusting God. How different from this way of faith, is the way of the law, which says that a man is saved by obeying every law of God, without one slip. But Christ has brought us out from under the doom of that impossible system by taking the curse of our wrongdoing upon Himself: For it is written in the Scripture, Anyone who is hanged on a tree is cursed (as Jesus was hung upon a wooden cross). Now God can bless the Gentiles, too, with the same blessing He promised to Abraham; and all of us as Christians can have the promised Holy Spirit through faith. Dear brothers, even in every day life a promise made by one man to another, if it is written down and signed, cannot be changed. He cannot decide afterward to do something else instead. Now God gave some promises to Abraham and his Child. And notice that it doesn't say the promises were to his children, as it would if all his sons—all the Jews—-were being spoken of, but to his Child, and that of course, means Christ. Here's what I am trying to say: God's promise to save through faith—and God wrote this promise down and signed it—could not be canceled or changed four hundred and thirty years later when God gave the Ten Commandments. If obeying those laws could save us, then it is obvious that this would be a different way of gaining God's favor than Abraham's way, for he simply accepted God's promise. Well then, why were the laws given? They were added after the promise was given, to show men how guilty they are of breaking God's laws. But this system of law was to last only until the coming of Christ, the Child unto whom God's promise was made."

It is very difficult to understand why any interpretation would lead to the belief that God has forsaken His chosen nation of Israel: or that the Church has displaced Israel. It must be remembered that the Kingdom of God is all inclusive. We have traced the building of the Kingdom of God from one man, Abraham, to Israel as a tribe, then as a nation, as a kingdom, as a divided kingdom, then as a kingdom scattered among the nations, then Israel restored as a nation and continuing as a kingdom on earth, expanding into the entire world. The Church became a large and growing addition to this kingdom in this age we are living in. The Church will continue to grow until the appointed number is met, then it will be taken to heaven: this is called the rapture of the Church. 1 Thessalonians 4:16-18: "For the Lord himself shall descend from heaven with a shout, with the voice of the archangel, and with the trump of God: and the dead in Christ shall rise first: Then we which are alive and remain shall be caught up together with them in the clouds, to meet the Lord in the air: and so shall we ever be with the Lord. Wherefore comfort one another with these words."

Following this event, which many think is the next important event in God's time-table, the remaining events of the end-times, will begin to fall in place, according to God's plan. We need to be careful in our study of these events because they are difficult. It doesn't pay to be dogmatic: there are many books and articles out there: and they vary from one extreme to the other. We need to remember that we aren't supposed to know every thing: And that as time moves on certain things will become clear, in the same manner as some things that were called mysteries, were later revealed. A mystery in, scripture, is a previously hidden truth, which is divinely revealed at a certain time. Matthew 13:17:

"For verily I say unto you, That many prophets and righteous men have desired to see those things which ye see, and have not seen them; and to hear those things which ye hear, and have not heard them."

The spiritual Jews believed the prophesies of the Old Testament, and one was of special importance to them: They were looking for their Messiah to come and a while after Jesus began ministering they realized He was the Messiah, but we know they were puzzled, by the question they asked in Acts 1:6-7: "When they therefore were come together, they asked of him, saying, Lord, wilt thou at this time restore again the kingdom to Israel? And he said unto them, It is not for you to know the times or the seasons, which the Father hath put in his own power." What they were expecting was far in the future, but in God's appointed time it will come to pass. We, like the Jews, would like to understand when and how certain things are going to happen, but we, like them will have to be patient and wait until God brings them to pass.

We considered how the human race at first was one great stream of humanity, which in Abraham's day divided in to two streams, the largest, the Gentile branch continued on, while the other branch became the Nation of Israel: Then after the Day of Pentecost the Church came on the scene: it was composed of both Jews and Gentiles. Then, in passing, we noted that Abraham's descendants exist in two distinct lines of descent: there is the line of Abraham, Isaac, and Jacob, which is the spiritual line, and the others which are Israel after the flesh, the natural posterity:

the descendants of Ishmael and Esau, who make up the Gentile nations that populate most of the world.

In order to interpret the end-time events it is necessary to find how all of these different groups fit in to the puzzle. It has been said that the book of Ezekiel tells of the future of the Jews: Daniel the future of the nations: And Revelation the future of the Church. All three of these are books of prophecy, which means they are not easy to interpret because among other reasons, they contain much symbolism, which in itself presents big problems: it is very difficult to determine when it is, and when it isn't.

Chapter 37

MIRACLES AND THE SUPERNATURAL

This is a subject that seems to cause some people problems. It is strange, but I suppose it is for the same reasons that some do not want to admit there is a God, and that He is alive and well. The human nature of man is to be in control: therefore, man has to cut God out of the picture. On the other hand miracles arouse curiosity; which Jesus uses to attract and get peoples interest. An example of this is King Herod "And when Herod saw Jesus, he was exceeding glad: for he was desirous to see him of a long season, because he had heard many things of him; and he hoped to have seen some miracle done by him." (Luke 23:8) Multitudes came to Jesus to be healed of diseases and to see other miracles; and many believed as a result.

Jesus was invited to a wedding in the village of Cana of Galilee. When they ran out of wine the mother of Jesus came to Him with the problem: Then she told the servants to do whatever Jesus told them. John 2:6-11in the Living Bible says, "Six stone water pots were standing there; they were used for Jewish ceremonial purposes and held perhaps twenty to thirty gallons each. Then Jesus told the servants to fill them to the brim with water. When this was done He said, "Dip some out and take it to the master of the ceremonies. When the master of the ceremonies tasted the water that was now made wine, not knowing where it came from (though the servants did) he called the bridegroom over. This is wonderful! You are different from most. Usually the host uses the best wine first, and afterwards, when everyone is full and doesn't care, then he brings out the less expensive brands. But you have kept the best for the last. This miracle was Jesus' first public demonstration of His heaven sent power. And His Disciples believed that He really was the Messiah."

Why did Jesus do so many healings, and miracles, and signs and wonders? Someone has suggested that the Apostle John used eight of these to reveal Jesus' glory and to prove His deity. This gives us two important reasons; and Hebrews 2:3-4 gives other information; "How shall we escape, if we neglect so great salvation; which at the first began to be spoken by the Lord, and was confirmed unto us by them that heard him; God also bearing them witness, both with signs and wonders, and with divers miracles, and gifts of the Holy Ghost, according to his own will?" Here God confirmed and endorsed the testimony of the eyewitnesses who heard the message of salvation that Jesus was preaching. What Mark says in his Gospel is similar except, that instead of Jesus it is the Disciples who were preaching. Mark 16:19 "So then after the Lord had spoken unto them, he was received up into heaven, and sat on the right hand of God. And they went forth, and preached every where, the Lord working with them, and confirming the word with signs following. Amen."

This has been God's method of building His Kingdom in the whole world. We know it is a good method because Christianity grew so rapidly as the Disciples and others went forth preaching the good news of Salvation. The plan has continued to work through the years: One hundred years ago Missionaries went to China, Africa, India and other countries where they preached the Gospel and helped start churches, as people became believers. Soon they needed preachers so they established Bible Schools to train them. Later Christians were persecuted in some countries and Missionaries were forced to leave, but Christianity continued to grow. Recently I heard that there are great numbers of Christians in Communist China and in parts of Africa Christianity is growing rapidly. This is true of other parts of the world. It is reported that this growth of Christianity is accompanied by miracles. God is still confirming the preaching of His word, with signs following, the same as with the Disciples in the beginning.

In Acts there is an interesting account: Peter and John were going up to the temple to pray; a crippled beggar asked them for money; Peter told him they didn't have money "but such as I have give I thee:

In the name of Jesus Christ of Nazareth rise up and walk." (Acts 3:6) The Man was healed: Then he went with them walking and jumping, and praising God. As a result: Peter and John were arrested and put in jail until the next day.

The next day the rulers had Peter and John brought before them and began to question them: "And when they had set them in the midst, they asked, By what power, or by what name, have ye done this? Then Peter, filled with the Holy Ghost, said unto them, Ye rulers of the people, and elders of Israel, If we this day be examined of the good deed done to the impotent man, by what means he is made whole; Be it known unto you all, and to all the people of Israel, that by the name of Jesus Christ of Nazareth, whom ye crucified, whom God raised from the dead, even by him doth this man stand here before you whole." (Acts 4:7-10)

Peter and John were released and went back to their people and reported what had happened to them. When they heard this they all joined in prayer to God. "Lord, thou art God, which hast made heaven, and earth, and the sea, and all that in them is: Who by the mouth of thy servant David hast said, Why did the heathen rage, and the people imagine vain things? The kings of the earth stood up, and the rulers were gathered together against the Lord, and against his Christ. For of a truth against thy holy child Jesus, whom thou hast anointed, both Herod, and Pontius Pilate, with the Gentiles, and the people of Israel, were gathered together, For to do whatsoever thy hand and thy counsel determined before to be done. And now, Lord, behold their threatenings: and grant unto thy servants, that with all boldness they may speak thy word, By stretching forth thine hand to heal; and that signs and wonders may be done by the name of thy holy child Jesus. And when they had prayed, the place was shaken where they were assembled together; and they were all filled with the Holy Ghost, and they spake the word of God with boldness." (Acts 4:24-31)

These early Christians realized the importance of healing and miraculous signs and wonders. But many misguided people today say these supernatural things passed away with the Apostles. My question is why? Christians today are endeavoring to accomplish the same identical mission as the early Christians. That mission is, to build the kingdom of God, and the best way to do it is God's way: Which is by speaking the word with the anointing and power of the Holy Spirit, accompanied by the Lord stretching out His hand to heal and perform miraculous signs and wonders. Try it any other way and you will come up short.

If you take the supernatural out of Christianity: what you have is a dead religion. Christianity started with a supernatural birth: Continued with a supernatural resurrection from the dead and then to a supernatural ascension in to heaven; with much supernatural in between. So let us be reasonable and obey the truth of God's word. Hebrews 2:1-4: "Therefore we ought to give the more earnest heed to the things which we have heard, lest at any time we should let them slip. For if the word spoken by angels was stedfast, and every transgression and disobedience received a just recompence of reward; How shall we escape, if we neglect so great salvation; which at the first began to be spoken by the Lord, and was confirmed unto us by them that heard him; God also bearing them witness, both with signs and wonders, and with divers miracles, and gifts of the Holy Ghost, according to his own will?

The Bible speaks of many antichrists in the world today and it speaks of "the antichrist" also called the beast, in the Book of Revelation, and another beast, called the "false prophet." These both receive power from Satan.

Rev, 13:11-14: "And I beheld another beast coming up out of the earth; and he had two horns like a lamb, and he spake as a dragon. And he exerciseth all the power of the first beast before him, and causeth the earth and them which dwell therein to worship the first beast, whose deadly wound was healed. And he doeth great wonders, so that he maketh fire come down from heaven on the earth in the sight of men, And deceiveth them that dwell on the earth by the means of those miracles which he had power to do in the sight of the beast."

This shows us that we need to be able to distinguish the true so we can reject the false. The Christian who is full of the Holy Spirit will have the help that is needed. So it is needful to walk in the Spirit, and not in the flesh, as the Bible tells us.

Chapter 38

EDUCATION

At the beginning we looked, in passing, at the subject of learning. But it is a big subject so we will consider some other aspects of it. Education is learning that takes place in schools or school like environments, this is called formal education; other learning takes place in the world at large. The object of education is the transmission of the values and accumulated knowledge of a society. The dictionary definition says it is a systematic training and instruction designed to impart knowledge and develop skill.

The United States has a good education system with many dedicated teachers. Much money has been spent and is being spent every year to make it possible for our citizens to become educated. Very early the settlers in the New England colonies began teaching their children: In most colonies the foremost reason was in order that they could learn to read the Bible.

Yale University the third oldest University in the United States was founded in 1701 and located in New Haven, Connecticut. It is a member of the Ivy League Association. Its initial curriculum emphasized classical studies and strict adherence to orthodox Puritanism.

Harvard University in Cambridge, Mass: The oldest institution of higher learning in the United States (founded 1636) was probably the most prestigious. Its schools of divinity, law, and medicine were established in the early Nineteenth century Harvard College was named for a Puritan minister, John Harvard.

What concerns me is the change that has taken place in our education system; whereas it was founded on Godly principles, it has deteriorated to the place where in many places God and most of His principles are not allowed. I understand that in some places that speakers of other religions are invited but Christians are not. In some of our Colleges it is a known fact that some Professors make it a goal to tear down the faith of the Christian students, and statistics indicate that they are quite successful. In the battle of good against evil; in this instance sometimes it seems that evil is winning, but we know that in the long run good will come out winner. If the above is true, and I am convinced it is, secular college is no place to send our Christian youth to be educated. This is something for Christian parents to seriously consider.

The way I see it our school system is unfair and under-handed. As an example, consider the issue of creationism and evolution, which, is a big issue. Darwinism is a theory, which has existed since 1858, but has yet to be proven. While creation is a recorded account of what happened thousands of years ago and has not yet been disproved. Evolution is taught as a fact in our schools, while the creation story is outlawed and belittled. Think about it. Is that Democracy? Not to me. It is more like indoctrination to me.

Another teaching is that there are no absolutes, which means that you can't tell whether a thing or action is good or bad; or that it depends on the circumstance. It is not hard to understand where this kind of thinking can lead. It means nothing is black or white. There is an expression, "every man was a law unto himself," which means anything goes: But it did not work out very good in the Bible.

Our good education system is teaching these kind of things, and more: Then we build more, and larger prisons because there is an increase in crime; more lying and cheating, robbing and stealing, and more corruption and fraud as well as other white collar crime. All of this costs the tax- payers much money, which could be used to a much better advantage. Another result is that it is becoming harder to know who can be trusted. There are still many good people out there, but it pays to read the fine print. Just this evening a man was telling me how he had refinanced his house. They told him it was straight interest, but later he found out that was for only three years, after which it shifted to variable interest. He didn't read the fine print. This present financial crises we are facing, January 2008, seems to be caused by some unethical maneuvering by some financiers.

Science is a branch of knowledge requiring systematic study and method. The definition of knowledge is all that is known, an organized body of information. The key word here is "known" but it seems that much we do is based on "theory" which is an opinion or supposition. It might be possible but there are not enough facts to be sure. A big illustration of this is the present theory of man made global warming, which is rapidly spreading over the world, This theory is costing big bucks with not much bang, except some people getting rich and other people and nations suffering financially. The cost of this undertaking will be tremendous at a time when it looks like the world is entering a financial slump.

In the world today we have an immense store of knowledge, which is growing rapidly, and much of it is readily available to the public. This is good, provided the information is used properly. Of course we all know that this will be true only part of the time. Because how knowledge is used depends on other things like wisdom and common senses, which are sometimes in short supply, especially with highly educated individuals.

Luke 11:52 says, "Woe unto you, lawyers! for ye have taken away the key of knowledge: ye entered not in yourselves, and them that were entering in ye hindered." Instead of entering the door of salvation they locked it so the others could not enter. Instead of taking the opportunity of repenting and being forgiven, they opposed Jesus and attacked Him. What fools! But they were the highly educated of their day. They had education and knowledge but they were not wise in spiritual things, and they missed the truth completely.

In the next chapter, Luke 12:54 NIV Jesus said to the crowd, "When you see a cloud rising in the West, immediately you say, it's going to rain, and it does. And when the South wind blows, you say, It is going to be hot, and it is. You Hypocrites! You know how to interpret the appearance of the earth and the sky. How is it that you don't know how to interpret this present time? Why don't you judge for yourselves what is right?" This is the important thing; to judge what is right and act accordingly."

1Corinthians 3:19-20: "For the wisdom of this world is foolishness with God. For it is written, He taketh the wise in their own craftiness. And again, The Lord knoweth the thoughts of the wise, that they are vain." From this we draw the conclusion that there is wisdom of this world, and there is the wisdom of God. 1Corinthians 1:20 "Where is the wise? Where is the scribe? Where is the disputer of this world? hath not God made foolish the wisdom of this world?" Here again mention is made of the wisdom of this world. As great as the natural wisdom of this world is, it is only useful in the natural realm; when it comes to spiritual things God's wisdom far surpasses it. This is demonstrated in Acts 6:9-10: "Then there arose certain of the synagogue, which is called the synagogue of the Libertines, and Cyrenians, and

Alexandrians, and of them of Cilicia and of Asia, disputing with Stephen. And they were not able to resist the wisdom and the spirit by which he spake." Stephen was up against some of the greatest Jewish minds of the day. The reason they could not out do Stephen was that he had divine wisdom and the help of the Holy Spirit, along with the truth on his side. Stephen was not an Apostle; the verses in the first part of this chapter tell us he was chosen as a deacon because he was a man full of faith and of the Holy Spirit; and another verse said, "Stephen full of faith and power did great wonders and miracles among the people." (Acts 6:8)

James 3:13-18: "Who is a wise man and endued with knowledge among you? let him shew out of a good conversation his works with meekness of wisdom. But if ye have bitter envying and strife in your hearts, glory not, and lie not against the truth. This wisdom descendeth not from above, but is earthly, sensual, devilish. For where envying and strife is, there is confusion and every evil work. But the wisdom that is from above is first pure, then peaceable, gentle, and easy to be intreated, full of mercy and good fruits, without partiality, and without hypocrisy. And the fruit of righteousness is sown in peace of them that make peace."

This shows the advantage of the wisdom from above over that which is here below. It is the same battle of good over evil. Many think evil is winning and sometimes that seems to be true but we must remember the battle isn't over yet. Colossians 1:9-10 "For this cause we also, since the day we heard it, do not cease to pray for you, and to desire that ye might be filled with the knowledge of his will in all wisdom and spiritual understanding; That ye might walk worthy of the Lord unto all pleasing, being fruitful in every good work, and increasing in the knowledge of God."

The truth is that we need both the wisdom of this world; and the wisdom that is from above. As followers of Christ we need all the wisdom that is available, of both kinds. Then we will be well equipped to go through life, and not be defeated by the many antichrists, and other opposition that we encounter.

"If any of you lack wisdom, let him ask of God, that giveth to all men liberally, and upbraideth not; and it shall be given him. But let him ask in faith, nothing wavering. For he that wavereth is like a wave of the sea driven with the wind and tossed. For let not that man think that he shall receive any thing of the Lord." (James 1:5-7) As Christians, we are most fortunate, because we have available to us, both earthly wisdom and heavenly wisdom. Unbelievers don't understand, and do not know this, so they belittle Christians because they believe a bunch of fairy tales; when in reality the true Christians are the ones who know the truth: And believe me that is what really counts in the end.

The simple truth concerning this whole matter of education and knowledge is, it is not critical how much you know, but what you know, and what you need to know is summed up in the words of Jesus, "Jesus saith unto him, I am the way, the truth, and

the life: no man cometh unto the Father, but by me."
(John 14:6) A short time before this Jesus said, "And
ye shall know the truth, and the truth shall make you
free." (John 8:32)

Chapter 39

ACTS OF THE HOLY SPIRIT

The great truth of the "Gospels" is the Son revealing and exalting the Father; and the great truth of "The Acts Of The Apostles" is the Holy Spirit revealing and exalting the Son: And also, it is the acts of the Holy Spirit working through the Apostles, and it tells what Jesus continues to do and teach, through the Holy Spirit, after He returned to heaven.

The ultimate goal for the church was to take the Gospel to the whole world. To accomplish this they needed all the help they could get and the Holy Spirit was to be that help. We shall attempt to examine all that is involved and how it is involved. In many respects the truth concerning the Holy Spirit has been glossed over and neglected by a large portion of Christianity because of ignorance and prejudices but when you put it all together it makes a lot of sense. Jesus stressed the importance of the Holy Spirit to

His followers before He ascended back in to heaven and it is plain that God's plan is for every Christian to be equipped with the help and power of the Holy Spirit.

John 7:37 NIV: "On the last and greatest day of the feast, Jesus stood and said in a loud voice, "If any man is thirsty, let him come to Me and drink. Whoever believes in Me, as the Scripture has said, streams of living water will flow from within him. By this He meant the Spirit, whom those who believed in Him were later to receive. Up to that time the Spirit had not been given, since Jesus had not been glorified."

In John 16:7 Jesus said, "Nevertheless I tell you the truth; It is expedient for you that I go away: for if I go not away, the Comforter (Holy Spirit) will not come unto you; but if I depart, I will send him unto you." These verses tell us that whoever believes in Jesus according to the Scripture will be eligible to come and receive the Holy Spirit.

Jesus said, "And I will pray the Father, and he shall give you another Comforter, that he may abide with you for ever; Even the Spirit of truth; whom the world cannot receive, because it seeth him not, neither knoweth him: but ye know him; for he dwelleth with you, and shall be in you. (John 14:16-17) These verses speak of Jesus leaving His followers and going back to heaven. He comforts them by telling them that He will send the Holy Spirit to them to be a comforter and helper. In the Old Testament the Holy Spirit was active; but in a different way, in that the Spirit was not in God's people: He would come upon them at times of special needs. Numbers 11:25

says, "And the LORD came down in a cloud, and spake unto him, and took of the spirit that was upon him, and gave it unto the seventy elders: and it came to pass, that, when the spirit rested upon them, they prophesied." Here are a few other examples, The Spirit of the Lord came upon Othniel, and he judged Israel. (Judges 3:10) "Then went Samson down, and his father and his mother, to Timnath, and came to the vineyards of Timnath: and, behold, a young lion roared against him. And the Spirit of the LORD came mightily upon him, and he rent him as he would have rent a kid, and he had nothing in his hand:" (Judges 14:5-6) Another was when Samuel took the horn of oil, and anointed David, and the Spirit of the Lord came upon David. (1Samuel 16:13)

In general we understand that the reasons for being full of the Holy Spirit are: To have the Holy Spirit as a comforter, which means, one along side to take the place of Jesus, and be a helper, and Jesus says, "for ever". To testify of Jesus, to reprove the world of sin, to make believers able ministers, and Romans 8:11-14 adds to that, "But if the Spirit of him that raised up Jesus from the dead dwell in you, he that raised up Christ from the dead shall also quicken your mortal bodies by his Spirit that dwelleth in you. Therefore, brethren, we are debtors, not to the flesh, to live after the flesh. For if ye live after the flesh, ye shall die: but if ye through the Spirit do mortify the deeds of the body, ye shall live. For as many as are led by the Spirit of God, they are the sons of God." To me, that makes it plain that God's plan is for all true believers to be filled with the Spirit and as Jesus said for ever. It is necessary now to see what actually happened in order for God's plan to begin to be carried out.

"And (Jesus), being assembled together with them, commanded them that they should not depart from Jerusalem, but wait for the promise of the Father, which, saith he, ye have heard of me. For John truly baptized with water; but ye shall be baptized with the Holy Ghost not many days hence."(Acts 1:4-5) Something to keep in mind is that those who were filled with the Spirit on the day of Pentecost were all believing Jews; and that the Holy Spirit did not come because they prayed but because the day of Pentecost came. They did pray and they were all of one accord but that wasn't the reason the Holy Spirit came.

Acts 2:1-6: "And when the day of Pentecost was fully come, they were all with one accord in one place. And suddenly there came a sound from heaven as of a rushing mighty wind, and it filled all the house where they were sitting. And there appeared unto them cloven tongues like as of fire, and it sat upon each of them. And they were all filled with the Holy Ghost, and began to speak with other tongues, as the Spirit gave them utterance. And there were dwelling at Jerusalem Jews, devout men, out of every nation under heaven. Now when this was noised abroad, the multitude came together, and were confounded, because that every man heard them speak in his own language." There are a few things to notice; first there were some supernatural things, the sound of wind, and the tongues of fire; but their speaking in other tongues is what confounded the multitude.

Notice closely that the "other tongues" were other languages, spoken by Galileans but every man of the multitude heard them speak in his own language: And what they heard them speak, in their own languages was the wonderful works of God. As a result they were amazed, and they were in doubt; some asked; "what does this mean?" And others mocked and said; "these men are drunk."

Peter, stood up and answered them "For these are not drunken, as ye suppose, seeing it is but the third hour of the day. But this is that which was spoken by the prophet Joel; And it shall come to pass in the last days, saith God, I will pour out of my Spirit upon all flesh: and your sons and your daughters shall prophesy, and your young men shall see visions, and your old men shall dream dreams: And on my servants and on my handmaidens I will pour out in those days of my Spirit; and they shall prophesy: And I will shew wonders in heaven above, and signs in the earth beneath; blood, and fire, and vapour of smoke: The sun shall be turned into darkness, and the moon into blood, before that great and notable day of the Lord come: And it shall come to pass, that whosoever shall call on the name of the Lord shall be saved. Ye men of Israel, hear these words; Jesus of Nazareth, a man approved of God among you by miracles and wonders and signs, which God did by him in the midst of you, as ye yourselves also know: Him, being delivered by the determinate counsel and foreknowledge of God, ye have taken, and by wicked hands have crucified and slain: Whom God hath raised up, having loosed the pains of death: because it was not possible that he should be holden of it. For David speaketh concerning him, I foresaw the Lord always before my face, for he is on my right hand, that I should not be moved: Therefore did my heart rejoice, and my tongue was glad; moreover also my flesh shall rest in hope: Because thou wilt not leave my soul in hell, neither wilt thou suffer thine Holy One to see corruption. Thou hast made known to me the ways of life; thou shalt make me full of joy with thy countenance. Men and brethren, let me freely speak unto you of the patriarch David, that he is both dead and buried, and his sepulchre is with us unto this day. Therefore being a prophet, and knowing that God had sworn with an oath to him, that of the fruit of his loins, according to the flesh, he would raise up Christ to sit on his throne; He seeing this before spake of the resurrection of Christ, that his soul was not left in hell, neither his flesh did see corruption. This Jesus hath God raised up, whereof we all are witnesses. Therefore being by the right hand of God exalted, and having received of the Father the promise of the Holy Ghost, he hath shed forth this, which ye now see and hear. For David is not ascended into the heavens: but he saith himself, The LORD said unto my Lord, Sit thou on my right hand, Until I make thy foes thy footstool. Therefore let all the house of Israel know assuredly, that God hath made that same Jesus, whom ye have crucified, both Lord and Christ. Now when they heard this, they were pricked in their heart, and said unto Peter and to the rest of the apostles, Men and brethren, what shall we do? Then Peter said unto them, Repent, and be baptized every one of you in the name of Jesus Christ for the remission of sins, and ye shall receive the gift of the Holy Ghost. For the promise is unto you, and to your children, and to all that are afar off, even as many as the Lord our God shall call. And with many other words did he testify and exhort, saying, save yourselves from this untoward generation. Then they that gladly received his word were baptized: and the same day there were added unto them about three thousand souls." (Acts 2:15-31) Now the believers were equipped to go forth and begin the task of evangelizing the world. That had been the first concern of Jesus when He told them to wait in Jerusalem until they were filled with the Holy Spirit.

The Day of Pentecost is said to be the birthday of the Church, however there were many believers; I say many and that may not be correct, and of course we have no way of knowing for sure, but my thinking is that we know Jesus had been speaking to multitudes for some time and of course the Apostles and other believers had been doing their part. These were all Jews and the ministry of Jesus was primarily to the Jews. From this day forth there was going to be a big change. Acts 1:8: "But ye shall receive power, after that the Holy Ghost is come upon you: and ye shall be witnesses unto me both in Jerusalem, and in all Judaea, and in Samaria, and unto the uttermost part of the earth." and that is what happened. Shortly after the Day of Pentecost the believers found themselves being persecuted at every turn. The persecution came from the leaders of the Jewish religious establishment, which was thriving, with Synagogues throughout the country. "Jesus came to His own, and His own received Him not," (John 1:11) They were waiting for their promised Messiah, but when Jesus came preaching the Kingdom of God, and claiming to be the Messiah sent from the Father they didn't believe Him, so they rejected Him. Because of this persecution the believers were scattered everywhere; except for the Apostles who remained in Jerusalem, which became their center of operation.

Acts 8:4-8, 14-15: "Therefore they that were scattered abroad went every where preaching the word. Then Philip went down to the city of Samaria, and preached Christ unto them. And the people with one accord gave heed unto those things which Philip spake, hearing and seeing the miracles which he did. For unclean spirits, crying with loud voice, came out of many that were possessed with them: and many taken with palsies, and that were lame, were healed. And there was great joy in that city....Now when the apostles which were at Jerusalem heard that Samaria had received the word of God, they sent unto them Peter and John: Who, when they were come down, prayed for them, that they might receive the Holy Ghost:" Notice that Philip preached Christ to the Samaritans who listened to what he had to say. They were impressed and overjoyed by the miracles and healings. When they believed Philip's preaching of the things concerning the kingdom of God, and the name of Jesus Christ, they were baptized both men and women. The Apostles were quick to send men to investigate, even though they were not on good terms with the Samaritans, and they prayed for them and then laid their hands on them and they received the Holy Spirit. Their receiving the Holy Spirit linked the Samaritans with the saints in Jerusalem and their long division was healed.

In the ninth chapter of Acts there is an interesting story about Saul of Tarsus, later known as Paul the Apostle. He was an educated Jew, who was very active in the persecution of Christians, by the Jews. He went from place to place arresting them and taking them bound to Jerusalem. On a trip to Damascus, suddenly a bright light shinned from heaven; "And he fell to the earth, and heard a voice saying unto him, Saul, Saul, why persecutest thou me? And he said, Who art thou, Lord? And the Lord said, I am Jesus whom thou persecutest: it is hard for thee to kick against the pricks. And he trembling and astonished said, Lord, what wilt thou have me to do? And the Lord said unto him, Arise, and go into the city, and it shall be told thee what thou must do. And the men which journeyed with him stood speechless, hearing a voice, but seeing no man. And Saul arose from the earth; and when his eyes were opened, he saw no man: but they led him by the hand, and brought him into Damascus. And he was three days without sight, and neither did eat nor drink. And there was a certain disciple at Damascus, named Ananias; and to him said the Lord in a vision, Ananias. And he said, Behold, I am here, Lord. And the Lord said unto him, Arise, and go into the street which is called Straight, and enquire in the house of Judas for one called Saul, of Tarsus: for, behold, he prayeth, And hath seen in a vision a man named Ananias coming in, and putting his hand on him, that he might receive his sight. Then Ananias answered, Lord, I have heard by many of this man, how much evil he hath done to thy saints at Jerusalem: And here he hath authority from the chief priests to bind all that call on thy name. But the Lord said unto him, Go thy way: for he is a chosen vessel unto me, to bear my name before the Gentiles, and kings, and the children of Israel: For I will shew him how great things he must suffer for my name's sake. And Ananias went his way, and entered into the house; and putting his hands on him said, Brother Saul, the Lord, even Jesus, that appeared unto thee in the way as thou camest, hath sent me, that thou mightest receive thy sight, and be filled with the Holy Ghost. And immediately there fell from his eyes as it had been scales: and he received sight forthwith, and arose, and was baptized." (Acts 9:4-18) In this account another element is added: The Lord is speaking to people, both believers and unbelievers, in visions. Peter mentioned this in his sermon on the Day of Pentecost when he referred to the prophecy of Joel the prophet, which spoke of both dreams and visions.

I have been hearing about Muslims becoming believers in this way: Jesus appears to them in dreams or visions and speaks to them and instructs them to go to a Missionary or a Christian who can explain the way of salvation to them. Muslims believe that Jesus is a prophet, this makes them more receptive, and I understand that a number of them are becoming believers on the Lord Jesus Christ as Savior. There is not much way of knowing how many. In many countries the lives of converts are in great danger, which is not conducive to letting just everyone know.

Another very interesting story is recorded in the tenth chapter of the Acts of the Apostles, which I am going to give to you from The Living Bible "In Caesarea there lived a Roman army officer, Cornelius, a captain of an Italian regiment. He was a godly man, deeply reverent, as was his entire household. He gave generously to charity and was a man of prayer. While wide awake one afternoon he had a vision; it was about three o'clock; and in this vision he saw an angel of God coming toward him. Cornelius! the angel said. Cornelius stared at him in terror. What do you want sir? he asked the angel. The angel replied, Your prayers and charities have not gone unnoticed by God! Now send some men to Joppa to find a man named Simon Peter, who is staying with Simon, the tanner, down by the shore, and ask him to come and visit you. As soon as the angel was gone, Cornelius called two of his household servants and a godly soldier, one of his personal bodyguards and told them what had happened and sent them off to Joppa. The next day, as they were nearing the city, Peter went up on the flat roof of his house to pray, it was noon and he was hungry, but while lunch was being prepared, he fell into a trance. He saw the sky open, and a great canvas sheet, suspended by its four corners; settle to the ground. In the sheet were all sorts of animals, snakes, and birds (forbidden to the Jews for food). Then a voice said unto him. Go kill and eat any of them you wish. Never, Lord: Peter declared. I have never in all my life eaten such creatures, for they are forbidden by our Jewish laws. The voice spoke again. Don't contradict God! If He says something is kosher, then it is. The same vision was repeated three times. Then the sheet was pulled up again into heaven. Peter was very perplexed. What could the vision mean? What was he to do? Just then the men sent by Cornelius had found the house and were standing outside at the gate, inquiring whether this was the place where Simon Peter lived! Meanwhile, as Peter was puzzling over the vision, the Holy Spirit said to him, three men have come to see you. Go down and meet them and go with them. All is well, I have sent them. So Peter went down. I'm the man you are looking for, he said. Now what is it you want? Then they told him about Cornelius the Roman officer, a good and godly man, well thought of by the Jews, and how an angel had instructed him to send for Peter to come and tell him what God wanted him to do. So Peter invited them in and lodged them overnight. The next day he went with them, accompanied by some other believers from Joppa. They arrived in Caesarea the following day, and Cornelius was waiting for him, and had called together his relatives and close friends to meet Peter. As Peter entered his home,

Cornelius fell to the floor before him to worship. But Peter said, Stand up! I am not a god! So he got up and they talked together for a while and then went in where the others were assembled. Peter told them, You know it is against the Jewish laws for me to come to a Gentile home like this. But God has showed me in a vision that I should never think of anyone as inferior. So I came as soon as I was sent for. Now tell me what you want. Cornelius replied, Four days ago I was praying as usual at this time of the afternoon, when suddenly a man was standing before me clothed in a radiant robe! He told me, Cornelius, your prayers are heard and your charities have been noticed by God! Now send some men to Joppa and summon Simon Peter, who is staying in the home of Simon, a tanner, down by the shore. So I sent for you at once, and you have done well to come so soon. So now here we are, waiting before the Lord, anxious to hear what the Lord has told you to tell us! Then Peter replied, I see very clearly that the Jews are not God's only favorites! In every nation He has those that worship Him and do good deeds and are acceptable to Him. I am sure you have heard about the Good News for the people of Israel, that there is peace with God through Jesus, the Messiah, who is Lord of all creation. The message has spread through Judea, beginning with John the Baptist in Galilee. And you no doubt know that Jesus of Nazareth was anointed by God with the Holy Spirit and with power, and went around doing good and healing all who were possessed by demons, for God was with Him. And we Apostles are witnesses of all He did throughout Israel and in Jerusalem, where He was murdered on a cross. But God brought Him back to life three days later and showed Him to certain witnesses God had selected beforehand; not to the general public, but to us who ate and drank with Him after He rose from the dead. And He sent us to preach the Good News everywhere and to testify that Jesus is ordained of God to be the judge of all; living and dead. And all the Prophets have written about Him, saying that everyone who believes in Him will have their sins forgiven through His name Even as Peter was saying these things, the Holy Spirit fell upon all those listening! The Jews who came with Peter were amazed that the Holy Spirit would be given to Gentiles too! But there could be no doubt about it, for they heard them speaking in tongues and praising God. Peter asked, can anyone object to my baptizing them now that they have received the Holy Spirit just as we did? So he did, baptize them in the name of Jesus, the Messiah. Afterward Cornelius begged him to stay with them for several days." (Acts 10:1-48)

Two main points are covered in this chapter, and the previous one, both have to do with the Gentiles. The Gentiles received the Holy Spirit just like the Jews had received before. The other important happening was the salvation of Saul and his receiving the Holy Spirit. Saul, later called Paul the Apostle, was chosen by God to be an Apostle to the Gentiles. Up to this time the Kingdom of God had been Jewish. But they rejected Jesus, their Messiah, and now God's plan is to take out of the Gentiles a people for His name, and Paul was to be a very important part of that process, which is still going on today, and will continue until the number is complete.

Christian character is not just moral or legal correctness, but the possession and manifestation of nine graces, which are listed as fruit of the Spirit, love, joy, peace, longsuffering, gentleness, goodness, faith, meekness, temperance. (Galatians 5:22) The Christian who is filled with the Spirit, and is walking in the Spirit has help in manifesting these fruit of the Spirit, in their life.

In addition to the "fruit" of the spirit, there are "gifts" of the Spirit, they are presented in 1 Corinthians 12:1-11. "Now concerning spiritual gifts, brethren, I would not have you ignorant. Ye know that ye were Gentiles, carried away unto these dumb idols, even as ye were led. Wherefore I give you to understand, that no man speaking by the Spirit of God calleth Jesus accursed: and that no man can say that Jesus is the Lord, but by the Holy Ghost. Now there are diversities of gifts, but the same Spirit. And there are differences of administrations, but the same Lord. And there are diversities of operations, but it is the same God which worketh all in all. But the manifestation of the Spirit is given to every man to profit withal. (for the common good) For to one is given by the Spirit the word of wisdom; to another the word of knowledge by the same Spirit; To another faith by the same Spirit; to another the gifts of healing by the same Spirit; To another the working of miracles; to another prophecy; to another discerning of spirits; to another divers kinds of tongues; to another the interpretation of tongues: But all these worketh that one and the selfsame Spirit, dividing to every man severally as he will."

All of these gifts are given primarily to enable the church, as the body of Christ, to accomplish its commission, which is to preach the word of God to the world. God has promised to confirm the preaching of the word with signs following, and that is the secret to seeing souls saved, however it is no longer a secret, for it is for every believer. Peter, in his speech on the Day of Pentecost said, "For the promise is unto you, and to your children, and to all that are afar off, even as many as the Lord our God shall call." (Acts 2:39)

In addition to the fruit of the Spirit, which are given to Christians in order that they might be like Christ, which involves a change of character, in which the old nature with its affections and lusts are replaced with the fruit of the Spirit. We now have the gifts of the Spirit also called spiritual gifts which are given to the Church, which is called the the body of Christ, in scripture.

We are concerned here with the Holy Spirit's relation to the Church, and that relationship is twofold. First, believers are baptized into the Church at the time of salvation, 1Corinthians 12:12-13: "For as the body is one, and hath many members, and all the members of that one body, being many, are one body: so also is Christ. For by one Spirit are we all baptized into one body, whether we be Jews or Gentiles, whether we be bond or free;" Another scripture speaks of being baptized into Christ, which is the same because Christ is the head of the Church. Galatians 3:26-28: "For ye are all the children of God by faith in Christ Jesus. For as many of you as have been baptized into Christ have put on Christ. There is neither Jew nor Greek, there is neither bond nor free, there is neither male nor female: for ye are all one in Christ Jesus." The thing to notice here is who is doing the baptizing. This is not the baptism of the Holy Spirit, the baptism with the Holy Spirit, or the filling of the Holy Spirit. This is the Holy Spirit baptizing (adding or putting believers into the body of Christ, the Church).

Now back to spiritual gifts, they are spiritual helps, which are given to the individual members of the Church. These gifts give them special ability to accomplish specific service. The Spirit acts in free sovereignty. It is the Holy Spirit who gives all these gifts and powers, deciding which gift each member should have. Something important to remember is that gifts are good, but only if ministered in love: And for the benefit of the whole Church, and under the guidance of the Holy Spirit.

Ephesians 4:11-13 NIV: "It was Jesus who gave, some to be Apostles, some to be Prophets, some to be Evangelists, and some to be Pastors and Teachers, to prepare God's people for works of service, so that the body of Christ may be built up until we all reach unity in the faith and in the knowledge of the Son of God and become mature, attaining to the whole measure of the fullness of Christ."

God's plan for man begins with his salvation from sin and, his freedom from the devil. Then He fills him with the Holy Spirit and power, and gives him the fruit of the Spirit, and gifts of the Spirit: Here in Ephesians, He gives to the Church, these men who are equipped with these spiritual abilities: For the perfecting of the saints; for the work of the ministry, and for the edifying of the body of Christ. These men are to be guided and directed by the Holy Spirit. Their ministry is not to do all the work of the Church: But to rather, to train the believers so they are capable of carrying out the work of the Church. The scripture says, for the edifying of the Church, which means to build up: Full development and growth into maturity in godliness. How many churches do you know like that? There seems to be two misunderstandings that cause some folks trouble. The first is confusion between being "born of the Spirit" and being "baptized with the Spirit." There are two verses that helped me with this. John the Baptist said in Matthew 3:11 "I indeed baptize you with water unto repentance: but he that cometh after me is mightier than I, whose shoes I am not worthy to bear: he shall baptize you with the Holy Ghost, and with fire:" Notice here that Jesus is the one doing the baptizing. This is "the baptism with the Holy Spirit" also referred to as, the filling with the Holy Spirit.1 Corinthians 12:13: "For by one Spirit are we all baptized into one body, whether we be Jews or Gentiles, whether we be bond or free; and have been all made to drink into one Spirit." Here the Spirit is doing the baptizing. These verses cleared up the question for me.

The other problem is a big one, it is "tongues" and I really don't know why. But let us see what we can find in the Bible. In Acts 2:4 on the Day of Pentecost, "They were all filled with the Holy Spirit, and began to speak with other tongues as the Spirit gave them utterance." They were speaking words in these languages, which were different from their own native language. And they were speaking of the wonderful works of God: They were worshiping God. In Acts 10:46. "For they heard them speak with tongues, and magnify God." In Acts 19:6 "When

Paul laid his hands on them, the Holy Spirit came on them; and they spake with tongues and prophesied."

1 Corinthians 12:10 when listing the spiritual gifts, gives divers kinds of tongues and interpretation of tongues. Divers kinds, means various kinds of tongues. Verse 28 mentions diversities of tongues, which is similar, and is translated different languages, in the NIV translation.

The interpretation of tongues is simply a gift, which gives the ability to tell the meaning of the message, which was given, in tongues, in order for the church to understand it, and be edified by it. 1 Corinthians 13:1 "Though I speak with the tongues of men and of angels and have not love, I am become as sounding brass and a tinkling cymbal."

"Moreover, be earnestly desiring, the spiritual gifts, and do this in order that you might more efficiently impart to others the divine revelation you have received. For the one who is uttering words in a tongue is not speaking to men but to God, for no one hears him as to understand what he is saying. And he utters with his human spirit (as energized by the Holy Spirit) divine revelations not explained. But he who imparts divine revelations to men is speaking with the result of up building the Christian life, and exhortation, and consolation. The one who utters words in a tongue builds himself up in his Christian life. But he who imparts divine revelation to others builds up the local assembly. Now I desire that all of you be speaking in tongues, but I prefer that you impart divine revelation to others, which you have received. Moreover, greater is the one who imparts divine revelation to others than he who speaks in tongues, except that he interpret, in order that the local assembly might receive, up building." (1 Corinthians 14:1-5 Wuest: An expanded translation.)

It seems that there was an excess of speaking in tongues, without interpretation, in the Church at Corinth, and Paul was teaching these new Christians. In another place he told them everything should be done decently and in order. For God is not a God of disorder but of peace. The main purpose of spiritual gifts is to build up, both the Church and the individual.

"Dear brothers, don't be childish in your understanding of these things. Be innocent babies when it comes to planning evil, but be men of intelligence in understanding matters of this kind. We are told in the ancient Scriptures that God would send men from other lands to speak in foreign languages to His people, but even then they would not listen. So you see that being able to speak in tongues is not a sign to God's children concerning His power, but is a sign to the unsaved, However prophecy (preaching the deep truths of God) is what the Christians need, and unbelievers are not ready for it. Even so, if an unsaved person, or someone who doesn't have these gifts, comes to church and hears you all talking in other languages, he is likely to think you are crazy. But if you prophesy, preaching God's word, (even though such preaching is mostly for believers) and an unsaved person or a new Christian comes in who does not understand about these things, all of these sermons will convince him of the fact that he is a sinner, and his conscience will be pricked by every thing he hears. As he listens, his secrete thoughts will be laid bare and he will fall down on his knees and worship God, declaring that God is really there among you." 1Corinthians 14:20-25 (The Living Bible)

Paul urges the Christians to use their intelligence in understanding spiritual matters. Then he points out that, although God spoke to Old Testament people in foreign languages they would not listen, because it was not a sign of God's power to them. Speaking in tongues is a sign to unbelievers; however it is the preaching of God's word that results in the conversion of sinners. This is the reason that the "gift of prophecy" is given prominence. Verse one of this chapter (14) says, "Follow after charity (love), and desire spiritual gifts, but rather that ye may prophesy" (inspired preaching). There is some thought that Paul is restricting the manifestation of spiritual gifts, while the truth is he is giving instructions so that every thing will be done decently and in order, and according to God's will and under His control. Some seem to want to belittle spiritual gifts by saying they will cease. Or have already ceased. But the truth is, the Lord will know how long they will be needed. The last three verses of 1 Corinthians chapter fourteen say, "But if any man be ignorant, let him be ignorant. Wherefore, brethren, covet to prophesy, and forbid not to speak with tongues. Let all things be done decently and in order." (1 Corinthians 14:38-40)

We have been looking primarily at how the Holy Spirit works in the church. But we don't want to miss the importance of the Holy Spirit in the individual's life. Romans 8:26, 27: "Likewise the Spirit also helpeth our infirmities: for we know not what we should pray for as we ought: but the Spirit itself maketh intercession for us with groanings which cannot be uttered. And he that searcheth the hearts knoweth what is the mind of the Spirit, because he maketh intercession for the saints according to the will of God." This kind of prayer is badly needed, because it is so effective, and it may be in operation much more than we know about, among Spirit filled believers.

In discussing tongues we mentioned that many times believers are worshiping and glorifying God. Some misinformed people condemn tongues, because they say that messages in tongues are adding to the Scripture, which is not true. God uses the supernatural gifts of the Spirit to speak mysteries; and to speak to edification, exhortation, and comfort. Probably most important of all the Holy Spirit teaches us of the things of Jesus Christ and bring all things to our remembrance; and He will lead us into all truth. These are areas where we need all the help we can get.

Here are some things no one should do. However, some are very careless, and are treading on dangerous ground by what they do and say concerning the Holy Spirit. Ephesians 4:30-32: "And grieve not the holy Spirit of God, whereby ye are sealed unto the day of redemption." (Other translations of grieve not, are, you must not offend, do not distress, never hurt, and don't cause the Holy Spirit sorrow) Verse 31 continues "Let all bitterness, and wrath, and anger, and clamour, and evil speaking, be put away from you, with all malice: And be ye kind one to another, tenderhearted, forgiving one another, even as God for Christ's sake hath forgiven you."

1Thessalonians 5:18-21: "In every thing give thanks: for this is the will of God in Christ Jesus concerning you. Quench not the Spirit. Despise not prophesyings. Prove all things; hold fast that which is good. Quench not means do not stifle, the manifestations of the Spirit. We need to let the Spirit be in control. That is hard for man to do. Many men want to be the one in control of everything.

Hebrews 10:28-30: "He that despised Moses' law died without mercy under two or three witnesses: Of how much sorer punishment, suppose ye, shall he be thought worthy, who hath trodden under foot the Son of God, and hath counted the blood of the covenant, wherewith he was sanctified, an unholy thing, and hath done despite (mocked and insulted) unto the Spirit of grace? For we know Him that hath said, Vengeance belongeth unto me, I will recompense, saith the Lord. And again, The Lord shall judge his people" This is speaking of disrespect, insult, and mockery toward Christ and the blood He shed on the cross, and toward the Holy Spirit and His supernatural manifestations.

Mark 3:28-30: "Verily I say unto you, All sins shall be forgiven unto the sons of men, and blasphemies wherewith soever they shall blaspheme: But he that shall blaspheme against the Holy Ghost (Spirit) hath never forgiveness, but is in danger of eternal damnation: Because they said, He hath an unclean spirit."In other words, whoever maliciously misrepresents the Holy Spirit never has forgiveness. The same thing is said by Luke in his gospel, Luke 12:10 "And whosoever shall speak a word against the Son of man, it shall be forgiven him: but unto him that blasphemeth against the Holy Ghost it shall not be forgiven."Some folks, if they understood the truth about these things, would be more careful with their attitude and actions.

How you relate to the Holy Spirit determines your spiritual life. Jesus is the central focus of all believers and the fundamental purpose of the infilling of the Holy Spirit is for a supernatural witness of Christ. Jesus told them, "ye shall receive power, after that the Holy Ghost is come upon you:" (Acts 1:8) The primary and continuing evidence that they had received the Spirit, was their becoming effective witnesses of Jesus Christ by the power they had received. It is the Spirit filled Christians privilege and duty to share in the work and ministry of the Holy Spirit, which is to present Christ and all He means, to a lost and dying world. That is the simple truth about the spirit filled life.

Anything that distracts from the central truth of Jesus and His crucifixion, and His resurrection are dangerous and even fatal. It is regrettable but there have been some excesses and abuses, which must be shunned. We are admonished by the Scripture to, "seek that ye may excel to the edifying of the church". (1 Corinthians 14:12) "For God is not the author of confusion, but of peace, as in all churches of the saints." (1Corinthians 14:33) "And they went forth, and preached every where, the Lord working with them, and confirming the word with signs following." (Mark 16:20) Some times people get carried away and get things all mixed up; they try to get the signs ahead of the word, and they forget that the Lord is the one in control of the signs and wonders. By doing foolish things they bring reproach and ridicule on the church and misunderstanding of the operation of the Holy Spirit. Much of Paul's teaching in the Church at Corinth was in the way of correction, because these new Christians had more zeal than wisdom. He started the twelfth chapter with these words, "Now concerning spiritual gifts, brethren, I would not have you ignorant." Any way you look at it ignorance can be troublesome, and if you get a shortage of love mixed with it you are in serious trouble. Paul must have had both, for in the following chapter he taught about love. He said, "But covet earnestly the best gifts: and yet shew I unto you a more excellent way. Though I speak with the tongues of men and of angels, and have not charity, I am become as sounding brass, or a tinkling cymbal. And though I have the gift of prophecy, and understand all mysteries, and all knowledge; and though I have all faith, so that I could remove mountains, and have not charity, I am nothing." (1 Corinthians 12:31-13:2) This is something to always remember; without love every thing else is worthless. Love heads the list of the fruit of the Spirit They are all important but love comes first: LOVE, joy, peace, longsuffering, gentleness, goodness, faith, meekness, temperance, against such there is no law.

After the Day of Pentecost the Lord of the Church was making it clear that He would build His Church when, where, and with whom he wanted. Whatever the Holy Spirit wants to do should be adhered to at all cost: At the cost of tradition, and at the cost of organization. The Church must contend for the faith, and respond to the leadership of the Holy Spirit. The main characteristics of the Spirit filled Church are: Stability of eternal truth: Essential doctrine will be clarified and proclaimed with power: The essential mission of the Church will be to witness to the world.

I guess the question is how do I receive the in filling of the Holy Spirit? I will answer with a question: How are we saved? Ephesians 2:8 tells us, "For by grace are ye saved through faith; and that not of yourselves: it is the gift of God:" And Galatians 3:14 says, "That the blessing of Abraham might come on the Gentiles through Jesus Christ; that we might receive the promise of the Spirit through faith." It sounds like both salvation and the filling with the Spirit both come the same way if man doesn't complicate things.

The Pentecostal pattern is, repent, receive the new birth, take on the character of Christ, be filled with power from on high, and be His witnesses in word and in action, because faith without works is dead.

Jesus came with a supernatural ministry of deliverance and redemption; He came to destroy the works of the devil and to build His Church, which the councils of hell could not destroy. When He went

362

back to heaven He left His followers with the task of continuing what He had started, and He promised to send the Holy Spirit to help us, and He fulfilled His promise.

True Pentecost and the miraculous are synonymous, however the ultimate goal of the miraculous is to glorify God, edify the Church, and draw people to Christ. The supernatural works of God have their greatest impact in the arena of evangelism. All of the Divine helps are given to perfect the Church, for ministry, and to empower it to impact the world with the claims of Christ. God has enough resources to build His Church so we can rest assured that it will be done. He will do it with people who will say, "here, I am, what do you want me to do?"

The early Church put faithful men in charge of the necessary duties so the Apostles could give themselves to a lifestyle of prayer and ministry of the word. Prayer must be the highest priority in the personal lives and public ministries of spiritual leaders.

The strategy of Satan is to turn Pentecostal truth into self-centered experience. Self-seeking, Pentecostalism is seeking for a blessing. It is seeking for spiritual gifts to impress, and these selfish endeavors short-circuit the Spirit controlled life. The secret of joyful living is in learning to find purpose beyond self. Think about others rather, than self-gratification. Seek the kingdom of God and mind the things of the Spirit. If Christians have the mind of Christ, they will soon have the motivation of Christ. Jesus came into the world to give His life, in order to do His Fathers will: He made the ultimate sacrifice.

Believers need to remember that manifestations follow, never lead, the visitation of God. It is the almighty, not men, who confirm the word, with signs following. Mark 16:20: "And they went forth, and preached every where, the Lord working with them, and confirming the word with signs following."

First we should leave miracles to God, and second we should follow the biblical rules. 1. They will be based on the word. 2. They will be decent and orderly. 3. They will bring sinners to repentance: Repentance is central to the preaching of the Gospel. Evangelism is twofold: preaching the Gospel, and bringing people to repentance. 4. They will exalt Jesus Christ; it must focus the glory on Him, not on anyone else. 5. They will build up the body of Christ. 6. They will nurture evangelism: When signs and wonders, within the Church, are breathed of the Spirit of God, the result is evangelism.

Believers must not seek physical and mystical signs, we are commanded to preach the word and leave the signs and wonders to the sovereignty of God. If we follow the simple biblical pattern, miracles of the living God will be present whenever they are necessary.

The Pentecostal Movement; has been embarrassed for years; by tongues talkers; who have long tongues, bitter spirits, and inconsistent life styles. This has caused much more than embarrassment: It has done serious damage, however; like many other things, the devil and his evil spirits have a hand in it. The truth of the matter is: There are evil spirits, and there is the Holy Spirit and unbelievers and sometimes, new believers, and immature believers, are unable to distinguish between the two.

There is a story in the eighth chapter of the book of the Acts of the Apostles, beginning in verse five, "Then Philip went down to the city of Samaria, and preached Christ unto them. And the people with one accord gave heed unto those things which Philip spake, hearing and seeing the miracles which he did. For unclean spirits, crying with loud voice, came out of many that were possessed with them: and many taken with palsies, and that were lame, were healed. And there was great joy in that city. But there was a certain man, called Simon, which beforetime in the same city used sorcery, and bewitched the people of Samaria, giving out that himself was some great one: To whom they all gave heed, from the least to the greatest, saying, This man is the great power of God. And to him they had regard, because that of long time he had bewitched them with sorceries. But when they believed Philip preaching the things concerning the kingdom of God, and the name of Jesus Christ, they were baptized, both men and women. Then Simon himself believed also: and when he was baptized, he continued with Philip, and wondered, beholding the miracles and signs which were done. Now when the apostles which were at Jerusalem heard that Samaria had received the word of God, they sent unto them Peter and John: Who, when they were come down, prayed for them, that they might receive the Holy Ghost: (For as yet he was fallen upon none of them: only they were baptized in the name of the Lord Jesus.) Then laid they their hands on them, and they received the Holy Ghost. And when Simon saw that through laying on of the apostles' hands the Holy Ghost was given, he offered them money, Saying, Give me also this power, that on whomsoever I lay hands, he may receive the Holy Ghost. But Peter said unto him, Thy money perish with thee, because thou hast thought that the gift of God may be purchased with money. Thou hast neither part nor lot in this matter: for thy heart is not right in the sight of God. Repent therefore of this thy wickedness, and pray God, if perhaps the thought of thine heart may be forgiven thee. For I perceive that thou art in the gall of bitterness, and in the bond of iniquity. Then answered Simon, and said, Pray ye to the Lord for me, that none of these things which ye have spoken come upon me." (Acts 8:5-24)

This portion of Scripture shows us the importance of the gifts and helps of the Holy Spirit: And the seriousness of being ignorant, and uninformed, concerning them. Paul expressed it very well when he said, "I would not have you ignorant brethren." But I fear that ignorance concerning the simple truths of the Holy Spirit; are rampant in much of the church world today.

Something else to notice is how the people of Samaria were bewitched by this man, even believing him to be a great man of God. He bewitched them, giving out that he himself was a great one; which is always a bad sign. Self-glorification is sin; God is worthy of all glory. Simon, it seems, had all of them bewitched; and for a long time; but notice something important: they all paid attention upon seeing and hearing Philip, and they believed, and their lives were changed. All of this shows the contrast between the true and the false. One of the gifts of the Holy Spirit, listed in First Corinthians, is, "discerning of spirits," which is helpful in distinguishing good spirits from bad. This shows us one of the weapons that God gives to Spirit controlled Christians, to help them destroy the works of the devil.

Many times we have a tendency to proceed in our own way, forgetting that God's ways are always better than our ways. The rapid success of the early Christians was largely due to the fact that many of them were unlearned: Consequently when they went out to spread the Gospel, they didn't depend on their own abilities; they let the Holy Spirit guide them, and work with them.

Of course, Paul the Apostle was an exception, in that he was well educated, however it seems that he had trouble, at times, keeping his natural abilities in their rightful place, but overall he was quite successful.

Chapter 40

BIBLE INTERPRETATION

The parables are a good place to start on this important subject. Jesus used parables in two ways in His teaching: The first way was He used them as illustrations, comparing natural, every-day things to spiritual truths, for instance He said, many times, "the Kingdom of God is like" and He compared it to many different things, such as weeds in the grain field, don't pull the weeds when the grain is small, because you will pull up the grain. Wait until the harvest, then separate the weeds and burn them. Another parable was the Kingdom of God is like a mustard seed, which is one of the smallest, but when planted it grows to be the greatest among the herbs.

Jesus used parables in another way at times when He was speaking to the multitudes. Jesus explains in Mark 4:10-11 "And when he was alone, they that were about him with the twelve asked of him the parable. And he said unto them, Unto you it is given to know the mystery of the kingdom of God: but unto them that are without, all these things are done in parables" By them that are without, He was speaking of those who were not followers of Jesus. Another scripture that ties in with this one is Matthew 13:34 "All these things spake Jesus unto the multitude in parables; and without a parable spake he not unto them:" Some have taken part of this verse, "without a parable spoke He not" and using this phrase as evidence they teach that all scripture is in parables: therefore it must be inter-preted accordingly. This gives the freedom to have God say what the interpreter wishes Him to say; or at least make it say some thing other than what God is saying. The mistake comes from not considering whom Jesus was speaking to. He spoke to the multi-tude in parables. But that does not mean that God always speaks in parables. In fact, the simple truth is, God usually says what He means, because He wants us to know what He is saying.

However, that having been said, it is important to realize that the Bible is a book of prophecy. The Bible is God's divine book and it is the sacred Word of the Christian faith, and it differs from the writings of all religions in one very important thing: Unlike them it contains many prophesies, some already fulfilled, others in the process of fulfillment in our day, and still others to be fulfilled in the future. Fulfilled prophecy and true and genuine miracles constitute the main proof of the inspiration of the Scriptures.

Prophecy in the Old Testament is a miracle of utterance and a miracle of knowledge, as well as a prediction of the future beyond the power of human ability. All scripture is profitable, 2 Timothy 3:16-17 "All scripture is given by inspiration of God, and is profitable for doctrine, for reproof, for correction, for instruction in righteousness: That the man of God may be perfect, throughly furnished unto all good works." Prophecy holds first rank as evidence of the authenticity and genuineness of Scripture: The major focus of biblical prophecy concerns the nation and people of Israel, and prophetic passages dealing with the following all focus on the nation of Israel and its important place in the end-time drama. 1. The tribulation period. Matthew 24:22: 2. The rise of antichrist: 2 Thessalonians 2:3-8: 3. The signing of a peace treaty: Daniel 9:25-27: 4. The invasion of Israel by Gentiles: Zechariah 14:12-13: 5. The battle of Armageddon: Revelation 16:16:

Here are some helpful guidelines for interpretation of the Bible and Biblical prophecies. 1. Interpret current events in light of the Bible; not the Bible in light of current events. 2. Fulfillment of most prophetic events related to Israel will not take place until after the rapture of the Church. 3. Does the biblical text provide enough data to draw a correspondence with current events? 4. Distinguish between the "last days" of the Church and the "last days" of Israel. 5. Avoid over-statement and excessive speculation about Bible prophesy; this has given critics of prophecy reason to reject prophetic fulfillment. Our only clear guide to the future is Biblical truth. Everything else is little more than speculation and man's ideas.

2 Peter 1:19 NIV "We have the words of the Prophets made more certain, and you will do well to pay attention to it, as to a light shining in a dark place, until the day dawns and the morning star rises in your hearts. Above all, you must understand that no prophesy of Scripture came about by the Prophet's own interpretation. For prophecy never had its origin in the will of man but men spoke from God as they were carried along by the Holy Spirit." Prophecy is made more sure by fulfillment in part. Fulfilled prophecy is a proof of inspiration because the Scripture predictions of future events were uttered so long before the events transpired that no human intelligence or foresight could have anticipated them, and these predictions are so detailed, and specific, as to be impossible to be man's fortunate guesses. Hundreds of predictions concerning Israel, the land of Canaan, Babylon, Assyria, Egypt, and many different people; so long ago and so improbable, as well as so detailed and definite that no one could have anticipated them, yet they have been fulfilled by the elements, and by men who were ignorant of them, or actually disbelieved them, or struggled to avoid their fulfillment. It is certain, therefore, that the scriptures, which contain them, are inspired. "For the prophecy came not in old time by the will of man: but holy men of God spake as they were moved by the Holy Ghost." (2 Peter 1:21)

Bible study is very important: The best is independent study because first hand knowledge is best. "Jesus answered and said unto them, Ye do err, not knowing the scriptures, nor the power of

God." (Matthew 22:29) These words are still as true today as they were when Jesus spoke them. There is a tremendous lack of knowledge of the Bible in the world today: even in the minds of many church-goers. Jesus told His followers He would pray to His Father to send the Holy Spirit to help them know the truth. The Holy Spirit illumines the mind, not the Scriptures. The scriptures have never been dark: the mind of man is where the darkness is. The Holy Spirit takes away the darkness from the mind so we can see the truth of God in the Scriptures. There is something about truth that makes it easily recognizable by all who are searching for it with open minds. It is of utmost importance to approach the Bible with an open mind: with no preconceived ideas, and with no intention of trying to prove any thing except the truth. When a person is sincerely searching for truth, some times all that is needed is just lifting the veil, or opening the door: And it is not necessary to be taught, For the mind sees, realizes, and understands. Comparing scripture with scripture is beneficial and can be done by the use of a concordance. I am not saying you don't need to listen to teachers and preachers, or others: learn from anyone possible, however it is always good to search the scriptures and see if these things you hear are true.

Another thing that is very necessary in study of the Bible is to strive to get the big picture. It seems that most of the time the Bible is treated different than any other book: It is studied in bits and pieces; a few verses here and a few there, or a chapter at a time, or book by book. All of this is profitable and necessary, but what I am trying to say is that reading it through from cover to cover, is probably the most profitable thing a student of the Bible can do as far as overall understanding is concerned: And is helpful in all other study of individual verses and portions of Scripture. It can be compared to a personal letter you might receive. To understand a particular sentence correctly you need to know what the rest of the letter says.

CONCLUSION

I had thought to consider the antichrist and some other end-time events but since those are quite extensive areas, I will leave them to a later time. They are not critical anyway: The important thing, for all of us, is to be prepared when those times arrive. Joshua 24:15 NKJ "And if it seems evil to you to serve the LORD, choose for yourselves this day whom you will serve, whether the gods which your fathers served that were on the other side of the River, or the gods of the Amorites, in whose land you dwell. But as for me and my house, we will serve the LORD." Shortly before his death, and after they had been in the promised land, for a while, Joshua gathered the tribes together because they were still in danger of not serving God in sincerity and in truth: He was trying to make them aware of the importance of being truly on God's side. Jesus said, "He that is not with me is against me; and he that gathereth not with me scattereth abroad." Matthew 12:30: Another scripture which expands on this thought is John 3:15-21 NKJ: "that whoever believes in Him should

375

not perish but have eternal life. For God so loved the world that He gave His only begotten Son, that whoever believes in Him should not perish but have everlasting life. For God did not send His Son into the world to condemn the world, but that the world through Him might be saved. He who believes in Him is not condemned; but he who does not believe is condemned already, because he has not believed in the name of the only begotten Son of God. And this is the condemnation, that the light has come into the world, and men loved darkness rather than light, because their deeds were evil. For everyone practicing evil hates the light and does not come to the light, lest his deeds should be exposed. But he who does the truth comes to the light, that his deeds may be clearly seen, that they have been done in God."

The point I want to make hinges on the phrase; "but he who does not believe is condemned already" in other words the unbeliever is condemned by doing nothing, because he is already on his way to destruction. With Abraham, years ago it was just the opposite; he believed God and he became saved: It was counted to him for righteousness, and multitudes have been saved, through the years, in the same way. The unbeliever can do absolutely nothing and be eternally lost: All Abraham did was believe and his situation changed.

An easy way to picture this truth is to think of being born on the road that leads to destruction: it is a wide road and many are traveling on it, all going in the same direction, all headed for the same destination. The only hope is that there is a fork in this broad road: a narrow road with a narrow gate forks off and goes up a steep hill. Jesus told His Disciples about these roads one day when He was sitting on a hill-side teaching them, "Enter by the narrow gate; for wide is the gate and broad is the way that leads to destruction, and there are many who go in by it. Because narrow is the gate and difficult is the way which leads to life, and there are few that find it." (Matthew 7:13-14 NKJ)

My desire is that many will understand how simple salvation actually is and will act accordingly: "The Simple Truth" is that it truly is simple. "But don't forget this, dear friend, that a day or a thousand years from now is like tomorrow to the Lord. He isn't really being slow about his promised return, even though it sometimes seems that way. But he is waiting, for the good reason that he is not willing that any should perish, and he is giving sinners more time to repent." (2 Peter 3:8 The Living Bible)

THE END

LaVergne, TN USA
17 August 2009
154998LV00001B/19/P